Praise for *Will She Do*

'She is the cur's cods, the terrier's testicles, the business. I will go farther and declare that Atkins is the finest actor appearing in the world right now' A. A. Gill

'There is something about those large eyes and that steadfast look that tells you that you are in the presence of a remarkable actor; and so it has proved in a career that has encompassed everything from Greek tragedy and Ibsen to Pinter and Albee, and that has led Atkins to be revered on both sides of the Atlantic . . . Vanessa Redgrave seems to have direct access to some other world. Judi Dench has the capacity to merge laughter and tears in a single moment. The greatness of Eileen Atkins, who is their peer, lies in her uncanny emotional direct-ness and her ability to make her eyes the window to her soul' Michael Billington, *Guardian*

'For some of us she cannot be on stage enough . . . she makes you feel the particular thing she is doing can only be for you . . . And I would give away all my West End tickets to again watch Eileen Atkins, peerlessly subtle, conjuring up Shakespeare's women – and one of his men – in her one-person show' Susannah Clapp, *Observer*

'Eileen Atkins's memoir *Will She Do?* is just a tiny bit better than the one I've recently published. It hurts me deeply to say that, but hers is a glorious book' Miriam Margolyes, *Radio Times*

'Atkins's [memoir] is bliss: so funny and atmospheric and true. It's not only that she has a way of bringing her more antic characters vividly to life (that goes for Laurence Olivier and Alec Guinness as well as the pretentious Madame Yandie). She's honest about herself, too, as content to relate her humiliations as her triumphs' Rachel Cooke, *Observer*

'From anyone else, this would be outrageous name-dropping, but actor Dame Eileen Atkins has gone toe to toe with them all over a career spanning seven decades and countless triumphs, the first few of which are documented in her richly enjoyable memoir, *Will She Do?*' *Radio Times, Book of the Week*

'*Will She Do?* displays the emotional intelligence, acute observation, wry humour and above all honesty that distinguish Atkins's acting . . . this is an exhilarating portrait of an actress who has surmounted seemingly insuperable odds to reach the pinnacle of her profession. The answer to the question in the title is self-evident' The *Spectator*

'Will there be a further volume? I hope so. Cross and impatient Eileen may be, but as an actress she is at the top of the pyramid, and as a writer she is very fine, with a wit drier than a martini' *Daily Mail*

'I really hope she's planning to write a few more volumes. She's a gifted storyteller, who writes evocatively about her childhood on a Tottenham council estate in the Second World War, and has a knack for a sharp anecdote. And oh, those anecdotes! . . . A rollicking ride through the early career of one of our greatest acting dames' *Evening Standard*

Made a Dame in 1991, Eileen Atkins who was born in Tottenham in 1934, has been on American and British stage and screen since 1957 and has won an Emmy, a BAFTA, been nominated for four Tonys and is a three-time Olivier Award winner. She co-created Upstairs, Downstairs and wrote the screenplay for Mrs Dalloway (for which she won an Evening Standard Award). Now in her eighties, this is first autobiographical work. She lives in London.

WILL SHE DO?

Act One of a Life on Stage

EILEEN ATKINS

virago

VIRAGO

First published in Great Britain in 2021 by Virago Press
This paperback edition published in 2022 by Virago Press

1 3 5 7 9 10 8 6 4 2

Typeset in Perpetua by M Rules
Printed and bound in Great Britain by Clays Ltd, Elcograf S.p.A.

Papers used by Virago are from well-managed forests
and other responsible sources.

Virago Press
An imprint of
Little, Brown Book Group
Carmelite House
50 Victoria Embankment
London EC4Y 0DZ

An Hachette UK Company
www.hachette.co.uk

www.virago.co.uk

For every actor who has waited for the phone to ring

Prologue

One evening, in the early 1950s when I was nineteen, I was walking from my shabby digs in Oxford to the theatre where I was an ASM, which meant that I was sweeping the stage, borrowing props, begging furniture, prompting and occasionally appearing on stage and saying a line or two if I was lucky. It was a dreary autumn evening with thin rain soaking right through to one's soul, and the last part of the journey took me down a very affluent, architecturally admired street of houses where most lower-ground floors had been turned into kitchen-diners and had their lights on, displaying the domestic scenes within. A woman cooking, laying the table for supper, often one or two children helping, and at one house I observed a man as he opened the front door, and I stopped to watch him as he entered the scene downstairs. The welcome, the smiles, the kissing, the laughing. And I was overwhelmed by the thought that I would never be that woman, because at this twilight hour I would always be on my way to the theatre. Standing in the seeping rain, I was drenched with melancholy. I trudged on to the theatre and pushed through the stage door, which immediately led to the green room, stinking of cigarettes, littered with dirty mugs and two sleeping actors sprawled on chairs. My melancholy vanished in seconds. This is my home, I thought as I happily gathered up the mugs. This is where I belong and where I'll always want to be.

1

My birth meant that three wishes had been granted. God had forgiven my mother, my father's manhood had been restored and the family became eligible for a council house.

My mother, father, half-sister, brother and grandmother had all been living in a rented house in Stoke Newington that was so damp they needed to move. While my mother was giving birth to me in the Salvation Army Mothers' Nursing Home in Clapton ('Costing two and six a night,' as my mother would proudly tell me. 'You weren't born on charity'), the whole family moved to 17 Courtman Road, Tottenham on the White Hart Lane council estate, which began a stone's throw from the Spurs football ground and stretched all the way to Lordship Lane. My mother, even though she was desperate to be rehoused, had refused two other houses because she wanted the open aspect of the allotments which stretched scenically behind Courtman Road. I, of course, had no idea that such grandeur awaited me.

Although my birth certificate says that I was born on 16 June 1934, my mother said it was 15 June. She remembered being told that she had a girl and asking fearfully if 'it was all right',

3

as she was almost forty-six, and at that great age was convinced there would be 'a bit missing', and the nurse telling her that I had 'lovely straight eyebrows'. She thought, What on earth must she look like if they can only talk about her eyebrows? Then she heard the clock strike midnight as I was wrapped and handed to her, and a moment later she noticed the doctor filling in a form and looking at his watch before putting my date of birth. It was always celebrated on the sixteenth, but at every birthday my mother would say, 'It was really yesterday.'

She was ecstatic that I was a girl. She was a dressmaker, and longed to make pretty children's clothes. She had had a hard life before she married my father. Not only did she work all day as a seamstress, but in the evenings she was a barmaid at the Trocadero Theatre at the Elephant and Castle, as well as having to help with the lodgers that my widowed grandmother was forced to take in. She was thirty-nine and had given up all hope of marriage when my father, three years younger, who lodged in the house in Stoke Newington, lost his wife Kitty in childbirth. He was left a widower with his three-year-old daughter, Peggy, and asked my mother if she would help him look after her. 'Only if you marry me,' answered my mother, and my father, always obliging, was dragooned into marriage.

This was not a love match. Neither my brother nor I ever noticed much affection between them, but they got on well enough together. Annie ruled the roost and Arthur clucked along. My half-sister, Peggy, told me that they had a good sex life, so maybe things got evened up in bed.

In less than two years after they were married they had two boys, Ronald and Reginald, and then my mother found that she was pregnant again. They couldn't afford another child. My father's wages as an electric meter reader were minimal, and even with my mother still working at home, sewing for a factory, there was hardly enough money. Having to look after her mother as well as two babies, she felt exhausted and unable to cope, so she had a backstreet abortion.

A year later her younger son, Reginald, known as Bubby, died of meningitis. My mother was convinced God had punished her, and her unhappiness cast a cloud over the whole family. Six years later my father had an illness that required the loss of one testicle, and my mother, who flew into terrible rages (which unfortunately I inherited), accused him of being a useless husband. Apparently he then threw her on the kitchen table to prove he wasn't useless, and the result was me.

That made us, with Grandma, a family of six and eligible for one of the newly developed council houses. So, as you can see, like a good fairy at my own christening, I granted three wishes. It was a promising start.

Our house was at the end of a row, and had a wide path that was the entrance to the allotments along one side of it, and the back looked over a longish garden that led to the several acres of these allotments.

The house had a living room with an open fire, a small kitchen with sliding doors behind which the council had oddly fitted a bath and a boiler – next to which my mother bred chicks – a hallway with a freezing lavatory, and upstairs three bedrooms. By the time I was born my brother, Ron, was five, and my half-sister, Peggy, eleven. After a year or so my mother thought it wrong that they shared a bedroom, so my grandmother had one room, my father and brother another, and my mother, sister and me the third. Quite naturally the only person who was happy with this arrangement was my grandmother, and after a year of frustration, with my parents unable to sleep together, and my grandmother becoming more demanding and difficult, my mother finally went to the local church and begged the priest there to help her find a home for my grandmother. And lo and behold, Father Waton of St Benet Fink Church, Lordship Lane, found a convent in Thames Ditton that would take her for no charge. As she was nineteen when she had my mother, she could scarcely have been seventy, and I'm pretty sure had only been to church for weddings, christenings and funerals when she went to live with the nuns. It was immensely good of the Reverend Father (he was High Church and not Catholic) to do anything, as no one in the family was remotely religious, and my mother wasn't even confirmed then. Later when I was ten or eleven I was obsessed by religion, and indeed was found in the church by Father Waton, dramatically stretched full length on the floor, arms out, prostrate in front of the altar. He was a severe, slightly frightening priest, but he listened to me and told me it was highly unlikely that I would want to become a nun when I grew up. Indeed, I didn't even get as far as confirmation as by then I'd discovered boys.

I was a toddler when Grandma left us, and only have an impression of a short, fat, red-faced woman who sometimes gave me sweets but was mostly cross and had all her meals served to her in her room in bed.

Later I was to learn that she had had three husbands, all of whom had died. The first one was my mother's father, a darkly handsome man who had married Grandma at eighteen and died when my mother was eighteen months old. Four years later she had married again, and sent my mother to live with cousins on the South Coast, as she was pregnant. I gather it was quite common for women then to send a child from a first marriage to live with relatives because the second husband didn't want to be bothered with another man's child. At least, my mother convinced herself that it was 'normal', and she wasn't invited back to the family until she was eight or nine years old and could be a 'help' and not a 'nuisance'. One can imagine what emotional stunting this might have caused a child.

With Grandma gone the atmosphere lightened considerably, although there always remained a huge, hideously badly coloured black-edged photograph of poor Bubby on the living room wall (the only adornment apart from a mirror) to daily remind us all of death.

I have only one memory of life before I was three, and that was of being thrown up in the air and caught again and again by my father, and I swear my small brain registered perfect happiness. I'm convinced that I felt I never wanted it to stop. I've told this to friends who have rushed to throw their babies up in the air, but so far no one else has reported a state of bliss. My father was a playful, affectionate, childlike man who doted on me, and when I was young I adored him.

The next thing I remember had a momentous effect on my life and I have a clear image of it. A gypsy came to the door. They would come in groups and word would get around that they were working their way down the street knocking at every door. My mother both feared and was fascinated by them, and she was very superstitious and always bought heather from them to prevent them putting the evil eye on her. Peering through the kitchen windows, we had watched their progress down the road and then the knock came at our door. Catching something of my mother's excitement and fear, I suppose, I went to the door with her, clinging onto her dress, and there was this exotic-looking woman, swarthy, bejewelled with bangles and earrings, and with a bright scarf round her head and a full, swishing skirt that showed coloured petticoats. My mother duly bought the heather, and the gypsy suddenly fixed her eyes on me. 'That little one there,' she said, pointing a bony finger at me, 'is going to be a great dancer – another Pavlova.'

That was it as far as my mother was concerned – the gypsy had spoken – I was to be a great dancer. She lost no time. I was taken to a dancing school the following week for my first lesson. I refused to 'join the other little girls' and screamed to be taken home. She tried a couple of other dancing schools but, refusing to follow my destiny, I screamed each time to be taken home. But my mother was persistent. I don't think that it was only because 'the gypsy had spoken'. She was a tall, overweight woman who had always thought of herself as plain and clumsy. There was no suppleness or softness about her – if you sat on her lap, her fierce whalebone corset was a buttress to prevent comfort, and she walked stiffly as if clad in armour. Maybe there was a dancer inside her that wanted to get out that would only be assuaged if I pranced and pirou- etted for her.

Finally she found a dancing school that had the somewhat snigger-inducing name of the KY School, and these initials were emblazoned on our practice clothes. Madame Kavos Yandie, the owner of these initials, purported to be Spanish and had eleven letters after her name, all of which she was barred from using twenty years later when it was revealed that she had been born Kathleen Smith from Peckham and had never passed a dancing examination in her life.

Although she managed to persuade me to stay for a lesson, as soon as my mother collected me I said I absolutely would not go again. 'Why not?' my mother asked. I couldn't think why not, and couldn't scream in front of children I'd just been dancing with. 'Why not?' repeated my mother. She'd got her foot in the door and was not going to give up. I had to have a good excuse. 'Because a horrible girl put my head down the lavatory and pulled the chain.' Where I'd heard of this minor torture I had no idea. 'What's this girl's name?' my mother demanded, fury rising at this unknown child. I searched about and tried to remember someone's name. Anyone's name. 'Doris.' I'd at last remembered one. My mother marched me back into the class, repeated my fantasy to Madame Yandie and poor Doris was banned from ever appearing at dancing class again.

I now had no excuse for not going, so I was dragged there a second time and this time my imagined treatment at the hands of Doris had made me notorious, and everyone in class had been told to be nice to me. So I began to enjoy being the centre of attention, and found that it was quite fun to learn to dance.

It had taken my mother two years to get me to go to dancing lessons, and in that time World War II had been declared. I was aware that this terrible and frightening thing might be going to happen, but it was eclipsed by the terror that I had turned five in June and would be attending Devonshire Hill Primary School the first week in September. The school was situated at the centre of the huge council estate in a road opposite the cemetery, which I thought a pretty place with all its flowers, and I enjoyed my first day there where I learned my first nursery rhyme:

> I love little pussy, her coat is so warm,
> And if I don't hurt her, she'll do me no harm.

And fell in love with a little boy with a shock of yellow hair called Gordon, who was willing to let me hold his hand. There were three blissful days of this heady stuff, before we were told that the school was closing and we were all going to be evacuated.

My brother had apparently already gone, but I wouldn't have noticed as I was scarcely aware of my brother or my half-sister. They were both at school by the time I was born, and shadowy figures who spent a lot of time in their bedrooms. I do remember my sister asking if she could take me for a walk when I was in a pushchair, but my mother wouldn't allow it, as she hadn't allowed the young teenagers in our street who had knocked on the door to ask if they could 'take baby for a walk' – as was the fashion on council estates in those days. She stood with clenched fists when my father put me on the crossbar of his bike in the mornings and rode proudly down the street, showing me off to everyone, then turned round and cycled back to deposit me safely at her feet. It's apparent to me now that until I was evacuated, I was never out of my mother's sight. She had at last got the girl she wanted (she didn't count my half-sister), and she wasn't going to lose me.

As soon as it was announced on the radio that war had been declared with Germany, I realised that the buzz of worry that had hovered over us for some months was now a real and dreadful happening. After the broadcast everyone went out into their back gardens and called out to one another. The Haywards next door, the Pritchards, the Mitchells, the Poulters, even Mrs Flowerday, our neighbour the other side of the allotment lane who for some reason we weren't normally allowed to speak to (probably because she 'used language'), all were clearly terrified though full of bluster. 'Who does Adolf think he is?'

'We'll show 'em.' 'When do you think the bombs will start?' The fear was certainly clear to me.

About a week later I was taken by my mother in my best clothes to a railway station where, on a platform, there was a group of children from Devonshire Hill Primary. My mother put a brown cardboard box on a strap across my shoulder and told me it was my gas mask, and someone gave me a bar of chocolate and an orange and I was put on the train, and before I knew what was happening, the train was leaving and my mother wasn't coming with me.

It wasn't a very long journey as we were only going to Essex. We were herded off the train at Chelmsford and put on a bus that took us to our new homes in Great Baddow. What they did with us then (and I found out later that they had done this with my brother's group) was to herd the children from door to door, where each owner came out and chose the children they would take. The children were ushered in and then the party moved on. In my brother's case, apparently, he and his friend Ken Bruton were the last pair to find sanctuary. The final door had been knocked on and the woman had come to the door and said, 'Oh, no, I can't take boys. I said I'd take girls. I've got three girls and I really can't take boys.' Ron was ten years old and desperate. 'Please take us, lady,' he said, 'we're ever so clean.' 'We don't have candles in our noses,' Ken added (he meant unwiped snot), and sweet Mrs Barham took them in. Ron was very happy in that family, and to this day still sees Margaret, the youngest daughter.

My experience was the reverse of my brother's. I was picked immediately by the woman who opened the first door. 'Oh', she beamed, 'I'll take the little blonde child. She'll be a perfect playmate for my girl.' I was ushered into the house and told to go into the first room on the right, where I would find 'Little Davina'. Little Davina was a very dark, square sort of child and she went red with fury at the sight of me. Then she ran at me, kicked me in the shins and snatched my chocolate from me. That kick released all my misery. I screamed and wouldn't stop screaming until they'd called back the Evacuation Officer, who took me out of the house. It was then discovered that I had a brother and that he was at Mrs Barham's. She said she would take me in for the night but suggested they send for my mother, who came the next day. I was put in the house next door with a sad, quiet woman who had no children, called Mrs Edwards. My mother stayed for a couple of days and we sat in a cornfield full of poppies, and I was enchanted with the countryside. 'Why can't we live in a place like this?' I asked. 'Well, your father has to work. There's his meter-reading job, and there's his soldier work' – being too old to fight, Dad had volunteered for the Defence Corps – 'and I have to look after him and Peggy.' Peggy had started work at fourteen as a telephonist at the GPO (General Post Office).

So I was left in the uneasy company of Mrs Edwards. Before she left, my mother asked me if there was anything she could bring me when she came again. It so happened that a baby panda had been born in the zoo, and the London shops had toy pandas. Someone in our street had had one, and although I never played with or even liked dolls (my father had made me a doll's house one Christmas and I just bounced on the roof and smashed it), I wanted that panda. The upshot of this was that, unable to afford such a toy, my mother had painstakingly got a knitting pattern to make a knitted panda and presented the result to me on her next visit. 'This is not the panda I wanted.' I was crying and threw the pathetically sad knitted animal at her. 'This is not a panda at all. It's horrible.' To this day I feel ashamed and sick remembering the look on her face.

I had to start school again, and Mrs Edwards did not accompany me to school. She took me to the front garden gate and asked some boys to walk me to the village school. As soon as she had shut the door they all started chanting, 'She's a Vaccy, a dirty London Vaccy,' but no one actually hit me, and I was so enchanted with the pretty country lane that we walked down that I started picking flowers. That caused hilarity. 'Barmy Vaccy,' they shrieked, 'you can't eat them.' Nevertheless, I arrived at the small infant school with a bouquet of weeds, which was snatched from me the moment I got there. I sat miserably through the day, understanding nothing. There was no 'Pussy whose coat is so warm', there was no gorgeous Gordon, just the rough, jeering boys and girls.

After some days of agony, I luckily caught head lice and was sent home. Mrs Edwards was horrified and had no idea that she had to buy some nasty black soap to get the nits out, so she asked for my mother to come and deal with the situation. When my mother saw how inept Mrs Edwards was and how miserable I was, she decided to take me back to London. There seemed to be 'nothing going on on the war front' (indeed, that period at the beginning of the war was called the Phoney War), so why not take me home? I think she was also missing me dreadfully – she certainly never sent me away again. So I spent the rest of the war in north London, which later was quite heavily bombed. Ron seemed happy, so she left him in Essex until she brought him home just in time for the bombing because he'd got a scholarship to the grammar school.

For some reason, I think probably fear that the authorities would force her to evacuate me again, she failed to send me to school; it just wasn't mentioned again, and it was at this point my mother had chanced on the KY School in Wood Green, and I was busy training three or four times a week to fulfil my destiny.

Madame Yandie, who I think was considered a very attractive, slightly exotic thirty-two-year-old, couldn't have children, and soon after I started classes she asked my mother if she could adopt me. The idea being, I suppose, that she could give me 'a better life'. (After all, she lived the other side of Lordship Lane, where the posh houses started.) But having received a firm refusal from my mother, she nevertheless petted me and made much of me, though there was something about her that always made me feel uncomfortable. I just couldn't like her, even though she was very good to me.

Soon after I started classes, she gave me her first great gift. She gave me a book called *More About Josie, Click and Bun* by Enid Blyton. I don't remember having seen a book before – there were none in the house, except maybe an almanac or possibly a household manual. There were no comics because expenses didn't run to them, and yet somehow I had learned to read, because when I was about four I was in my father's arms, waiting for a bus outside the Regal Cinema, Edmonton, when I looked up at the huge Bovril advertisement on a hoarding and read slowly and clearly: 'BOVRIL PUTS BEEF INTO YOU'. I knew immediately that I had upset my father as he turned miserably to my mother, saying, as if having to admit to a sad defect, 'She can read.'

I think I probably knew those five words because I had been brought up on Bovril and had looked at the jar daily. The only other way I think I might have picked up a bit of reading was at Sunday school, which I'd attended since I was three (my mother had to keep on the right side of Father Waton), and there had been lots of picture books of Jesus, my favourite being one of a very handsome, very blond Jesus holding out his arms and saying, 'Suffer the little children to come unto me.' I was slightly worried about the suffering bit, but intrigued to see that many of the children in the semicircle around Jesus weren't the same colour as me.

My father's misery at my being able to read was because he made up stories to tell me from his own imagination, and he saw all that ending.

I was never quite sure just how well he *could* read. I never saw him with a book. He read the newspaper in the evening, but as I grew older I suspected that he just read headlines and the comic strips. He had received very little education as he had left school at twelve years old, although he did have beautiful copperplate handwriting. His father had been a carpenter in Glasgow and at some point had moved the whole family down to Birmingham. My father was the youngest of thirteen children: three had died in childbirth, five boys and five girls had grown to adulthood. Soon after he left school he was employed as under-chauffeur (my father always pronounced it with a French accent) to the Marquis de Soveral, the Portuguese ambassador, at his house in Surrey. Most of his brothers and sisters were in service, and I suppose one of them got him the job. He wasn't allowed to drive and the chauffeur refused to teach him – he was there to clean the car and keep the driver awake when they were waiting for the ambassador to leave a party. I believe the ambassador was a friend of Edward VII and was quite a party man. At fourteen my father thought he'd like to have a go at driving, and thinking that the chauffeur was well out of the way, backed the car out into the mews. He was reported and sacked immediately.

After that he did various jobs, but was mostly in service until World War I started in 1914, when he joined the London Irish Rifles, a territorial unit that was not intended for action abroad. However, the war was going so badly that they were asked to volunteer – which they all did. After one year in France he was invalided out, not because of a bravely earned wound but because a doctor at the front thought his feet too deformed for action. Back in England, he was put in charge of German prisoners.

After the war he had met and wanted to marry his first wife, Kitty. So if, as I believe, he had gone back into service he would have had to give in his notice, as you could only be married if you were both servants in the same house.

His marriage to Kitty was clearly for love, as the wedding photographs show, and sometime after Peggy was born in 1922 the little family moved into Grandmother's house as lodgers. But my father, finding it difficult to get regular employment, took off to New Zealand, where he hoped there would be more opportunity, on the understanding that Kitty with Peggy would follow.

He had scarcely set foot in that country when news came that his wife was pregnant again and would not be coming to join him. How long he stayed there I don't know, but he was certainly home for his wife's death in childbirth. My brother says that things didn't go well in New Zealand, but when our father died I found a photograph of a young Maori woman sewn into one of his jackets. After Kitty's funeral he managed to get a job with Hackney Borough Council as a meter reader, and having waited a year for propriety's sake, he married my mother. Though he was working class and clearly feckless, my mother must have thought that she could pull him into shape.

He was certainly considered a good-looking man. He was a keen gymnast and entertained at parties, singing songs from the music hall, which he followed faithfully, and he loved making people laugh. Children adored him – my dancing friends called him 'Uncle Funny Man'. But as I grew older I realised that not only was he totally uneducated, but that he had weird blanks in his brain. For instance, when the first motorway was built, my father insisted on calling it the MI (pronounced 'eye'), even when I explained that there would be an M2 and an M3, and so on.

Other people laughed, but I was sometimes ashamed at these lapses, though I admit there is something odd about my own brain. My old friend Jean Marsh once described it as being like Gruyère cheese – full of holes – and there is no doubt I have him to thank for my imagination.

He told me the most wonderful stories. They would start something like this: 'There was this boy, you see, about twelve he was, and he'd just started work at the Metal Box factory, but he soon got fed up of it, so he went down the docks and worked down there a bit, got himself some muscles, then thought, why not stow away on a boat – see the world, go to Timbuctoo – so he hid himself under a tarpaulin, and then wha' d'ya think happened?'

So I never got to read *Winnie-the-Pooh*.

My love for my father was unconditional until the beginning of the war, when the terrible possibility entered my head that he might be Hitler. It happened almost overnight. Someone must have told him that he 'looked a bit like Adolf'. This encouraged him to trim his moustache to look exactly like Hitler's and start to slick his hair across his forehead. He also wore a dark uniform with a peaked cap for his work. Everyone who came to the house remarked on the likeness. One day he came home very proud of himself and told us, 'I was on my knees reading the meter just off the Lower Clapton Road and this big woman, Jewish she was, I reckon, came up behind me, pushed me in the cupboard, locked the door, got the police in and told them she'd got Adolf Hitler, disguised as a meter reader, locked in her cupboard.' The police had evidently arrived and let my father out. He was thrilled at what had happened, and repeated the story to impressed neighbours without a hint of humour, just great pride at causing such a stir. It sounds absurd, but I was only five when this happened, and a little worm of doubt entered my mind that maybe, possibly, he really *was* Adolf. People laughed and admired him now, but when the Germans came and he was revealed as the terrible dictator I would be dragged out into the street and have my head shaved – I'd seen that happen on the Movietone News in the cinemas when my sister had taken me to see *Random Harvest*. Of course, I'd got a bit muddled there – if the Germans had arrived in Tottenham it would have meant that they had won, so I would have been in rather a good position as daughter of the Führer, but I worried away at the problem quietly, and spent a great deal of time working out how my mother, sister, brother and I could all squeeze into the lavatory to hide, as it was the only room with a lock, so that we could be safe from the baying hordes in the street.

The fact that my father's metamorphosis happened at the same time that I was given a book and started to read and didn't need my father's stories any more, didn't help the lack of trust I was beginning to have in him. Reading *More About*

Josie, Click and Bun had encouraged me to find the local library, and although my mother approved, my father just couldn't bear to see the books about the house, and said if I even once got a fine for not taking them back in time, he would forbid me from going to the library. That would have been terrible, for in the local council library I had found paradise. As I went up the steps to enter this hallowed hall, my excitement was so intense that I nearly always had to go to the lavatory, and to this day a bookshop can bring on the same feelings.

Of course, the worry about him being Adolf came and went and finally disappeared, and he replaced telling stories with teaching me cribbage, which we played night after night in the Anderson shelter when the bombing raids finally started. I've wondered often since why my father should have enjoyed looking like the most hated man of our time. It wasn't till reality shows started happening on television in the 1970s that I began to understand. He wanted to be a celebrity, and he would do anything to be noticed. I hope his 'dream of being famous for five minutes' was fulfilled when, years later, my parents went to holiday camps for their holidays (never Butlin's – that was 'too common', my mother would say when she really meant 'more expensive than the others'), and my father, in a grand gathering of contestants from various camps, held at a packed Lyceum in London, was crowned winner of the Mr Debonair Contest.

2

The first eight months of the war were strangely quiet. No church bells could ring, and ambulance sirens and car horns were silenced; not that the latter made much difference in Courtman Road, where hardly anyone had a car and the children, me included, played in the street unbothered by traffic. Cars and buses would swish down the Great Cambridge Road, but you rarely found either on the council estates.

The adults seemed a mixture of jittery and cross. They had been told that they were at war and they had sent their children away, had dug their gardens up to put in the Anderson shelters, kitted them out, and had put up their blackout curtains. But nothing seemed to be happening. People began to think that nothing would happen, and my mother wasn't the only one who had brought a child back to London. Eileen Poulter at number nine was back, and Pam Mitchell at number eleven.

The day war had been declared, my mother and Mrs Hayward next door at number fifteen had decided that they would like a gap made in the back garden fence. It was just stakes joined with wire, and the wire was ceremoniously cut by my father so that the two women, without having to dress up to go into the street to knock on each other's doors, could walk across the gardens in their pinnies and go through their back doors. It also meant that I could easily play with the Haywards' adorable three-year-old daughter, Dorothy. Six years later, the day that peace was declared, the fence was firmly wired back into place. Although the women had seen each other most days of the war for a chat and a cup of tea, and seemed to get on famously, and Dorothy had joined the KY School as well, all the friendly camaraderie that had prevailed during the war had to stop. Standards had to be kept up again. Mrs Hayward wasn't quite up to scratch, and her husband was 'not only a layabout but a *communist*', and 'if he likes the Russians so much, why doesn't he go and live there'.

I loved Mrs Hayward. My own mother was fat, but Mrs Hayward was enormous. She sashayed across the two back gardens with the grace of a South Sea Islander, her apron held together with large safety pins, her hair escaping from her victory roll hairstyle and falling round her face, always singing softly to herself. Playing in her house was preferable to ours because you didn't have to 'be careful'. There were two collapsed armchairs in her living room with stuffing hanging out (*we* had a vinyl three-piece suite), a table on which were spread newspapers when they ate (which I thought an excellent idea, as you could read at the same time as eating), and their lino was so worn you could see the concrete underneath. The Haywards chose, instead of an Anderson shelter, to have a Morrison shelter, which took up a large part of their living room. They were made of steel and about four or five people could crawl under them. Later, when the raids started, my mother and I were in their house one afternoon when the bombs were dropping even as the siren went. So our mothers literally threw Dorothy and me under the Morrison, then tried to get under themselves, but they were too fat and both only got their top halves under and had to leave their bottoms sticking out. We were all hysterical with laughter, but when finally the all-clear went and we got up, we found that a house just up the road had had a direct hit and two people had been killed.

I had settled back home happily. I was going to dancing lessons now three or four times a week, but still nobody seemed to have remembered that I should be at school. It's possible that, Devonshire Hill Primary School being closed down, with everyone evacuated, the only school left was Risley Avenue, in a rather rough part of the estate, and my mother couldn't bring herself to send me there.

For several months after I'd been brought back from Essex I was mostly at home alone with my mother, playing with Dorothy next door and going to dancing classes. My father, being too old to fight, had volunteered a year before the war started, when things weren't looking good, to join the Defence Corps. To my mother's fury this patriotic gesture now meant that he was billeted at Mill Hill guarding a gunpowder factory. My sister did long hours at the GPO, and I was in bed by the time she came home, and my brother was still in Great Baddow.

My mother had added to her skill as a dressmaker and learned to smock, and she became very fast at delicately embroidering the tiny pleats that decorated upmarket children's clothes. It meant that she could work at home for a local factory, and as I grew older I was dispatched to collect and deliver the bundles of cloth. She did this work for several hours a day and she did it until she was ninety. There was no way we could have lived on my father's wages as an electric meter reader, and even with two wages and Peggy's contribution coming in we knew that it was pointless to ask for a bun or cake on a Thursday – there wouldn't be enough money till Dad's Friday pay packet. Then there would often be a celebration as I was sent to the fried fish shop in Lordship Lane for fish and chips for five.

My mother was never idle. She was either sewing, cleaning or cooking, though her efforts at the latter were disastrous. It's true that everything was rationed, but what we did have she mostly managed to ruin. My father would grow delicious fresh vegetables and my mother would boil them until they were mush. Early on in the war there were tips on the wireless on 'How to make your rations go further'. One of these tips was to take the small amount of meat allowed and roast it on a Friday afternoon, let it cool in the larder until Sunday morning, when you would then be able to cut it into very thin slices because it was so cold, and lay these slices at the bottom of a Pyrex dish, make gravy with a few spoonfuls of Bisto in hot water, pour it over the grey meat and stick it in the oven to warm up. It meant that everyone had two very thin, leathery, vile-tasting slices of meat instead of one delicious slice of freshly cooked lamb or beef, and of course no roast potatoes. For years I didn't understand why anyone looked forward to 'A Lovely Sunday Roast'.

Only on a Sunday did we eat at the table in the living room. Every other day of the week we ate at the oilcloth-covered kitchen table where, often at the same time you were eating, someone was washing themselves at the kitchen sink (the only sink we had), getting ready to go to work or school or just to 'go out'. Which meant that you were often splashed while eating or knocked on the head by someone reaching over the table to get the towel which hung on the larder door.

An average weekly menu would be:

SUNDAY: The horrible non-roast

MONDAY: Another pale blue-grey slice of the horrible meat with chips

TUESDAY: The final remains of the meat made into a practically all-potato cottage pie

WEDNESDAY: Spam and boiled potatoes

THURSDAY: Egg and chips. (We were lucky that there were plenty of eggs because we kept chickens)

FRIDAY: With luck, fish and chips from the shop

SATURDAY: A tin of Fray Bentos corned beef and mash

Only in the summer when I could eat fresh lettuce, tomatoes and radishes from Dad's allotment did I eat much.

My not eating was a problem from the beginning. Also my not sleeping. I was taken 'round the corner' to see the GP – everything was 'round the corner', a ten-minute walk that followed the bend in the Great Cambridge Road that took us to the shops, the library, the post office and the lovely soft-speaking Indian doctor. He told my mother that to get me to eat she was to give me my breakfast (a bowl of porridge and a jam sandwich) in bed and let me read a book while eating. This she did, and I began to eat. (I have had breakfast in bed whenever possible ever since.) But he also suggested that there might be something wrong with my digestive tract and gave us a letter for the hospital. There I was given what was called 'sunray treatment', which meant that I just had to lie naked under a warm lamp, which was quite enjoyable, and the doctors told my mother I was never to be given the white of an egg, only the yolk. She thought that diagnosis utterly ridiculous so she took no notice of it, and we never went back to the hospital. I was taken to the doctor several times because I didn't sleep much. I would wander from room to room hoping that someone wouldn't be asleep and would talk to me, and would always end up waking my mother. The doctor had no cure. He just said, 'She has too much imagination.'

Insomnia is a horrible affliction and when, finally, as an adult, I took myself to a sleep farm in the States and it was proved that, even when apparently sleeping, I never went down into the deep sleep we all need but stayed in REM (rapid eye movement) all night – which means that you are dreaming continuously and keep waking – and I was given sleeping tablets, that I at last could sleep. It was like starting a new life. I could take a pill and sleep. Absolute bliss – and I was no longer exhausted half the time. I've been taking them steadily for over fifty-five years. I'm sure there are other treatments today, but it's too late for me to try anything else, though I'm really glad that the work on sleep deprivation has totally proved that we all have different sleep patterns, and if I was allowed to go to sleep at 4 a.m. and get up at twelve noon, I probably wouldn't be an insomniac. Maybe my ancient forebears did the night shift.

After a year at the KY School I had become Madame Yandie's star pupil. I don't think this was because I was a better dancer than the others (Maureen Kean, with whom I did duets, was first-rate), but because I had blonde curly hair and big eyes everyone fancied I looked like Shirley Temple. In fact, by the time I was six my hair had lost its curl; but my mother couldn't bear me to have straight hair, so every night she would soak my hair in Amami setting lotion and roll my hair in rags, and I had to try to sleep with these tight little knots all over my head. Nevertheless, the trick worked and I had curly hair each morning, so there was still a possibility that I might become

Tottenham's own Shirley Temple – which was what Madame Yandie had in mind. It was a far cry from Pavlova. She suggested to my parents (she flirted outrageously with my father, and in later years I wondered if they had had an affair) that they have cards printed saying

---

BABY EILEEN
SOUBRETTE AND DANCER

ENQUIRIES MR ATKINS   OR MADAME YANDIE

17 COURTMAN ROAD   THE K.Y. SCHOOL

TOTTENHAM   65 BOUNDARY RD, WOOD GREEN

I never did know what 'soubrette' meant. I've just looked it up in the Concise Oxford English Dictionary to find that it means 'maidservant or similar character implying pertness, intrigue and coquetry'. God knows what Madame Yandie thought it meant, and my parents certainly never had a clue.

I was to perform a solo song and dance act at working men's clubs. I would be paid, Madame assured us, fifteen shillings an engagement for just one number in an evening along with other artistes (it was always pronounced *arteests*) and I would become a little star. Both parents were very happy with the idea. I was told that a third of the money would be put away in the savings bank for me, and I wanted a bicycle, so I was up for it too. I was six.

There are still plenty of working men's clubs in existence, and I think that they are useful, friendly places and these days are much more inclusive of women, but in the 1940s, though they may have had a 'ladies' night' occasionally, they were really exclusively male.

My first gig was at a working men's club in Finsbury Park, and both my mother and father were excited at the prospect, but I disliked everything about it. I didn't like being hauled away from the living room fire in the evening to go out in the cold, and down into the tube, which already had groups sleeping on the platform, and was soon to be so packed with people sheltering there that you had to step over sleeping bodies. I didn't like the fog of smoke that hit you as you entered the hall of the club, the strong smell of beer and the overpowering odour of male sweat, and I didn't like the way the other 'arteests' looked at me.

There seemed to be only one protective rule for child performers and that was that they must be kept separate from the other performers. This in most cases meant that a curtain was hung across the corner of a dressing room – mostly one room for both sexes – and I was shoved behind it with my mother, zipped out of my siren suit and dressed in fancy little outfits, mostly with frilly knickers. I don't know if the word 'paedophilia' was known in Tottenham – but one of the other performers would mutter, soon after my arrival as I disappeared behind the curtain, 'Well, there's a treat for the dirty old men out there tonight then.' 'I hate working with bloody kids.' 'Yeah, they don't have to bother with talent – just show their arses.' Throughout this talk my mother would get flustered and try to distract me, and later, when she got more confident, she would put her head round the edge of the curtain and tell them to 'be quiet, you'll upset the child'.

That first night 'Baby Eileen' was announced, and as the pianist struck up with my number I walked up the steps to the platform dressed in a white cotton swimming costume with big red spots painted on it and a pair of flimsy wings attached to my back and to the middle fingers of both hands, and sang:

> The Love Bug will get you if you don't watch out
> If he ever bites you then you sing and shout
> You shout a-hidey-hidey-hi, and a-hidey-hidey-ho
> And that's what love is all about

And I tap-danced. My audience knew the song and were ready to join in with the 'hidey-hi's' and 'hidey-ho's', and the applause was generous. I couldn't sing for toffee but I could 'put a song over', as Madame Yandie called it, and I tap-danced well, so Baby Eileen's career was launched.

My repertoire moved on from 'The Love Bug' and 'Animal Crackers In My Soup' to 'Shine On Harvest Moon', 'Sunny Side Of The Street', 'Mairzy Doats And Dozy Doats' and dozens more, as I tapped my way across Tottenham.

Then, when I was seven or eight, Madame gave me her version of two 'French' songs to do. The first was 'I Got Ze Eye', the chorus of which was:

> I got ze eye, I got ze wink (wink at audience)
> Ze wink that makes ze fellows think
> I got ze mouth zat goes like zis (kiss the air)
> Ooh là là I am French and a Frenchy girl can kiss
> I got ze smile (smile) I got ze style (hand on hip)
> Zat makes ze old men young la la (look naughty)
> Zey hug and squeeze me like a sheik (cuddle yourself)
> Zen zey kiss me on ze (pause) cheek
> Oh là là comme ci comme ça

The second 'French' song was called 'Fifty Million Frenchmen Can't Be Wrong', most of which I didn't understand and which I now know was a modified version of lyrics written by Cole Porter. The last few lines were:

> And all over France, they're full of romance
> They say policemen wear embroidery on their pants
> And all the best married men in France they say
> All blot their copy books each day
> Fifty million Frenchmen can't be wrong

All done with suitable (or unsuitable) gestures.

But although I did these gigs regularly in working men's clubs, with my mother in tow, as I grew a little older I began to feel embarrassed, even though I wasn't the only child doing it. A girl called Shani Wallis (the first 'Nancy' in *Oliver*), who had a wonderful voice, was beginning to be quite famous from doing clubs, but she really could sing and didn't have to waggle her bottom.

I always felt when I was doing my 'sexy' numbers that there was something slightly wrong, but I really didn't know exactly why until at a party at a schoolfriend's house I was encouraged to do one of my numbers. I did Carmen Miranda's famous song 'I Yi Yi Yi Yi I Like You Very Much', shaking my non-existent breasts and gyrating my bottom in an exaggerated fashion because I thought it would make the girls laugh – which it did. My friend's father was a vicar, and he sent me home with a note for my mother saying that what she was encouraging me to do was disgusting. I was ashamed for myself and ashamed that my mother was criticised, and upset that she was upset. 'What a prude,' she fumed. 'It's just a bit of fun.'

But my instinct told me the vicar was right. It was a

muddling situation to be in. I liked going to class and tapping with the other girls and learning routines; I liked the ballet dancing we did and I loved doing daring acrobatics, but when it came to going to the clubs with only my parents, and doing the so-called sexy songs, the fun went out of it.

It wasn't until after the war when I was thirteen that I finally rebelled. There were terrible arguments with my mother then, but luckily my grammar school had discovered my sleazy secret and told my mother that she was exhausting me and it should stop. So not only could I stop parading myself, I could stop having my hair curled every night, as she'd advanced from putting my hair in rags to learning to twirl my hair (soaked in Amami) round her middle finger and putting two hair grips either side of each curl, which was even more painful than sleeping in rags. At my grammar school hair had to be tied back if it was long, so I had bunches of curls which were easy to release for my night work.

But before then, as well as clubs I also performed at what my mother called 'Masonic Do's', which I found somewhat creepy as there was no stage, just a lot of men, often sitting round a table, while I sang and danced in a corner, but my mother insisted that it was a great honour to perform for the Masons and spoke in a hushed voice whenever I did a gig for them. There were also 'shows' put on by the KY School – lavishly cheap affairs that went on for hours, in which the finale always featured an older girl as Britannia and a patriotic line-up of tapping soldiers and sailors (we didn't do air force numbers). My mother made money by making clothes for almost every-one, and she had to be inventive as clothing coupons couldn't be spent on dancing dresses. The worst costume she ever made for me was an orange plastic affair and I can remember the sweat dripping on the floor as I danced. There were also competitions, talent shows and ballet exams.

When I was six, Madame Yandie put me on my blocks. These are ballet shoes with a wooden block at the end so that you can stand on your curled-up toes. In any decent ballet school you would never be put on your blocks before you were twelve or thirteen, when the bones in your feet had set. Till then you would only do soft-shoe ballet, but Madame Yandie had heard of this clever thing called toe tap. You put the metal that was used for tap shoes on the end of block-toed ballet shoes and stood on your toes and tap-danced. It must have looked very ugly, but it was thought to be clever, and Madame considered that I was just the child to bear a bit of pain to show off – and I was. I was so keen to be clever that I was soon toe-tap-dancing on three drums of different heights, jumping from one drum to another while dancing on my toes. This was the beginning of the massacre of my feet. Madame assured me that all great dancers had terrible feet, and though it is true that classical dancers tend not to have pretty feet, they are not as deformed as mine. After a year or two I was in such pain that my mother took me to a chiropodist in Tottenham High Road. He was shocked when he saw my feet, and appalled when he heard what toe tap was. He said I must stop doing it immediately, and block-toe ballet, and wear a corrective in my shoe, but I would probably need an operation on both feet. My eyes welled with tears. 'Look, you see, she's crying at the thought of not doing her toe-tapping.' 'You can still do ballet in flat ballet shoes,' the chiropodist said encouragingly, 'that is good for you,' and added to my mother, 'and let her walk about in the house barefoot.' 'Well, he doesn't know what he's talking about,' exploded my mother when we got outside.

'You'll catch your death of cold if you walk about barefoot.'
But I knew she was worried. Could this dancing be ruining
my feet? Should she stop the toe tap? But secretly we both
knew that the toe-tapping was what made me a star turn and
people were impressed by it. The next day she spelt out what
the chiropodist had said to Madame Yandie. It was received
with scorn. 'Mrs Atkins,' she said, 'do you really think that
they would *make* block-toed ballet shoes in small sizes if they
harmed little girls' feet?' So any qualms my mother had were
squashed and I continued to toe-tap.

It would be easy to say that they forced me to go on with
it, but although I realised that my feet were growing horribly
out of shape and I soon had to wear sandals all year round
(Bata sandals from a factory in Czechoslovakia, where Tom
Stoppard's father was employed as a doctor), as shoes were so
uncomfortable. I didn't complain because I knew that being
able to toe-tap was what made me extra special, and of course
I enjoyed the praise I got for it.

In September 1940 the bombing started in earnest. We were
all packed into the Anderson shelter, and the first time I heard
a bomb drop nearby I imitated the noise: 'Wheee . . . BANG!'
I shouted, clapping my hands. 'Thank God she's going to find it
funny,' my mother said to my father. I never found it funny again.

Night after night when the Blitz began we would trail down
the garden to the 'dugout', as my father called it. He was now
at home, as he had been discharged from the Defence Corps
because of his flat feet and bunions (my mother remembered
this when my feet were in trouble: 'It's her father our Eileen
gets her bad feet from, it's nothing to do with dancing', so it
was totally acceptable to continue to ruin feet that were ruined

anyway). My brother (now back home) and my sister would climb into their bunks, and my father and I would play cribbage with a little wooden scoreboard with matchsticks. 'Fifteen two, fifteen four, fifteen six and a pair's eight!' I would cry triumphantly, and my mother would sit absolutely terrified, sewing or knitting. I suppose we slept intermittently, and my insomnia was easier to bear with us all being squashed together in one small space and no one sleeping well anyway.

One evening when my sister was doing a late shift and the bombing had been continuous, word went round that St Paul's Cathedral had been hit. The GPO was close to St Paul's, and as it got later and Peggy didn't come home, our fears grew. She finally arrived just as dawn was breaking. She had had to walk all the way from the blitzed City, but she was triumphant that the GPO was still standing.

That winter was hard. I know that all big cities in England were bombed, but nothing like the endless bashing London withstood.

Suddenly one Sunday, to our amazement, my mother announced that we were not going to sleep in the Anderson shelter any longer. 'It's cold and damp down there,' she said. 'We've all got colds, and before we know where we are we'll be dead of pneumonia. We might as well take our chance and stay in the house.' So we arranged ourselves in the house. My mother and I slept in the alcove by the fire (chimneys were often left standing in bombed houses), my brother by the door that led to the passage, my sister under the door frame from the living room to the kitchen and my father in the bath, which was of course in the kitchen.

Three nights later, on the Wednesday night at about 3 a.m., our Anderson shelter had a direct hit from a high-explosive bomb. We would certainly all have been killed had we been in it. As it was, although the windows and doors of the house had been blown out and bits of ceiling had come down, no one was actually hurt. My father had a few cuts from the glass in the bathroom window, but that was all.

The ARP (Air Raid Precautions) wardens came to help us out of the house immediately as it was deemed unsafe, and one of the neighbours opposite us, Mrs Cannell, took us into her house with her twins for the rest of the night, and made us tea and found some biscuits. At one point when we were all crowding into the Cannells', it was noticed that my brother was missing – then we saw him walking across the road with his school uniform on a hanger. He had eluded the ARP and gone back into the house and upstairs to get it. He was proud that he'd got into Tottenham Grammar School, and there was no way he wasn't going to save his uniform.

In the morning we were moved down to St Benet Fink's church hall, which was packed with people who had been 'bombed out' all sitting and lying around on camp beds. It was horrible, as everyone was squashed together and it was too cold to go outside. Children were crying and the grown-ups were sitting miserably on the camp beds, or pestering any officials that came in, while the WVS (Women's Voluntary Service) handed out endless cups of tea. Suddenly into this melee came my determined saviour, Madame Yandie, looking tremendously glamorous in a fur coat, fur Cossack hat and brilliant scarlet-lipsticked lips. She lived near the church, and my father (I'm sure at my mother's entreaties) had walked to the house and told her what had happened. She offered to take me to her home immediately – no one else in the family – just me. Horrid as the atmosphere was in that church hall, I didn't want to leave my mother, but she assured me that it was for the best, and unwillingly I went back with Madame to her house. It was in a row of mock-Tudor houses set well back from the road with a huge grass verge and a front door that had stained glass. It made me nervous. Everyone else I knew lived in a council house or over a shop.

Madame Yandie who was also Mrs Slade had a husband called Leslie who played the piano at our shows. A small, bad-tempered-looking man (although he wasn't, actually) who my father dismissed as 'a bit of a nancy boy, not in Madame's league at all'. We all called Madame Yandie 'Madame', so it came as a bit of a shock when she took me to stay with her that she asked me to call her Auntie Kathleen. I can't have had to stay with her more than a few days, but it felt like months, and I was deeply uncomfortable the whole time. As soon as I was inside the house, she gave me some food and said she was sure I would like to have a nap after such a dreadful night.

It felt odd going to bed in the daytime, but I thought I should say yes. After about half an hour she got into bed with me, lifted my pyjama top and started lightly scratching my back with long, slow strokes. I was rigid with fear and embarrass-ment. Then she asked me if I liked her doing this. I couldn't speak. I had come from a family where no one hugged or cud-dled. The only affection any of us received was a kiss on the cheek when you went to bed. That she was lying in bed with me seemed weird, and that she should touch me in any way made me very uneasy. She went on for a bit longer, then got up and went away.

I didn't like it and I really didn't want to stay in her house. She had no idea what to do with me, and one day spent the whole afternoon teaching me to do 'a frayed edge' on a piece of silk as if I were a rich Victorian child. I remember thinking, Is this what she thinks children do at home?

Very soon after this she adopted a child of three, Wendy, and then went on to adopt two boys, so she must just have been desperate to have children, but I was horribly uneasy with her, and for all her generosity to me could never like her very much. My instinct told me she was a phoney. Everything about her was pretentious. Her made-up name, her made-up honours, her talk of working with the great Italian ballet master Cecchetti, the often ridiculous dances she dreamed up – when the actuality was that she was mainly teaching me how to shake my ass on stage.

Though the windows were still boarded up downstairs and we had to have the light on all the time, I was very happy to be home again. Then one afternoon an official-looking man knocked at our door. My mother answered it.

'Is this number seventeen?' he said briskly.

'Yes.'

'And was this house bombed recently?'

'No,' said my mother with great sarcasm. 'We like living like this.'

He soon wiped the smile off her face.

'It seems from the ARP report that there are two children in the house, one a boy who apparently attends Tottenham Grammar School, but the girl doesn't seem to attend any school. Or can you put me right on that?'

In the dark living room by the fire, I froze. I was going to have to go to school.

3

Risley Avenue School was a vast, ugly, Victorian building with high railings round it, and my first day there was horrible. It was pouring with rain, and although I was seven years old and certainly should have known how to tie a bow (I would have been putting on my own tap shoes for a couple of years), for some reason my mother had tied the thin string of my pixie-hooded mackintosh and she had done it in a double bow. As she did it I said, 'I won't be able to undo that knot,' but she assured me that I just had to pull the longest string and it would come undone.

It was about half an hour's walk to the school and my mother was smart enough to know that she mustn't take me, it would be too shaming at seven, so an older girl in the street was asked to look after me. When we arrived, somewhat bedraggled, she pointed me towards the infants' entrance and disappeared through the door marked in stone JUNIORS.

I followed the crowd to the cloakroom, where I pulled the long string of my pixie hood – and it just tightened. I tugged and tugged and all that happened was that the hole for my face got smaller and smaller. The bell was ringing and children were rushing off to classrooms, and I just sat on a bench still in my mac with just a nose and two half-eyes showing. Finally someone found me, extricated me from my raincoat, took me to a classroom and handed me over to the teacher there.

The teacher was called Miss Dear, but sadly she didn't look a dear – she looked very severe. She had a long face, with her hair in a centre parting and dragged firmly back behind her ears into a low bun. She looked a perfect caricature from a children's book of a frighteningly strict teacher. She was told why I was late and I managed to give my name, and a desk was found for me in the class of about thirty-five children.

I was cold and frightened and for the next several minutes I didn't understand a word that was said. It was all to do with making a table for subjects. The only tables I knew had four legs, and subjects were what kings and queens had in stories in books. I sat doing nothing while everyone else copied the hieroglyphics the teacher chalked on the blackboard. She finally noticed me. Where was my exercise book? My what? I was dumb. Where are your pencils? Rather than admitting that I had no exercise book or pencils, and that so far I hadn't followed a thing she had said, tears started to well in my eyes. I absolutely knew that it was the wrong move, but I couldn't stop them. She briskly found an exercise book and pencil for me and told me to copy what was on the board. But I paid for those tears at 'break', when as soon as we had finished drinking our obligatory small bottle of milk we were pushed out in the still-drizzling weather to play. 'Crybaby!' they all yelled round me as I tried to hide in the doorway. 'Stupid crybaby.' I climbed back up a couple of steps to try to get back into the building when someone caught a glimpse of my knickers. My knickers were a trial for me throughout the whole of my school life. My mother made them out of whatever she had left over from what she had been making. Any material was used that wasn't 'see-through'. So I had anything from scarlet satin, candy stripes to highly coloured flowered cotton, all with a high leg cut à la a 'bunny girl' outfit (sans tail). I longed for the soft navy bloomers that other girls had, but no matter how much I begged, my mother was adamant. She 'wasn't going to waste money on those ugly navy drawers'. At dancing class we all wore the same red cotton knickers, so I hadn't been bothered.

There was a great shout of 'she's got funny knickers on', and then no matter which way I turned or ran a boy would flick up my skirt and a shriek would go up. I was poked and pinched till the bell went, then it was back into the classroom where once again I sat, shaking from the playground ordeal and unable to take in anything that was said to me at all. At dinner time I ran home and said I wasn't going back. My mother said I had to go back, but that she would come for me after school and talk to the teacher. I didn't think that was a good idea either, but she was there at four o'clock and dragged me back into the class to see Miss Dear. When it was explained to her that I had only had a few days' schooling, Miss Dear turned out to be quite a dear after all, and promised that she would try to help me in the limited time she had with such a large class. But I couldn't tell them about the horrible teasing at the sight of my knickers because I was ashamed, not only for myself, but for my mother's poverty that I wore such strange underwear.

At the end of the week I told my mother there was no way I was going there again. I said I'd run away if she sent me.

I don't know whether my mother asked Madame Yandie for help or she just offered – all I know is that I would have had a very different life if she hadn't decided to pay two guineas a term (six pounds and six shillings a year) for me to go to a small private school called Parkside, which was sometimes referred to as a 'dame' school, literally only a three-minute walk from Risley Avenue.

I was taken by my mother and Madame the next Monday afternoon to meet the headmistress, Miss D. M. Hall (Dorothy Margaret).

I was enchanted by Parkside. It came as a wonderful surprise to find that at the end of Risley Avenue you suddenly came into the quiet calm of Church Lane, which not only had a beautiful church – All Hallows – but led straight into Bruce Castle Park, a park that looked like wild country to me, not a bit like the recreation ground where we played on the council estate, and there, in the lane opposite the park, behind a tall hedge, was the most lovely house I had ever seen. It sat elegantly back from the road behind a large, pretty garden. As we walked to the front door there were masses of small, gaily coloured upright little flowers either side of the path that I learned later were autumn crocus. To this day I can't see a flowering of autumn crocus without being transported back to my first magical footing into Parkside.

We were welcomed by Miss Hall herself. I loved the whole cut of her jib. She looked like Charlton Heston's younger sister. The same cheekbones and jawline, but her cheeks were rosy and her smile was wonderfully warm. I realise now that I'd never seen such an 'open' face. The people I lived among mostly had closed, tight faces. My mother's was taut much of the time, tense with worry. Dorothy Margaret Hall had had just enough education and just enough money to find her true place in life, and was totally fulfilled by her work. It could have sounded a sad story – a spinster lady having to earn her money by turning her own home into a school, which she ran with her seventy-year-old mother and a friend – but it wasn't. You knew immediately that Dorothy Margaret enjoyed life enormously.

We were ushered into her study, a sunny room overlooking the garden with a desk, a piano and two or three comfortable but upright chairs. As she offered my mother and Madame Yandie seats, a girl of about ten or eleven in a pretty peach-coloured dress with dark brown binding (the school uniform) knocked and came into the room, and Miss Hall said, 'Oh, Eleanor, have you finished your organ practice?'

'Yes, Miss Hall.'

'Then before you go home, would you like to show Eileen round the house? You wouldn't mind doing that for me, would you?'

Eleanor looked as though she wouldn't mind walking through fire and water for Miss Hall – Eleanor with a badge saying 'Prefect'; Eleanor who could play the organ – oh, why wasn't I called Eleanor, it sounded so romantic. And Eleanor took my hand (a girl I didn't know just taking my hand!) and gave me a tour of the house.

What had obviously been a garden at the back of the house was now cemented over – only a huge elm tree was left to spread its branches over the playground. All the schoolchildren – it catered for no more than sixty – came in down a pathway at the side of the house and entered via the playground by the back door. To the right of the door there was a large kitchen. 'That's mainly used by children who bring their own lunch.' 'Lunch', what was lunch? Then on the other side of the passage was a cloakroom. 'You'll have your own peg and a place to keep your plimsolls.' 'Plimsolls', what were plimsolls? 'And through here is the big classroom for the older children.' It was a huge room with an enormous window at either end where creamy-yellow cotton curtains gently moved with the breeze. It contained desks for about twenty children, a blackboard, and there was an organ in one corner. But best of all was a huge stove in the middle of the room with a big fireguard round it. 'So when it gets cold and wet, as it soon will,' said Eleanor, 'you dry your gloves and things round the stove.' It was the most inviting and exciting room I'd ever been in. It may have contained desks, but it was nothing to do with school as I'd known it so far. Upstairs there were two more lovely light classrooms. 'Mrs Hall's class, where I expect you'll be, and Miss Person's class for the babies – the five- and six-year-olds.'

Well, I couldn't wait to start.

I was given permission to not wear a uniform for the first few days, as my mother would have to make it because we couldn't afford to buy anything except the brown felt hat with a peach and brown band round it and a blazer, both bearing the school crest. My mother's copy of the school clothes, including a brown unpleated gymslip and creamy-peach blouse, were so accurate that I didn't look different in any way, though I had to beg her not to make the gymslip short. My knickers *had* to be kept a secret. I was to do the fifteen-minute bike ride four times a day as I was to go home for my dinner – or lunch, as I would learn to call it.

The first morning I was nervous but also excited. I was shown my peg and hung up my coat, then everyone went into the big classroom. The children whose classroom it was stood at their desks, the rest of us faced them. When we were all assembled, Mrs Hall went to the organ and we sang a hymn. That was easy. I knew my hymns. Then Miss Hall said a short prayer followed by a brief speech, which she ended by telling everyone that they were welcoming a new girl today who would be in Mrs Hall's class upstairs. Eileen wasn't in uniform yet but she soon would be, and she hoped that they would all make me welcome. Everyone was looking at me. I was the centre of attention. I lolled on one foot and hung my head down, simpering. Then I was marshalled upstairs by old Mrs Hall. She was short and plump with grey hair in a jolly bun on top of her head and half-glasses hanging on a string round her neck. She was dressed in a high-necked blouse and a skirt down to her ankles. Miss Hall's skirts were mid-calf, and she wore pretty silk blouses, soft jackets and sensible flat shoes. Old Mrs Hall looked Edwardian, but there was a lovely 1930s swing to Dorothy Margaret. I thought their clothes were beautiful in comparison to the ugly, knee-length utility clothes worn by everyone else that I knew.

'Arithmetic books out, please,' said Mrs Hall. 'We're going to attack division and multiplication this morning.' She could have been speaking Greek. Everyone opened their desks, took their exercise books out, and Mrs Hall chalked some sums on the board, and they all started to copy them down and work out the answers. It didn't take long for Mrs Hall to notice that I wasn't moving. I was staring at the board like a rabbit caught in headlamps.

'You'll find an exercise book for arithmetic in your desk, Eileen, and pens and pencils.'

Two treacherous tears gathered in my eyes. She came over and sat next to me.

'What's the matter?'

I couldn't speak. She put her arm round my shoulder and the tears splashed down. She handed me her handkerchief.

'We don't like tears at Parkside,' she said quietly. 'I want to help you, but I can't unless you tell me what is wrong.'

43

'I don't understand,' I choked out. 'I don't understand any-thing.' And I managed to explain that I'd only had a few days at other schools and had learned nothing. (Why had my mother not told them this?)

She suggested that I could come to school earlier or stay later every day and she would teach me on my own, and assured me that I would pick things up very quickly. She turned to the rest of the class.

'Eileen has had the hard luck not to have been to school before, so she has to catch up – but we'll all help her, won't we?'

So when milk break came, the children in my class were very friendly, and Angela Davis, a girl with wildly frizzy hair and a big round face with a watermelon smile, told me what sums were, and I realised that it was just what I did when I played cards with my father. By the end of the day, I was feeling that everything was going to be all right, and was happily putting my coat on to cycle home when an older boy came over to me.

'Miss Hall did an imitation of you when you left the class-room this morning,' he said slyly. 'She stood like you did' – he stood coyly on one leg – 'and said in a little girl voice, "Oooh look at me, I'm a *neeew*" – he drawled it out – "girl".'

Of course, it was totally out of order. I realise that had Miss Hall been working today she would probably have been sacked on the spot for doing such a thing, but it really was one of the best things that could have happened to me.

The shock was only momentary. My next thought, as I went to get my bike, was, Miss Hall is right, that was a silly way to behave. I behave like that because people seem to like it and think I'm cute, but I don't want to be a girl that Miss Hall thinks is a simpering show-off. I want her to admire me. I wanted that more than anything in the world. I already knew that she liked 'sensible' children with 'self-control'. She had said that in the morning talk. So I mustn't be silly, I mustn't cry and I mustn't, mustn't, mustn't simper and show off. I was aware that I possibly was a show-off – I'd already been called one by some boys on the estate one day when I'd insisted on cycling home from a dancing show in a red velvet cloak – I really fancied myself in it – and the boys had chanted at me, 'Show-off, show-off', and I never wore it in the street again.

But of course at dancing class I was instructed to show off all the time. 'Show them your nice big smile.' 'Show them how clever you are.' 'Show them your pretty knickers.' 'Show them how cheeky you are.' That was what they liked in the clubs.

I prayed that Miss Dorothy Margaret Hall never found out that I went to dancing class and did the clubs for fifteen shillings a go. I knew that I had entered a new world under her roof, and I didn't want to be thrown out of paradise. There would have to be secrets.

The next morning I was cycling past Risley Avenue School looking forward to my second day when I felt a sharp pain in my ankles and quickly realised that I was being pelted with large, sharp stones. Arthur Bartlett and his gang – my knicker tormentors from Risley Avenue were the perpetrators – yelling as they threw the stones – 'Stuck-up', 'Stuck-up bitch. Ain't we good enough for you?' They must have found out that I was now at Parkside.

I knew straight away that I mustn't complain about this incident at Parkside. Some of the children wouldn't like it that I'd been to the 'rough' school, and I didn't want to look a sissy. So when Mrs Hall noticed the cut on my leg, I said, 'I fell off my bike.' But I told my mother when I got home at lunchtime. She told my brother to cycle in with me the next morning, and

Arthur Bartlett and his gang stood on the pavement and glared, but didn't dare to throw a stone. Then I realised that if I went a slightly longer way round, I could cycle through All Hallows churchyard and cemetery and down Devonshire Hill, which was lined with cherry trees, which was a prettier route. I was beginning to be aware that the council estate was *not* pretty, it was just functional.

I happily settled in at Parkside. Jolly, sensible Angela became my best friend (and stayed a good friend till her death in her seventies). I finally admitted to her that I went to dancing classes. She immediately wanted to come as well. Amazingly, her mother, a young, attractive, good-natured woman, thought it was a good idea, and Angela turned out to be a wonderful acrobat. We both intended to join a circus as soon as possible, and spent much of our time together training for the trapeze by swinging from trees in Bruce Castle Park, contorting our bodies into unlikely positions, endlessly doing backflips and cartwheels in the air, and even rigging up a rope between our two beds at Angela's house to practise tightrope walking. God knows how, but we never really hurt ourselves.

I stayed at Angela's house often. I loved it there. They had a semi-detached house the other side of the park; she had a younger brother who was fun and her father was a travelling salesman. The whole atmosphere in the house seemed incredibly jolly to me, especially when her father was at home. I expect it was just that they were affectionate with each other. In my own home we all seemed to be leading different lives, and apart from sometimes managing to eat together there was very little 'family' life. Something told me not to ask if Angela could come to our house, and my mother never suggested it. She didn't want to have anything to do with Parkside. I don't think she ever went there again after that first meeting with Madame Yandie. She was probably nervous and thought it way out of her class, and luckily during the war there were no parents' meetings or open days. If I was at home with a cold, wrapped up in an eiderdown in an armchair by the fire, she would let me prattle on about school as she sat quietly smocking and saying little. But I would soon bury my head in a book, and with no one to irritate or annoy her, and nothing demanded of me, there would be a contented, sweet calm between us. These were the happiest times I spent with my mother.

My desire to be the kind of girl Miss Hall would approve of wasn't to be fulfilled easily. After a year I was moved into her class, and I became entirely addicted to her performance as a teacher. She was quite a turn. Charismatic, funny and sometimes joyously outrageous. If anyone said that they couldn't do something, she tended to say, 'Can't do it? Can't do it? Well, I might say I can't climb that wall out there round the playground, but if there was a German behind me with a bayonet at my bottom, I'd be up and over it in no time.' We loved it.

Another day, one of the very young children was weeping at the morning assembly because a bomb had dropped on a house in her road in the night and killed people that her family had been friendly with. I had passed the bombed house on my way to school on my bicycle, and stopped to watch as a body was pulled out and put on a stretcher. I knew it was a dead body and cycled on quickly, not wanting to see more.

When the child had gone upstairs with Miss Person to her class, Miss Hall said, 'Now, I don't want to hear anyone call Joan a crybaby. That was a very dreadful thing she had to see this morning.' In the pause that followed, an overexcited boy made the noise of a plane and crashed his hand on his desk, saying, 'Smash them to pieces.' Miss Hall surveyed him for a moment or two, then said, 'Simon, go into my study. I want to have a little talk with you. Everyone else, I'm going to give you paper, and I want you to put on the paper something that you feel about this war. It can be a drawing or painting or you can write about it.' She disappeared and paper was given out. We were all very silent. I would have liked to have drawn a picture of what I'd witnessed that morning, but I was hopeless at drawing, so I just wrote a bit piously but nevertheless full-heartedly: 'Please God, give us peace', and coloured the words ornately.

When she came back with a thoughtful-looking Simon, she walked all around the room looking at what children were drawing or writing. I think most were crude drawings of bombs and ruined houses. Then she collected them and, one by one, burnt them in the stove. As we watched, she said, 'I'm sure that all those brave men fighting for us will soon bring us peace and will be grateful for those little flames of prayers, but let us burn all these thoughts of hatred and fear, because the best way to fight the Germans is to forget those nasty thoughts and think cheerful ones instead. And the first cheerful thought *I* have is that it's a lovely day, and why don't we all put our plimsolls on and run round the park?'

We went into the park to play games each week, and it was there I first saw a beam of approval from her. I was the fastest runner, and although I wasn't much good at hitting the ball in rounders, I was good at catching.

One day in the park she walked me away from the others and asked me if I slept well. I admitted that I didn't. 'I don't like those dark circles round your eyes. What's keeping you from sleeping? What are you worried about?' At eight or nine you don't say, 'Well, life, death – the whole damn thing', so I said I didn't know. 'You try and work out what's keeping you awake and tell me, would you? Because I would be interested and I might be able to help. We don't want you to be a nervy girl, do we?' So it was good that I could run fast and catch, but I mustn't have 'nerves'. I often heard my mother say I had 'nerves'. Well, I would try very hard not to have 'nerves'. I wanted to be like Geraldine Holmes, the golden girl of the school, who looked like the advertisement on the Ovaltine tin – blonde, pink-cheeked and blue-eyed, without a trace of a dark circle, full of smiling confidence.

By the time I was eight or nine my hair was no longer blonde – if you were kind you called me 'fair'. If not, 'mousy'. And it would have been straight if I wasn't being tortured at night with the knotted rags.

I had a slight envy of Geraldine, who was clearly Miss Hall's favourite. She had two best friends, Sheila Whitford and Pauline Daly. When we were ten, Geraldine was Head Girl and Pauline was Vice Captain (a title we were too innocent to find funny). Geraldine Holmes finally admitted me into her magic circle when I bumped into her as I was coming out of Totterdells, the bookshop in the High Road near the Spurs football ground. I would save up my pocket money, which was easy as there were hardly any sweets to spend money on they were so strictly rationed, and I didn't have much of a sweet tooth anyway. So every six or eight weeks I would buy a new book – mostly at that age by Enid Blyton – as a new book gave that extra thrill a library book couldn't. I think Geraldine was impressed that I had the money to buy books, and I saw her sizing me up and thinking, Maybe she's not quite what I thought. Maybe she'll 'do' after all (I can't tell you how many

hundreds of times I've seen that look on people's faces throughout my life), and she invited me back to her three-storey house
across the road.

I'd cracked it. I was 'in'.

Angela was still my best friend, but we were now invited to
Sheila and Pauline's houses, as well. (It was at Sheila's house,
the Rectory, that I had shocked her father, the vicar, by doing
my Carmen Miranda act in a bid to entertain my new friends.)

And it was at Pauline's house that I was first given powdered eggs and realised I liked cheese. My mother had told
my brother and me that we didn't like cheese and would eat
our ration every week. So when I came home saying that I
liked cheese, she went into a fury. 'No, you don't. You know
you don't like cheese.' (And then her guilt clearly making her
angrier, she turned her rage on the reconstituted egg.) 'And
why on earth are you saying that you like *powdered egg* when
we have real eggs at home?' But I think her anger was mainly
because I was enjoying going to other people's houses and she
was afraid that in comparison, 17 Courtman Road wouldn't
come up to scratch.

By the time I was ten I was definitely one of the elite top girls
at Parkside, but felt that Miss Hall still had some reservations.
There was still something suspect about me. Was I really made
of the right stuff? And then one day she stopped me as I was
going home and said would I like to come to school at six fifteen
the next morning and sell yellow flags for Princess Alexandra
Rose Day with her and Geraldine? We had to start early to
catch people going to work. Mrs Daly had evidently refused to
allow Pauline to do it. 'Yes. Yes. I would like to. Yes, of course
my mother will let me do it.' I raced home to demand permission. Grudgingly my mother gave it. At six the next morning

it was cold and raining quite heavily. 'She won't go out on a morning like this,' my mother said. 'She will. She will,' I said, and raced off into the filthy rain and sleet on my bike.

Miss Hall looked quite surprised to see me. 'I didn't think you would come in this weather,' she said. 'Geraldine's mother has phoned to say she's not coming.' (Thank God we didn't have a phone.) So here I was, ready and willing and one up on sissy Geraldine. I was given the tin for the money and Miss Hall had the tray with the yellow cardboard flowers on a pin. We walked together under her big umbrella to the main road and placed ourselves by a bus stop. For nearly two hours we sold flags, and I was blissfully happy. I was pleasing Miss Hall. I behaved politely but not shyly with people and thanked them for their money. I didn't complain once about the cold or wet, and Miss Hall was treating me like a grown-up. Soon after eight she said that we would walk back and have some break-fast. 'You deserve it,' she said. 'You've really surprised me this morning, Eileen. I'm very proud of you.' I nearly broke the first rule of Parkside and cried with joy. And then to sit at the table in the lovely kitchen, all tiled and pretty, after we had been given warm towels to dry ourselves, and eat eggs and bacon with Miss Hall – well, my cup runneth over.

I didn't make one mistake. Although when Geraldine Holmes arrived at a quarter to nine and saw me finishing my breakfast, and said she was sorry her mother hadn't let her come, and Miss Hall said, 'Never mind, Geraldine. I had Eileen to help me, and she was champion at it', I had to make a huge effort not to smirk and look triumphant.

Dorothy Margaret Hall was my first saviour. I dread to think what an obnoxious child I would have been without her influence. Until I was seven I had been totally spoilt at home, and

Miss Hall grounded me. Her charismatic magnetism made me want to behave well (although I certainly haven't always kept to Parkside standards), and I'm grateful to her to this day.

The eleven-plus examination – or the scholarship, as it was called – now loomed over us. Miss Hall didn't make too much fuss about it, but at home I was made very aware that I was expected to pass the examination. Both my brother and sister had, therefore I, with my private education, *had* to pass. My mother was tense with anxiety. Although I was going to be a dancer and it wouldn't matter if I wasn't academic, I would shame her if I had to go to an elementary second-ary school or the technical school. My brother had been to Tottenham Grammar School for Boys, and my sister had been to Tottenham High School for Girls. I wanted to go to the con-vent school that Angela hoped to go to, but my mother didn't want me to go there for some reason, presumably because she didn't want me to become a Catholic. You had to name your first three choices of school that you would like to go to if you passed, and my mother took it into her head to visit a woman in Edmonton who was, apparently, my godmother, to ask her advice. I had never seen or heard of this woman, and she cer-tainly had no desire to meet me. I was taken to her house but told to stay in another room while she talked with my mother. It was a gloomy room filled with china and I sat not moving till my mother took me home, the woman having spoken not more than a few sharp words to me. However, my mother had been convinced by this woman that my first choice of grammar school must be the Latymer School in Edmonton, which took both boys and girls.

We took the exam – reading, writing and arithmetic – and then had the anxious weeks waiting for the results. On one of those days, as we weren't doing much serious work, Miss Hall said, 'Why don't you girls amuse yourselves by doing a play together?' A play? I had no idea what a 'play' was. I knew about 'shows', I knew there was music hall and once I'd seen a pantomime, but a play . . . ? Miss Hall suggested that we do *Little Women*. Well, I'd read the book, so I was all prepared and knew that I had to play Jo – clever, courageous, witty Jo. I was perfect. The other girls wouldn't hear of it. 'No, no, Eileen, you're Amy. You have to be Amy.' Oh dear – the spoilt, silly one who behaved quite badly. Is that how they still saw me? But all was forgotten when we started to learn our lines and rehearse, which we were left to do by ourselves. I had never had so much fun in my life. I found that I loved being Amy, and when we finally performed the play to the three teachers and half a dozen older children, and they laughed at some of the things that Amy said, it gave me a thrill that I had never experienced when dancing for an audience. I immediately wanted to experience the thrill of it again, and straight away suggested that we do another play. The others weren't so keen, but I wasn't to be put off. Miss Hall gave me a few more plays to read (they were all no more than a few scenes put together to last about half an hour), and there was one about a king and queen and two servants that I thought was very funny, and I fancied playing the queen.

Opening scene:
    The Queen is pacing back and forth in a room in the Castle. She is clearly very cross. Enter the King, very dishevelled, with his crown sitting crookedly on his head.

QUEEN: Danilo, where *have* you been?

Well, I could see a laugh already, so I rounded up two boys and a younger girl and we performed the piece to the whole top classroom. It went down a treat. Then the exam results started to come through and there were no more plays.

Geraldine was the first to come in triumphantly and say that she had passed. Then Pauline, then Sheila, then Angela, and still I heard nothing. The atmosphere at home was horribly tense. Then early one morning, when I had given up all hope, the brown envelope came. I had passed. And I had passed for my first choice (well, my godmother's first choice): Edmonton Latymer.

The post had come very early and I leapt on my bike, forgetting breakfast, and cycled as fast as I could to Parkside. It was so early Miss Hall hadn't yet opened the back door. I stood alone in the playground, willing her to see me and open the door. At last she did. 'What are you doing here so early?' 'I've passed,' I said, waving the brown envelope at her. 'I've passed.' She looked momentarily surprised, then very, very pleased. 'Well, well,' she said, putting her arm round my shoulders and taking me inside. 'I think that deserves a cup of cocoa.'

Had I not become an actress I would almost certainly never have seen Dorothy Margaret again, but thirty-one years later, when I had been tricked into playing Shaw's *Saint Joan* at the outrageous age of forty-two, Miss Hall came to the Old Vic to see me. She was now in her mid-sixties, but to me she looked exactly the same as she had done all those years ago.

I had by then played leading parts in many plays in London, and I might have wondered why she had left it so long before coming to see her old pupil. I think she had finally ventured out because she felt that *Saint Joan* was a safe play. The first hit play I'd done was about a lesbian couple, *The Killing of Sister George* (the first British play about a female gay relationship), and I'd been in a lot of avant-garde plays that I think would have frightened her off, but she must have been sure that *Saint Joan* would be acceptable. I was thrilled that she had bothered to come. She walked into my dressing room with all the assurance of someone who spent their life backstage, saying, 'You naughty girl, you made me cry.' Laurence Olivier had said the same thing, but actors often lie backstage. I knew that Dorothy Margaret would only tell me the truth. We talked a little and I promised to visit Parkside with my new husband who I'd married during the run of the play.

So when the production had finished its run, I took Bill with me to have tea with Miss Hall. She made the tea in the kitchen and then we sat in the big classroom, the breeze still billowing the creamy-yellow curtains, the stove still there (unlit that day), the organ still in the corner, and we talked and talked.

She was upset at what she thought were ridiculous rules laid down for teachers by government ministers who had never taught in a classroom. 'I mean,' she said indignantly, 'this idiotic rule that you must no longer ask the children to read out loud in class, as those who are not good at reading are ashamed. Don't they *realise*,' she said with great emphasis, 'that I've sat the evening before working out exactly who will read what section and made *absolutely sure* that a boy or girl who finds it difficult gets to read an amusing paragraph, and they get a laugh and that makes them feel good and so they think it's worth sticking at it?' I could see that she was frustrated by the new rules and regulations, and she had my sympathy.

I could also see that she was proud of me, and that meant more to me than prizes and praise from anyone else, although of course she wouldn't have been so proud if she had known the life I had led in the thirty-one years since she'd seen me. I think she would have been shocked at much of what I'd done. But that afternoon I basked in her approval and could only be grateful that I'd been influenced by her. I certainly don't always *listen* to her, but there is her voice in my head every so often saying, 'Now, where is your self-control?' and, 'Are you really being sensible, Eileen?' and her face, with that raised quizzical eyebrow, looking at me thinking, Is she going to come up to scratch? Will she do?

4

We had a map of the world on the wall that had tiny flags on pins – red for the Russians, blue for Britain and her Allies, and black for the Germans (I don't remember us bothering much with the Japanese, but I fear that those flags would have been yellow) – and I could see the world growing blacker and blacker as the Germans advanced across Europe.

Everyone was very aware that we were likely to be invaded, and even I could understand that there was only a narrow stretch of water that flowed between us and France – after all, there were people who could *swim* it. Surely that nasty Hitler and his army would find it quite easy to invade. But every time I got really frightened, Mr Churchill would come onto the wireless with his stern but somehow comforting voice and tell me that I had to be brave. The weird thing was I always *did* feel brave after he had spoken to us, even though he didn't promise anything but a good fight. The whole mood of our house would change after he had spoken. Everyone would be cheerful, and the next day all the neighbours would be talking about 'What Winnie said last night'. It was as if God had spoken, and although he hadn't said anything good, somehow everything would be all right. I loved Mr Churchill. Even when I became an adult and realised that he hadn't always been wonderful, nothing that anyone said about him could change the fact that I loved him. And although, thanks to a bit of luck and a lot of bravery, we never *did* get invaded and Hitler decided to go to Russia instead, the war in England wasn't exactly a picnic. Not if you lived in a city.

At one point my mother attempted to get my brother and me out of London again and we went to stay with one of my father's sisters in a very pretty village in Oxfordshire called Minster Lovell. I simply loved it there, but my aunt lived in a sort of wooden shack with no running water, and after a few weeks my mother couldn't stand it. 'Hitler's not going to make us lower ourselves to living like that,' she said firmly as she bundled us into the train that would take the three of us home.

There would be quiet patches, sometimes for several months, and then the raids would start again. Then on my tenth birthday the first doodlebug or buzz bomb, as we called them, fell and one fell on Tottenham. I remember the excitement of waking that morning and then realising something terrible had happened. A new kind of bomb had dropped that was far bigger than anything we'd had before. What was worse was that it didn't drop from an aeroplane – the bomb itself was a plane and it somehow got under the radar so we didn't get an air raid warning. It was a vile bomb. Its engine would drone, then pause, drone, then pause, then there would be a horribly long pause and down it would come. You would hear it coming in the distance and you prayed it didn't come your way, and if it did, you prayed that it didn't stop anywhere above your head, and if it did you then prayed that it did a swerve and fell on someone else, because sometimes you were thanking God that it had passed over you and some other poor devil was going to get it when it turned, after you heard the engine stop, and fell backwards. They were terrifying, and I had such feelings of guilt at the relief when I heard the bomb fall on other people. The rockets, or V-2s, that came next were more powerful than the buzz bombs, but as there was absolutely no warning of them at all, by the time you heard the crash it was all over – some people were dead, some were injured, but it wasn't you. I remember being in Bruce Castle Park with Angela when one dropped not far away. There was an enormous explosion and we both leapt into some bushes. Then we became so hysterical with relief that it wasn't us that we couldn't stop laughing. We lay in the prickly bushes with tears streaming down our cheeks, and every time we tried to get up we fell over again. I suppose that was the terrible excitement of the war – the kick of adrenaline as you realised that you hadn't been killed. It made you feel very alive.

In our family my father was too old to be in anything but the Home Guard, and my brother was too young. The only relative who was killed was a cousin, Roland – my Aunt Esther and Uncle Harry's son. He was a pilot, and it was early in the war that he was shot down, so I must have been about six years old and my mother had invited Uncle Harry and Aunt Esther to Sunday dinner (that is, lunch). Everyone was sitting down at the table when my mother noticed that Aunt Esther was still in the garden and she sent me to tell her we were about to eat. Esther was a small, frail-looking woman who had had three children die in infancy and only a daughter, Joy, and Roland had reached adulthood. She looked incredibly sad perched on a deckchair, gazing blankly over the allotments. 'Aunt Esther,' I said, 'Mum says please come and sit down.' There was a long pause and I began to wonder if she had heard me. Then she turned her head and focused on me and I realised that she was angry. 'They know nothing,' she said, 'and they tell lies. I've lost three babies and now my Roland has been taken from me. There is no God. All that stuff about Heaven is rubbish. Don't listen to them.'

I was tremendously shocked that anyone should say such a thing. I felt that if I told anyone Aunt Esther would be punished in some way – maybe even put in prison – and I liked her and felt sorry for her, so I never told anyone. But it had opened up in my mind a nagging question mark. Was it possible she might be right? Suppose it *was* all rubbish? Another story – like Father Christmas. For a moment my faith in both God and grown-ups wobbled. As a child I continued to believe (and even today I don't want to totally disbelieve and am an agnostic). But Aunt Esther had sown a seed of distrust, and it didn't fall on stony ground. A green shoot of suspicion whispered that maybe my parents weren't always to be totally relied upon.

Despite the bombing I was always busy. There was school, and there were dancing lessons at least four times a week and always on Saturday mornings. There were my performances late at night at clubs, all made so long by transport to the venue and back in a blacked-out Britain – hardly anyone had cars – and yet I remember I spent a great deal of time playing in the street and up at the recreation ground with the council estate kids. I suppose 'going out to play' mostly happened in the school holidays, but I don't remember any of the local children bullying me for going to a private school – rather the reverse. I seemed often to take the role of leader even when there were boys in the group.

One sunny summer's day in the holidays about a dozen of us

from the street who had bicycles decided to go on a long bike ride to Enfield, which we thought of as 'the country'. Off we set with a picnic – slices of bread and jam or bread and dripping (my favourite) with the odd apple or tomato between us. I felt very much in charge and pleased with myself, as I knew the way and had led them up the arterial road to a good spot in a field by a stream. We had eaten our food and were all having a good time, the girls paddling in the water and climbing trees with some of the bigger boys, while the young ones roared around the field pretending to be aeroplanes. Suddenly there was a scream. One small barefoot boy had trodden on some hidden rusty barbed wire and it was well embedded in the sole of his foot. He sat on the ground terrified and in pain, and we all rushed in a circle round him looking at him in horror. Someone said, 'We 'ave to pull it out,' and then everyone looked at me. It was my outing and I had taken the lead, but I was paralysed with fright. After what seemed a horribly long time one of the Nutting boys, who came from the poorest family in the street, and who I'd been a bit annoyed had come with us on the ride and wondered where they had pinched their bikes from, stepped over to the small boy, took hold of his ankle and pulled the barbed wire out. Then one of the girls wetted a rag she was using as a hanky in the stream and someone else had some string they tied the foot up with. He couldn't cycle home, so one boy took him on his crossbar and another cycled with his empty bike. I don't think I said a word all the way home. I felt so ashamed that I hadn't had the courage to pull the barbed wire out, or had any idea how to deal with the accident at all. I was a failure. A wimp. I wasn't made of the right stuff, and Miss Hall certainly would have been very ashamed of me. When we reached our houses dear little Dorothy, my friend next door, said, 'It wasn't your fault.' But I'd been a coward. I was always being told how brave I was to go out on the stage and that I was brave to do such dangerous acrobatics, but when it came to helping someone in pain with a simple act of taking some barbed wire from a bloody foot, I'd bottled out. I discovered I couldn't do it. It was important in those days of war to feel that you could be brave if the moment came. I'd let England down.

After Pearl Harbor was bombed, the Americans came into the war. The GIs descended gloriously on this country and the women of Britain perked up immediately. These servicemen had a famous club in Mayfair where Madame Yandie had some-how secured me a prestigious gig. It was called the Stage Door Canteen. There was even a song about it:

I left my heart at the Stage Door Canteen,
I left it there with a girl named Eileen.

No, the song wasn't inspired by my performance. As I remember it was inspired by a girl selling doughnuts.

Doughnuts! We didn't *have* doughnuts till the Americans came – or nylons or bananas or gum – at least, I'd never seen them.

These American soldiers cheered the women up enormously and infuriated the men who were still at home, who had to watch as girls fell in love in droves for these exotic, attrac-tively uniformed men. Ethel Hayward to the left of us fell for a Canadian, and Ada Flowerday to the right of us for an American. My father would stand with clenched fists at our back window, glowering at them both lying in the gardens with their boyfriends, 'canoodling' as he called it, and say with a great sneer: 'They don't smoke, they don't drink, but can't they luuurrve.' The furious chant was, 'They're overpaid, oversexed and over 'ere'.

I was in a train with my mother going down to Torquay to visit my grandmother, whose nursing home had been evacuated down there, when I first became aware of them. The carriage was packed with these very different-looking soldiers. They all seemed more attractive and healthier than the British – and they were. They had better food and their uniforms were a better cut than those of our men, and they didn't have to wear forage caps, they had really sexy peaked caps . . . and they had more money. I must have been about eight at the time, but as soon as one of them in our carriage offered me some gum, I was off my mother's knee (where I'd been forced to sit because of the crowding) and onto his lap in no time, and I refused to get off. She was furious with me, though he assured her that he was very happy to have me on his lap as he had left two young kids back in the States. The whole carriage spoilt me and I lay back in that man's arms, listening to the soft, lazy twang of their voices and their easy camaraderie, and I didn't want the journey to end. Three or four hours later, when we arrived in Torquay, my mother was still cross with me. 'You made me ashamed. You wouldn't leave him alone – why did you behave like that?'

'He smelt so lovely,' I said, 'I didn't want to move.'

Of course, they *did* smell lovely. Deodorants for a man in those days in Britain were unheard of, and apparently only the upper classes wore aftershave, and I'd never met an upper-class man.

Starry as it was, my gig at the Stage Door Canteen was a bit of a disappointment. I was hoping to meet a lot more American soldiers, but I was backstage, and most people there were

English. I was on the same bill as Anna Neagle and Randolph Scott. I had no idea who the latter was, but I knew that Anna Neagle was a film actress and she was very sweet to me and told me not to be afraid of the big audience. I wasn't. I sang 'I'm A Yankee Doodle Dandy', dressed in a short pleated red silk skirt and top with a military touch of epaulettes and a red pillbox hat, and carried a swagger stick under my arm, then gave them my speciality of toe-tapping on three different-sized drums and leaping from one to the other while staying on my toes. The audience roared their approval. I wanted to go and meet them, but no, I was bundled into a car immediately afterwards and taken home. It was infuriating. I had wanted to join the party I'd glimpsed going on in the Canteen, where there were lots of pretty women, and dancing, and everyone seemed to be having a good time, unlike the stale-smelling, seemingly joyless atmosphere of the working men's clubs, where there were no women.

Our own family parties didn't have music and dancing like this. Not like this at all.

I was given enjoyable birthday parties every year, where we had jelly and cake and played games that usually involved a treasure hunt in the garden, arranged by my sister, which were always very imaginative and fun, but this was the only time she was allowed to 'help' with me in any way. My mother would never let me go out with her at all.

And then there were family parties, which were always with my mother's half-sister, Aunt Edie's family.

We hardly ever met Dad's brothers and sisters (the Aunt Esther lunch was a one-off because she'd been bereaved). As I've said, my mother looked down on them because they had nearly all been in service (the only two that hadn't had worked on the railway, and both were killed in World War I; one is remembered on the wall at Waterloo Station, the other at Baker Street). In snapshot albums there were photographs of them in their best clothes in the grounds of beautiful houses, and even one shot of Uncle Harry on a horse, and I was very impressed and asked my mother how it was that they lived in such grand houses and went horse riding. She said, 'They are just being silly.' 'How are they being silly?' I asked. 'They're pretending,' my mother would say crossly. 'I don't want to talk about it.' It was years before I realised that they had been in service, and years later when I realised how much it angered her when I mentioned in interviews that my father had been an under-chauffeur while still a boy. My father saw absolutely nothing wrong in being 'in service'. I think he would quite like to have stayed in service. He loved wearing a uniform and he never questioned a world made up of the rich and the poor. He knew that he didn't have the brains to make money and was perfectly happy to work for those who did. My mother thought service was demeaning and yet she made clothes for, if not exactly rich customers, those with a lot more money than we had. The difference was that she wanted the people she worked for to understand that she was as good as them, and my father was happy to be subservient. So my mother made sure we didn't see his family unless it was unavoidable.

Aunt Edie and Uncle Will, who we saw quite often, ran a newsagent's at 1, The Parade, Crayford in Kent. They had a boy, Peter, who was three years older than me, and a girl, Gladys, who was about seven years older than me. I liked staying there because they let me serve in the shop, which I enjoyed enormously, as between customers I would read all the comics and magazines. To me it was a treasure trove.

At home the only comic or magazine I got to look at was *Enid*

Blyton's Sunny Stories, which were given to me by a wealthy customer of my mother's who had three daughters. I would take the clothes that my mother had made for the children in a parcel to the house, which was a thirty-minute walk. I would hand them over to Mrs Bristow, who would ask me to sit in a separate room while she tried them on the children. When this was done she would give me the piles of *Sunny Stories* that her girls had finished with and I would stagger happily home. I never saw her girls.

I was allowed to read anything in the shop that I wanted, and the only thing I can remember being 'a bit rude' was the cover of *Tit-Bits*, which wasn't even Page Three stuff. I don't remember any pornographic magazines. I suppose they must have existed – perhaps they hid them.

Another great joy of staying in Crayford was that it was the countryside. There was a heath a two-minute walk from the shop, and I could ramble about there on my own for hours as long as I came back for meals.

The only fly in the ointment about these visits was that my Aunt Edie, a furiously jolly woman with a volatile temper, thought I was spoilt and indulged by my mother (which of course I was) and was determined to dislike me.

I wouldn't eat chicken because I'd seen my father wringing our chickens' necks at Christmas, and it had put me off ever wanting to eat one. But every Christmas Aunt Edie would put the chicken on my plate and my mother would say, 'You know she doesn't like chicken', and Aunt Edie would say, 'You've let her get too finicky', and plonk the plate in front of me. 'Just tell her she's not getting up till she's eaten it.' She hardly ever spoke to me directly. The meat would sit on my plate till the end of the meal when Uncle Will or Peter would happily eat it for me and my aunt would glare at both of us.

She was both glad and furious that I worked in the shop. Glad that it gave her some spare time and furious that at eight or nine I did it so well. She would say with great venom: 'Perhaps she'd like to get up at six o'clock with me and mark up the delivery papers?' 'If you like, Auntie,' I would say angelically, knowing that my mother would come in with, 'I'm not getting her up at six to do your dirty work.'

I quite enjoyed these confrontations with my aunt. I totally understood why I annoyed her. I *was* indulged – even my uncle spoilt me and I enjoyed the explosions of fury it produced. She used to bang saucepans about, and once threw a whole plate of food that I had only picked at onto the floor where it smashed, saying to my mother, 'Milady will have to get her servant to pick that up.' I knew she couldn't really hurt me, and I liked the drama.

Years later, my sister told me that there was a lot of jealousy between the sisters and that Aunt Edie's fury at me was mainly directed at my mother. She died in her fifties when I was a teenager, and my mother took me to the hospital to see her. She was very near death. She just looked at my mother and said, 'Did you *have* to bring the girl with you?' I left the ward – hurt by her words for the first time.

We never went anywhere else – only to Crayford, which, incidentally, was often bombed as there was an arms factory, Vickers-Armstrongs, behind the shop. Most celebrations were spent there, and sometimes relatives of Uncle Will joined us.

I didn't think there was anything odd about these celebrations until I was very much older. We would put on our best clothes and a running buffet would be laid out of sausage rolls, cold cuts, pickles, bowls of tomatoes and bowls of radishes with not a single green offering. This would gradually morph as the day went on into home-made jellies and trifles (they were very big on trifle) and cakes.

Soon after the food, the first round of games would start. Every single game seemed pointless to me, the worst involving a cake-like shape made only of flour with a matchstick set at its centre, being brought in on a plate. Then everyone would sit crouched round it in a circle and a knife would be passed round, and when it was your turn you had to 'slice the cake', and the person whose cut made the matchstick fall in the flour had to pick the matchstick up with their teeth and as they tried to do that, everyone pushed their face in the flour. Then there was 'Murder' with the lights out, and various other childlike games like 'Stone, Scissors, Paper', but the point of most of the games was that someone would be humiliated.

Then, as the women moved back to the kitchen to change the food to teatime, there was a rustle of excitement and the men disappeared into a bedroom. When the women were back in the living room, the men would return dressed very much in the style of Monty Python, as women. They didn't perform in any way, they just stood giggling and struck poses. This made the women helpless with laughter. After that was over my father, who never dressed as a woman, but had always found some kind of fancy costume, and would be dressed as the Pearly King or a Chelsea Pensioner, would sing his repertoire of music hall songs, and finally, many sherries, shandies and beers later, there would be a sing-song of mostly war songs: 'The White Cliffs Of Dover', 'Run Rabbit Run', 'Roll Out the Barrell' or 'We're Going to Hang Out the Washing on the Siegfried Line', and then they would wind up sentimentally with 'Lili Marlene', and by then I was probably in bed. As they went to bed one of the boys would start up the jingle:

> Hitler has only got one ball
> Goering has two, but rather small
> Himmler has something similar
> But poor old Goebbels has no balls at all

And then the party really was over.

When I was about eleven, with the help of my cousin Peter who I adored, in an effort to join in, I dressed up in his clothes and wore my uncle's trilby and presented myself as a man. I thought I looked great, but nobody laughed and Aunt Edie told me not to be 'so damned silly'.

I was beginning to cast a beady, detached eye on my family. They certainly didn't conform to the books that I read and my mother had very different opinions from Miss Hall, made clear to me by an incident with my sister.

Peggy had been engaged at the beginning of the war, when she was seventeen, to a fresh-faced, good-looking young man called Eric, who was immediately called up and was fighting in Egypt. After a year of much-longed-for and eagerly sent airmail letters (many of his blanked out by security because they were thought to be letting out secrets that enemy agents might intercept), she found herself having to write him a 'Dear John' letter because she had fallen in love with a sweet-natured man called Bill who hadn't been called up because he had TB. ('Dear John' letters were the ones that forces abroad received from their sweethearts at home who had tired of waiting for them and had met someone else.) Bill had supposedly recovered from his tuberculosis but was not fit enough for active service. He and Peggy became engaged and the marriage date was fixed (people didn't hang around during the war). Three weeks before the wedding Bill's lung suddenly collapsed and he died. My poor sister, as well as being grief-stricken, was also racked with guilt that she was being punished by God for her behaviour to Eric. I sometimes heard her crying at night in the bedroom we shared, but my mother had kept me so much to herself, and there was such a lack of affection or at least the ability to show affection in our family, that I just stayed silent in my bed and didn't like to show that I was even awake. The feeling in the house was that something unpleasant had happened and it was best not spoken about. Peggy was still only nineteen, but it was many months before she went out again, even with her girlfriends.

Then one Sunday afternoon, my parents were in the garden and there was a knock at the door (none of us were allowed keys) and I went to open it. My sister had brought a GI back home and he was black. I had never seen a black person before and just gazed at him open-mouthed as my sister said, 'This is Homer. Say hello,' and hustled him in. I said, 'Are you from Africa?' 'No,' he smiled, 'I'm from the US of A.' They were both laughing and I was glad to see my sister looking happy, and was looking forward to a jolly tea with this exotic man, when Peggy said, 'You'd better come out into the garden and meet my mum and dad.'

If my mother hadn't been sitting in a deckchair I think she would have collapsed at the sight of Homer. I saw at once that my sister had done something very wrong. 'Get back indoors,' my mother hissed as she heaved herself out of her chair to practically push them in. He was allowed a quick cup of tea in a very hostile atmosphere, and then I could see my mother making signals to my sister to get rid of him. Peggy finally said that she would walk him to the bus stop, at which my mother nearly choked and my sister pretended not to notice. When she came back my mother was incandescent with rage. My father was told to take me into the garden, but I could hear most of what they said. 'What on earth did you think you were doing bringing one of them back here?' 'He was friendly and good fun,' my sister said firmly, 'and he told me he hadn't been invited into a British home, so I thought I'd bring him back with me. I don't see anything wrong in that.' 'If any of the neighbours have seen you, we're finished. How could you have done such a damn silly thing? I'm thoroughly ashamed of you.'

There was a terrible pall over the house after this. My sister stubbornly refused to apologise, my mother was tight-lipped with fury, my father so embarrassed he couldn't look at anyone and my brother, having missed it all, looked at us furtively, wondering what had happened, and got out of the house as soon as possible.

I was confused. Why was it wrong for Peggy to bring Homer home? It had to be that the trouble was he was black, but Miss Hall (and indeed the Sunday school teacher) had made it clear that the colour of your skin made no difference to God and that everyone should be treated equally. In fact, a boy at school had been heavily reprimanded for talking about 'those yellow bastards' (he meant our then enemy, the Japanese) and it was made clear that it wasn't just because he'd sworn. Miss Hall had explained that it was a very wrong and foolish thing to judge someone by the way they looked. 'Do you want to be known as the pink spotty English boy? It's the way people act that counts. Don't come to conclusions about people till you've got to know them even if their skin is purple, they only have one eye in the middle of their forehead and a nose shaped like a banana.' Of course she got her laugh but she'd made her point. I came to the shocking conclusion after the Homer incident that my mother had behaved badly and could definitely be wrong about other things. Dorothy Margaret Hall I never doubted.

As I grew older I realised that my mother knew that the neighbours would not have welcomed a person of colour in their midst, and we would have been looked down on by the whole street. Nevertheless, I wished she had had the intelligence to know that they were ignorant to think that way and the bravery to show them she was different. I was beginning to be rebellious.

One ridiculous argument was over a bowl of gooseberries, my favourite fruit, which she had placed on the table as a treat after tea.

'Yippee,' I said, 'goosegogs.'

'Gooseberries,' my mother said.

'Goosegogs,' I insisted. 'Everyone calls them goosegogs.'

'Only common children. You won't get any until you call them by their right name.'

'Goosegogs, goosegogs, goosegogs,' I chanted stubbornly as my mother gave everyone a portion except me. They were the last of the season and I knew it was unlikely there would be any more that summer, but I sat there saying 'goosegog' under my breath until they were all gone, then ran upstairs to cry. After a while she came to the bedroom and tried to put her arms round me, but I wouldn't give in and moved away from her. 'Everyone in the street calls them goosegogs,' I said again sullenly.

'But I don't want you to be like everyone in the street,' said my mother. 'Why not?' I asked. 'Because I want you to be different.' There was silence, then with great effort she managed to say, almost in a whisper, 'because I love you.' She could barely squeeze the word out. It was the only time in her life she ever said it, and it had embarrassed us both.

But of course, this was quite normal. It wasn't until the 1960s that most people started saying 'I love you' to their children. It might have occurred among the middle classes, but certainly not among working-class families, and I'm pretty sure not in the upper classes either. Then television came along and told everyone that they should be saying it. To this day my brother can't even write 'Love Ron' on a birthday card.

I find it hard to remember any close family life – anything that we did together. I checked with Ron and he couldn't remember anything either, and then I said, 'The wireless, we all listened to the wireless.' 'Yes,' he conceded, 'there was that.'

The wireless was pure magic, the most favourite programme being *ITMA (It's That Man Again)* with Tommy Handley. We'd all sit round laughing and chorusing the catchphrases like, 'Can I do you now, sir'.

There was *Monday Night at Eight*, and Bebe Daniels and Ben Lyon in *Life with the Lyons*, and Arthur Askey, who I didn't find funny at all, and *London Calling* and *Much Binding in the Marsh*. These disconnected voices brought us together for the odd half hour in the evening without the necessity of communicating with each other. But then a huge percentage of families today only come together around the television.

I was taken to the music hall by my parents but my brother and sister never came with us. I suppose they were both in their teens by the time I was taken at seven. My brother has no memory of going at all.

My favourite act by far was Nat Mills and Bobbie. The act was always the same. Bobbie was a blonde woman in evening dress who came onto the stage to play the grand piano, and then indicated that the piano was in the wrong position. The rest of the act was Nat Mills trying to move the piano. I think the only words spoken were 'I'll move it', and I cried with laughter every time I saw them.

One evening I left the house with my father to go, I thought, to the Wood Green Empire to see Wilson, Keppel and Betty, a strange act where two men and a woman did a comic dance in sand dressed as Egyptians. But when we were on the bus to Turnpike Lane my father said very confidentially to me, 'We're not actually going to Wood Green Empire, we're going to Finsbury Park Empire because they've got a much better show on there, but you must never, ever tell your mother. All right?'

If my father thought there was a better show on somewhere else it was fine by me, but I was intrigued as to why we had to keep it a secret.

The attraction at Finsbury Park was Miss Phyllis Dixey, who was a striptease artist. Striptease was allowed in music halls only if the stripper was absolutely motionless. I knew none of this. I just saw, as we went in, that that was the name at the top of the bill. 'Does she sing or dance, or is she funny?' I asked my father. 'You'll see,' he said. There was tremendous excitement in the audience when finally the light at the side of the stage gave the number for her act and the voice boomed, 'And now we present Miss Phyllis Dixey.' The curtains parted and there was a tableau of two or three girls scantily dressed, pointing to a woman sitting perfectly still on what looked to me like a posh wheelchair, holding a fork and stark naked, except for a helmet. 'BRITANNIA,' the voice boomed out, and then Miss Dixey uttered a couple of rhyming couplets about Britain and how great we were, scarcely even seeming to move a muscle, and the audience applauded. The curtains closed and there was some music, then slowly they opened again and there was Miss

Dixey, starkers again, except for a fig leaf and hair cascading down her back, holding out an apple to a handsome man wearing only a slightly bigger fig leaf. 'EVE,' boomed the voice. Then Miss Dixey gave us a couple of seductive couplets, urging the man to eat. Neither of them moved. The final curtain revealed Miss Dixey in a shell as 'THE BIRTH OF VENUS'. That was it. I thought it was the dullest act I had ever seen, but the audience, mostly men, were very appreciative, and I understood completely why I mustn't tell my mother. I never did.

Once America had joined us to fight against the Germans and Japanese there was a feeling that we had a chance, but it wasn't until 1944 that the tide seemed to turn in any way and then we seemed to win more battles, and suddenly after Christmas everyone was saying that we were going to win, and it would all be over. Then suddenly it *was* all over, and on 8 May, a month before my eleventh birthday, we all celebrated VE Day. Victory over Europe. The Japanese still wouldn't surrender and were holding out. There were parties everywhere, long trestle tables were put out in the streets and I don't think there was a single child who didn't get to a party somewhere. You've seen it on the newsreels. There really was dancing in the streets – even the young princesses crept out of Buckingham Palace and joined the throng to be part of it all.

I can't remember whether or not I knew that I'd got the scholarship by then because every worry was pushed away by this huge national celebration. We had won. We were battered and exhausted, but we had won. We could sleep in peace in our beds at last.

5

So there was a national sigh of relief that the war in Europe was over, and a family sigh of relief at 17 Courtman Road that I hadn't shamed them by not winning the scholarship.

I'd said a sad farewell to Parkside. It was hard to keep the tears back, but Miss Hall made it clear that we should be nothing but excited at the prospect of our futures, and we were excited. And then to cap it all my father had a win on the football pools.

He did them with great care and consideration every week and often won small amounts, but this time he had won a hundred pounds. A hundred pounds! I thought we must be one of the richest families in England. I'm told that a hundred pounds in 1945 would be worth about £4300 today, and I imagine that anyone living now on a council estate in Tottenham would be pretty chuffed at getting a cheque for £4300. We were all over the moon. When the cheque came in the post my mother became near hysterical as to where to safely put such a precious thing. She finally put it inside the upright piano (no one played it, it was just a status symbol) – not just under the lid, no: she opened the top of the piano and dropped it down among the strings. When my father came home from work and she rushed to get it, it had dropped right down and there were moments – terrifying moments – when they couldn't see it, then finally my father fished it out.

The question was, how should it be spent? My mother wanted a new three-piece suite and my father wanted us all to go on holiday. It seemed we could have both. Apparently I'd had a holiday before the war as a baby at Littlehampton, which I couldn't remember – now we were going to the seaside. I couldn't believe it. I was going to see the sea.

'We'll have a week at Southend,' said my father.

'Westcliff,' said my mother. 'Southend is common.'

Plans were made. My sister couldn't get time off work, but the four of us would stay at a boarding house in Westcliff-on-Sea for a whole week at the end of August.

Then something happened that made me feel so sick, I felt that we shouldn't be celebrating in any way about anything.

The Americans dropped the first atomic bomb on a place called Hiroshima. I saw the pictures of that terrifying mushroom cloud and heard on the wireless about the devastation and horrors it caused, and it filled me with a fear that was worse than anything I'd felt about the war that had just ended.

I was old enough to understand why the Americans had done it. I knew that the Emperor of Japan had said that they would never capitulate and made a speech telling his people to commit suicide rather than surrender, and this of course meant that the war would go on and on and the Americans and the British and our Allies wanted to finish it. But I still thought it was a very terrible thing to do. It wasn't until they dropped a second bomb on Nagasaki that the Japanese finally surrendered.

The war with Japan was over on 15 August, which coincided

with the last day of our holiday and we went into Southend where all the celebrations were being held. But for me, glad as I was that finally the war was completely over, I couldn't get the image of that mushroom cloud and what it could do out of my mind. It remained a background worry throughout my teenage years, and it was why in my twenties I ended up on an Aldermaston March.

The holiday was a bit of a disappointment, I think, for everyone. The boarding house we stayed in was run by an incredibly gloomy woman who served up our meals (which were nearly as bad as my mother's) always singing the same song: 'Please Don't Talk About Me When I'm Gone', which, as I never heard all the words and she sang it in such a doleful voice, I took to be about death. It was many years later that I found out it was a love song. Then we had to be out of the house from ten thirty till five thirty when she gave us our high tea – and she liked us out in the evening as well, and as there was only the depressing room we ate in to sit in, we wanted to get out.

It rained much of the week and we were forced to go to the cinema a lot, which I loved, but as we walked out after *A Connecticut Yankee at King Arthur's Court*, which I quite enjoyed, my mother said to my father, 'What a load of tosh. We're having to spend this money on tosh. We're never having a holiday like this again,' and we never did, as from then on we always went to holiday camps. On the days that were fine I was happy enough to mess about in the sand, paddle (I couldn't swim) and walk along the pier, but my brother, now seventeen, was bored stiff and deeply embarrassed at being on holiday with his parents. He had left school at fifteen and was a trainee draughtsman, and he and I had no relationship whatsoever, so it was odd to be thrown together all day and every day – and with our parents, who also weren't used to being with each other all day and every day. Of course, this is the story of many a family vacation. It can show up the cracks when you have nothing to do but talk to one another. Mrs Gloomy didn't even have a wireless we could listen to together. But there is an upside to a holiday like this – everyone is very happy to get home.

I was excited now at the thought of going to Latymer's, and for once there had been enough money for the uniform and everything had been bought in a shop, and I was all kitted out. Navy gymslip, a pale blue square-necked blouse, a navy blazer with the school crest and motto on it, *Qui Patitur Vincit* – He Who Endures Conquers – and most exciting of all, a pair of navy shorts for games and gym with a mauve stripe down the side of each leg, which was the colour of my house. I was to be in Charles Lamb House, whose colour was a pretty pale lavender. The shorts, which were like American Bermudas, tight-legged and down to the knee, were necessary as the school was mixed, and though we wouldn't actually do gym with the boys, there would be games and athletics, and it was not thought a good idea that the boys should see the girls anywhere in navy-blue knickers. It was a relief, as I knew my mother would have made a fuss if she had had to buy me those 'horrible bloomers'.

The new school would be a longer journey for me of about forty-five minutes. I would cycle on fine days and take the 144 bus and then walk on wet days. Latymer Grammar was enormous. At the time I attended it was one of the three largest schools in England with 1350 pupils. To go from a school that had sixty pupils to one of this size was daunting. On the first day as I entered the gates thronged with children, past the stone that said 'Founded by Edward Latymer for eight poor boys of Edmonton', I did wonder if Edward Latymer would approve of all these girls his school now educated as well as boys.

At the first assembly in the Great Hall, the headmaster asked any new boy or girl who didn't live in the County of Middlesex to report to his study as soon as assembly was over. I had never heard the word Middlesex – was Tottenham in Middlesex? It was a long bus ride. I decided I probably didn't live in Middlesex, and stood nervously outside what I was told was his study with about four or five other children. The headmaster, Mr Davis, was a quietly comforting-looking man with a ready smile. When I told him that I lived in Tottenham and it was a long way away, he put his arm round me and said, 'It's a good thing you've come to see me because I can tell you that you *do* live in Middlesex, along with most of the school. Just a few of them who live in the countryside and come a very long way don't come under Middlesex County Council.'

'Oh, you mean like Enfield,' I said.

He found this amusing.

'No,' he said, 'Enfield is less than half a mile up the road.' I was confused. 'Don't worry, you'll soon get your bearings. Now, do you know the way back to your classroom?' I didn't, so he took me to the door and gave me directions. I waved goodbye and he waved back.

Each year was divided into six streams, A, B, C, D, E and F. I was in stream D. That was fine by me. I was pretty sure I wasn't brainy, and I was relieved that I wasn't in F. A, B and C streams learned French as their foreign language, D and E learned German and F learned Spanish. To this day I tend to think that if you put an A and the odd O at the end of English words, you're speaking Spanish. I was thrilled that I was learning German as, although the war had now finished, I was quite sure spies would still be needed. I'd seen quite a few spy films, and although I wasn't that keen on having my fingernails pulled out, it did seem a very glamorous job.

When I can't go to sleep at night, I can still recite my form register. We sat in alphabetical order, boys on one side of the classroom, girls on the other, starting with the As in the front. Beryl Ansell paired with Eileen Atkins, then Norah Bradley and Sheila Bride, then Janet Bryan behind me, starting the next row. Janet Bryan was one of the prettiest girls I'd ever seen. She barely came up to my shoulder and had masses of chestnut-coloured curly hair, a heart-shaped face with the merriest brown eyes and an enchantingly mischievous smile. We took to each other on the first day and remained close friends through-out our school lives. We drifted apart when we left school, but found each other again in our forties and remained close until her death a few years ago. Jan as she was always called (and she called me Eil) was always 'up for a laugh', as she put it, and I only saw her sad when she was made to leave school at fifteen, and later in life when her husband was ill with leukaemia.

One of the first things our form mistress told us we had to do was to choose a Form Captain. As no one knew anyone, I don't know how we were meant to judge characters for this so-called responsible position. I was voted in pretty unani-mously, I think simply because I was the noisiest person in the class. I suppose dancing classes and Parkside had taught me to be very sociable, whereas apart from Jan, the children in my class seemed almost taciturn – they certainly didn't want to be 'picked out' in any way or have any responsibility. So there I was, Form Captain in the first week with a badge to prove it. My only job seemed to be to keep the class quiet when we lacked supervision between classes and to walk home anyone who became ill at school. This latter was a real treat as I got a break from lessons, had an interesting walk with my sick classmate and was usually thanked profusely by their mother and given a drink and possibly a biscuit or cake of some sort. Then I'd meander back to school happily having missed a boring lesson.

I quickly learned that none of the teachers seemed to have Dorothy Margaret Hall's charisma, and that doing only English and maths made life a lot easier than doing all those other boring subjects – geography, history, science and German, which I found I only enjoyed when we sang German songs, 'Ich bin nur ein armer Wandergesell, gute Nacht liebes Mädel gut nacht', or 'Sag' mir Darling, sag' mir Liebling, sag' mir Du', sung flirtatiously to the girls by a stern-looking but good-humoured teacher who had just come back from fighting in the war. Over seventy years later when I was filming *The Crown*, playing Queen Mary, I had a scene that required me to speak German. I was thrilled that for once I knew a language and didn't need to ask for help. I read smoothly at the reading and was immensely pleased with myself when we shot the actual scene. Being able to speak the lines so fluently and with such confidence made me feel clever and well educated. A few months later we did the ADR (additional dialogue recording) that you sometimes have to do for technical reasons. Once more I was ready to show off my knowledge of German when Stephen Daldry said, 'Before we do this scene again, Eileen, you've got to have a word with the dialogue specialist.' A nervous woman took me to one side and, almost unable to look at me from embarrassment, said, 'Your German is very low-class, and of course Queen Mary would have spoken High German.'

I was too old to be mortified, but it made me suddenly realise that the German Mr Edwards had taught us he had probably learned from German prisoners.

Most of our male teachers had just been demobbed, and these were the men who had voted Churchill out. They had been through hell for Britain, and they now wanted their country to be well worth the fight. Though some of them, I'm sure, must have been mentally harmed in some way by the war, they all seemed to me to be enthusiastic and idealistic, and I don't think I could have had a better bunch of teachers.

Only one of them slightly frightened me. He was a tall, cadaverous-looking man who flew along the corridors with his gown billowing, reminding me of an eagle. He had a sardonic face with a nose that looked as if you could cut cheese with it, rather beautiful pale grey eyes and lips always set in an ironic smile as if finding himself a teacher at Latymer's was a huge private joke. He was known to lose his temper and throw chalk and even the wood-backed blackboard cleaner at pupils in his classes. His name was Mr Burton and he took us for religion – which was called divinity.

The first time he took us for a lesson he picked on me immediately to read the Bible, Psalm 33. Quite confidently I stood up and read, 'Rejoice in the Lord, oh ye righteous *for* praise is comely for the upright' (a piece of chalk flew past me – I continued). 'Praise the Lord with Harp, sing unto him with the psaltery *and* an instrument of ten strings.' He exploded, 'What the hell are you doing those weird stresses for? And the "p" is silent in psaltery.' There was, of course, laughter from the boys and more chalk was thrown.

'Because they're in italics, and that means you're supposed to stress the word.'

'Not in the Bible,' he said wearily. 'The italics used there are because there is a question about the translation.'

Always chatty and used to the informality of Parkside, I said, 'Oh, that's interesting. I've always thought it was a bit odd. I mean, I wouldn't say, "Mr Burton *has* come into our classroom and *is* cross". A few of the boys tittered. Mr Burton waited until their reaction had died away, then said:

'Mr Burton *is* glad that you understand stress and *isn't* cross,' and smiled at me.

I felt an immediate connection with him. I thought, I think he likes me, and I'm no longer frightened of him.

Soon after I'd gone to Latymer's, Madame Yandie had suggested to my mother that I enter a poetry competition, presumably because she wanted to show off the results of the elocution lessons she had given me. The competition was held in a big hall somewhere near Archway tube station. The room was packed with girls, most of them in their school uniforms, their hair tied back or plaited, whereas my mother had dressed me in one of the frilly frocks that she made me, and my Amami'd curls were all let loose for the event. I think the age group was eleven to fourteen years old. I know that I was eleven and everyone else seemed older. Madame Yandie, having gone through the poem with me (I'm pretty sure that it was 'Romance' by Robert Louis Stevenson), for some reason couldn't come with us, and my mother and I went alone.

I was immediately aware that these girls were very different from any I'd met so far. They all seemed tremendously confident, and there was no doubt that I was the odd one out. My mother was nervous but very pleased she had put me in a dress. 'Look at them in their school uniforms – they haven't even tried,' she said contemptuously. When it was my turn I tried to remember what Madame Yandie had told me to do, and thought I had done quite well.

When all thirty or so girls had performed, there was a short break while the adjudicator sorted out his notes. Normally a very sociable child, I sat close to my mother and didn't attempt to join in the buzz of chatter around us. Then he took the floor to give his opinion on each performance. His name was Clifford Turner and he taught at RADA (the Royal Academy of Dramatic Art). He was a very impressive, handsome-looking man who I discovered later was much admired by actors.

He made a few remarks about each performance and gave a mark to each girl. The marks hovered between 76 per cent and the high nineties for the girl who won. When it came to my turn, he said, 'Now, contestant number seventeen. Well, what can I say? Who would have thought we would have a little cockney in the competition? I don't know how it happened, but there she was – a little cockney. I can only say that whoever suggested she should enter this competition gave ill advice. Those vowel sounds quite upset me. Fifty-three per cent.'

I think the audience were too well brought up to snigger, but I, nevertheless, felt a snigger. My mother was so mortified she couldn't move. When we were asked to come up and collect our certificates with our marks – but, thank God, not his remarks – I rushed up to take mine as quickly as possible and got us both out of the building. When we were outside, we sat on the nearest public bench in silence. Then, after a while, my mother almost whispering, said, 'A little cockney . . . how could he?' And I was very afraid that she was going to cry. After a bit she said, 'It wasn't your fault,' and then, 'Give me that certificate. We're going to change that mark.' She fished for a pen and changed the 53 per cent to 88 per cent. 'There,' she said, 'that looks all right. We won't tell anyone.' I didn't argue. I too, of course, was mortified.

There was a part of me that knew I might be a bit of a cockney, and for a long time I'd thought Madame Yandie's elocution lessons something of a joke, as I would repeat a phrase from the classes in Dorothy Margaret Hall's presence and she would correct me. Mum brazened it out at home, saying I hadn't won but that I'd done very well, and waved the certificate in front of the rest of the family who weren't in the least bit interested anyway.

But she had got the message. Madame Yandie's elocution lessons were no good. She clearly wasn't as upper class as she pretended to be. But if I was to be the kind of dancer Mum imagined, I would have to speak well. None of us had ever seen a musical, but we knew that in pantomime you wouldn't get the part of principal boy or girl if you had a cockney accent. As we had no acquaintance with anyone 'posh', she decided there might be a teacher at Latymer's who could help.

So she gave me a note to take to school to give to my form mistress, asking if there was any teacher at Latymer's willing to give me elocution lessons. Miss Kaye, an English teacher, said that she would be willing to do it. It would cost seven and six for a half hour lesson each week. My mother couldn't afford that, so I had to knock on the teachers' common room door and ask for Miss Kaye and say, 'Thank you very much but Mum says it's too expensive.'

A few weeks later I was walking along the corridor when Mr Burton swooped down on me. 'You. I want to talk to you,' he said, and he pulled me into a niche in the corridor. 'I hear that you want to learn to speak properly.'

'Well, my mother wants me to learn to speak properly,' I answered.

'Listen. I can teach you. I don't want any money but you'll have to come to me after school whenever I feel like it. All right?'

'All right.'

A few days later I had my first lesson.

Ernest James Burton was a clever, intense, fascinating and tortured man who was passionate about the theatre. He had gone from university into the priesthood, but celibacy hadn't suited him, and whether he was thrown out or he just walked out it was never clear. What was clear was that religion and lusts of the flesh tormented him. He took to teaching and married and had two children but had divorced by the time he got to Latymer Grammar, and was living alone in a small flat off Marylebone High Street. Although he taught divinity he was also the drama teacher and directed the school plays. He was thirty-two years old.

For the next five years he tutored me in the empty art room after school, mostly two or three times a week. He didn't just give me a new accent; he gave me a completely new view of life.

I'd never heard anyone talk the way he did – not just about the theatre but about the arts and life in general, including politics and religion and psychiatry and yes, sex, and somewhat naturally the relationship didn't go totally unnoticed and caused some consternation in the staffroom. I had no idea at the time, but after I had left Latymer's I was told that certain members of staff took it in turns to patrol the corridor outside the art room. He must have been aware of this but nevertheless always, though remembering my age, tried to treat me as an equal and encouraged me to respond in the same way. I loved these sessions, and couldn't get enough of him. The last bit of his journey to school involved getting the same bus as I did when it was raining. Before the end of the year I had agreed to give up cycling to school and to always wait till the bus came with him on it so that we could talk together all the way to school. We mutually split at the left turn that took us into Haselbury Road where the school was, and Jan would be waiting for me and I'd walk the rest of the way with her.

The change in me wrought by my tutoring from Mr Burton (or E.J., as he liked me to call him, but I was careful to use it only when we were alone) began to make my mother uneasy. I didn't want to go to dancing lessons any more; I didn't want to *talk* about dancing. I started to spout Shakespeare at home, and she looked at me and chewed her long, thin lips.

My introduction to Shakespeare by E.J. had been very clever. He handed me a speech that he had typed out of Helena's in *A Midsummer Night's Dream*, not telling me it was Shakespeare, and not typed out in verse form. So I just read, '*How happy some o'er other some can be! Through Athens I am thought as fair as she. But what of that? Demetrius thinks not so; He will not know what all but he do know.*' And so on, for the whole speech.

'What do you think this is about?' he asked me when I'd read it.

'Well, this girl loves this boy, and they'd bin going out together and now he's fallen for someone else and she's really fed up and blamin' Cupid.'

'Anything else you noticed about it?'

'Well, it's sort of verse, isn't it?'

'Did you understand it all?'

'Yeah, yeah, I think so. It's just old language, isn't it?'

'Yes,' he said. 'It's Shakespeare.'

So I never had a moment's fear of England's greatest poet and playwright.

After a school day and then an intense hour or so with Mr B.,

My mother's mother

My father's mother

My mother when young

My father in his meter-reading uniform

My mother all dressed up for a wedding

My father all dressed up, at the age of seventeen

Horribly coy on my father's knee with my brother Ron behind

Top: On holiday at Westcliff aged ten and flirting with the photographer
Bottom: One of my uncles in service pretending to be 'a gentleman'

Aged four-and-a-half

The evacuees – Ken Bruton, Ron and me in my best clothes eating a sweet

Left: Dressed to sing 'Burlington Bertie from Bow'
Right: Me, Derek and Pam

Ron, the drummer for the KY School

I was told that I was Peter Pan with his pipe!?

Top and right: With Maureen Kean

Above: Me aged twelve
Centre: With Madame
Yandie
Right: I believe it was
called an elbow stand

Me at four, eight and twelve with Ron and my half-sister, Peggy

Left: My father dressed as a Chelsea Pensioner

Above: Janet Bryan, aged fifteen, with her hair cut, ready to start work

Right: Me dressed in my cousin's clothes

Right: E. J. Burton, my teacher at Latymer Grammar School

On the beach with Angela Davis

At my sister's wedding. Left to right: Me, the best man, Howard Lewis, Peggy, my father, cousin Gladys, my mother and Mrs Lewis

As Lucy in *The Rivals* at Latymer Grammar School

Playing Sister Bonaventure with Judith
Dawson in *Bonaventure* at the Guildhall
School of Music and Drama

With Trevor Martin in *The Leading Lady*

I looked forward to a very roundabout route home with Jan, to include a visit to the tuck shop and the hope that we might catch some of the boys from Enfield Grammar on the bus back for 'a bit of a laugh', as Jan would say. As we climbed up the stairs to the top deck, full of testosterone-fuelled boys starved of the companionship of girls, and sashayed down the aisle, our hair now loose and flowing, our gymslips hitched up as high as we dared, we aroused a great deal of comment. Our exchanges weren't exactly Wildean, but we thought we were brilliant, or 'brill' as we called it. Our favourite words were 'brill' and 'tric' (terrific).

The boys would always comment on our arrival.

'Oh, look what's just got on the bus.'

'What a bit of all right.'

'What you two doin' tonight, then?'

'Not standing outside the fish shop with you lot,' Jan would say grandly.

'No, we've got better things to do.' I would toss my hair back.

'Oh yeah? What's better than meetin' us then?'

'Washing our hair,' we'd both say with great scorn, and then sit and giggle and whisper to each other about who we thought was best-looking.

The odd thing was that we took no notice at all of the boys in our own class. I think we waited for the Enfield Grammar bus because at that later hour we got mostly boys older than those in our class, and I think we just had an instinct to tease them because they had no girls at their school and were excited and nervous when two such obvious little tarts were sitting among them. Though we did sometimes meet 'just for a laugh' in the evening and cycle together to the fish and chip shop where some of them usually hung out. We leaned against our bikes, sharing a bag of chips and throwing out the odd inane remark to them and giggling. Neither of us ever went out with them.

At the end of my first year at Latymer's I came bottom of the class of thirty-four children and Jan came second from bottom. It didn't bother either of us, but my form mistress asked to speak to my mother. I thought I was going to be in trouble, but apparently Miss Cullimore had suggested to my mother that this had come about because I was clearly tired a lot of the time, and maybe it would be a good idea to cut down on the dancing, and in particular that I shouldn't be out late at night dancing in clubs. My mother was angry at being told what was best for her daughter but didn't show it and agreed to cut the dancing back a bit. She was very amenable, I realised, because at the end of that school year I had my twelfth birthday, and was now old enough to be in pantomime that coming Christmas.

The first day I went back to school in September I was stopped in the corridor by Miss Nagle, the Discipline Mistress. Miss Nagle, like Aunt Edie, had taken against me at first sight. She also just saw 'a show-off'.

'What form are you in this year?' she asked slyly.

'2D, Miss Nagle,' I said with great pride. It was thrilling to be back and now a second-former on the first floor of the building.

'But they were supposed to put you down to E,' she said, 'after your shameful exam results.'

'No,' I said nervously. 'D. I'm still in D.'

She looked annoyed. 'If I'd had my way you would have been put down,' she said, disgruntled. 'All right, you can go.'

I was in shock. The thought that I might have had to leave Jan and my class and Miss Cullimore and start over in the E stream was horrific. I would have to try to do better.

*

As she had promised my mother, Madame Yandie got me into pantomime. She got me an audition to be one of 'Vane's Juveniles', who were to appear in *Cinderella* that Christmas at Clapham Empire for two weeks and Kilburn Empire for two weeks, and they accepted me. As the school holidays were only three weeks, I would have to have two weeks off school as there was a week of full rehearsals as well. Permission was granted. It also meant that I had to do a lot of rehearsing after school in Cheam, as that was where Vane's Juveniles were based and where we worked on the routines.

Most pantomimes then had a troupe of little girls who tapped their way through a panto. I discussed it with Mr Burton and after a despairing smirk or two he said, 'I don't suppose it will do you any harm, and you'll get used to being in a theatre, which won't be a bad thing.'

I enjoyed the experience enormously. I was the tallest of a very jolly group of girls and we were all excited to be performing in a real theatre. My height had stopped me getting picked for the top shows in the West End, as they liked the child dancers to be all roughly the same height and as short as possible. Some mothers even gave their girls gin in the hope of stunting their growth so that they could be child performers for a few more years. I had to be thankful my mother hadn't stooped to that trick. Though Mr Burton had dashed up to me one milk break and taken my free milk away from me, yelling at me, 'You'll grow too tall.' Not that he cared about panto. He just thought it was better for an actress to be shorter than her leading man. But as I'd only had a jam sandwich for breakfast, I wasn't going to give up my milk.

When we finally got to a rehearsal with the whole cast and met the adults, it turned out that there was an exchange with

Buttons that required one of Vane's Juveniles to say three lines. It ran thus:

SMALL GIRL: Buttons, what is it that has six legs, six arms and five eyes?

BUTTONS: I don't know, I don't know. What is it that has six legs, six arms and five eyes?

SMALL GIRL: Three sailors.

BUTTONS: Three sailors? Wait a minute. Wait a minute – six legs, six arms and *five* eyes?

SMALL GIRL: One of them was Nelson.

I was picked for this witty repartee. I can't say that I brought the house down every night, but I did always manage to somehow get a laugh.

Of course it also meant that as far as my mother was concerned, Mr Burton was doing his job properly, and she was satisfied. She was very happy throughout the whole run of the pantomime. She had secured the position of chaperone for all the children, so she felt included. I think I earned three pounds or three pounds ten shillings a week for two shows a day, and she would also have been earning, and it was all beginning to look as though her dreams were coming true. Here I was, dancing on the stage in a proper theatre and speaking lines, and she could luxuriate in the bright lights, the music and general bonhomie backstage. She was in 'show business'. This was going to be my life, and she was part of it. Everything was coming up roses.

6

When I went back to school a week late after the pantomime, I was full of myself and probably quite unbearable. I was put in my place by Miss Cullimore with a talk she gave to the whole class. 'I would like to believe,' she said, 'that anyone in my class would behave well out of school as well as in it, but I was horrified by the antics I witnessed of a member of this class waiting for a train on the Underground at a late hour just after Christmas. She was jiggling about, talking loudly, clearly to draw attention to herself, wearing make-up and most unsuitable clothes. I hope never to witness such behaviour from any of you again.'

Obviously I recognised myself, and so did the rest of the class. I suppose she did the ticking off in public to make me more ashamed. It certainly worked. In the morning milk break Jan took my hand and squeezed it. 'She's an old cow,' she said, 'I expect you were only having a laugh.' But I *did* feel very ashamed.

In the weeks I'd been away, Jan had become friendly with two other girls in our form – Sheila Bride and Gladys Turville – and although Jan was still my best friend, and Gladys Sheila's, we became a foursome, and as we were all pupils unable to afford school dinners, we would sit in the domestic science room to eat our packed lunches (mine white sugar sandwiches or sultana sandwiches, with a very occasional apple), and chat and giggle companionably together. Sheila and Gladys both came from families where TB (tuberculosis) was rife, and they both knew that it was very possible they would get it as well. Gladys came from a family of about ten children and two of her brothers had already died of it. She was an angry, stoic child who came into school one morning and marched up to Miss Cullimore, as soon as she came in, with a note which Miss Cullimore read and then told her to go home. She left the class without looking at any of us. Miss Cullimore said, 'I've sent Gladys home because her father died last night. I hope that when she comes back tomorrow you'll show your understanding of the situation.'

Poor Sheila died within eighteen months of leaving school, and Gladys herself was hospitalised as soon as she left, but she survived. I remember visiting her in hospital when I was at drama school and us both roaring with laughter because she had to drink bottles of Guinness – it was believed to be a good way to build up strength – and she pretended to be drunk. Of the four of us she was the poorest and the cleverest, and certainly should have gone to university.

In my father's *Evening News* once a week there was a piece called 'Fieldfare' where they suggested a walk you could take in the countryside near London. It was always within a forty-mile radius of the centre of London and between five and ten miles long. I suggested we four do one of these walks together on Saturdays or Sundays when we could get away. I don't know where we got the money for the fare to a station like

Godalming, but we let ourselves loose in the countryside in shorts and plimsolls with a sandwich of sorts and a bottle of Tizer, and had enormous fun – laughing most of the way but also lapping up the countryside. Those walks gave us a great feeling of accomplishment, a relief from our drab surroundings, a taste for scenic beauty and for all our chattering and giggling, a sense of peace.

Soon after getting back to school I was cast as Alice in *Alice in Wonderland*, and as with *Little Women* I simply loved doing it. Totally by accident I looked more like Tenniel's drawings than most small girls as my mother had suddenly decided, before I did the panto, to take me to the hairdresser's and have my hair permed. I hated the idea, but was ready to put up with anything that would stop her torturing me with the strips of hair wound round her fingers into curls and then secured by two uncomfortable hairgrips each night. The perm didn't work, so I still had to put up with the discomfort. But when the panto was over I begged her to try just washing it and leaving it to dry, which of course gave me long frizzy hair – perfect for Alice – and I refused to let her curl it again. I had long, straight, mousy-coloured hair and I was happy, but my mother never stopped mourning those curls.

I was now totally settled in my mind – of course being nurtured by Mr Burton – that I would be an actress, not a dancer. At nearly thirteen I told my mother I would do no more dancing in clubs. The offers for that had been slowing down anyway, as it was child performers who were found cute, not a pubescent young woman. I'd all but given up Madame Yandie. I just did one or two classes a week, and the occasional 'show' if it was demanded of me.

My mother saw me becoming a chorus girl as soon as I left

school, and then progressing because of my good enunciation to parts in musical comedy. She never seemed to accept the fact that I couldn't sing a note (I couldn't even get into the school choir) and had no desire to spend my life dancing. I wanted to act.

Latymer's had a wonderfully advanced curriculum, and in our third and fourth years you could choose an extra four periods a week of gardening, music, drama, carpentry, another language, extra science or maths, or cooking. I, of course, chose drama and so did Jan. I realised later when I got to drama school how advanced Mr Burton's drama classes were – his ideas were way ahead of his time. He talked to us about Stanislavski and method acting, and we did a lot of improvisation, and at one point he took it into his head to give a public performance of improvisations. I can remember Jan and I both thinking this was a very daring and possibly ridiculous idea, and deciding not to tell our parents that they could attend.

The parents who did come were treated to an odd evening. Mr Burton first gave a speech about the theatre and his teaching method, and then said that we would start with some breathing exercises, and humming, and we all had to repeat tongue-twisters like 'Peter Piper picked a peck of pickled peppers'. Then he started to throw out ideas for us all to improvise. He said, 'You're all in a jungle, you're hot and sweaty' – and we all acted accordingly – and, 'You're animals in the jungle.' By the time we got to the verbal improvisations, the audience were totally mystified and quite bored. The improvisations were performed in pairs, and when Mr Burton asked me and Jan to come centre stage and said, 'Your improvisation is "news",' Jan whispered quickly to me, 'We're neighbours,' and so we both folded our arms and leaned towards each other as if talking over a fence. We were meandering on a bit, not getting anywhere when Jan said, 'That poor Mr Harris at number eighteen is looking very tired these days.'

I knew I was taking a bit of a chance, but I said, 'Well, I hear she's very demanding.'

'D'you reckon?' Jan said. Then I saw her decide to take it further. '*I* think he's two-timing her with her up the street at number forty-two. You know – her that's all fur coat and no knickers.'

The audience had certainly livened up, so I thought I'd go with it.

'Well, he'll be paying through the nose for that,' I said. 'She's been on the game for years, and apparently gives a "special" that costs a fortune.'

'What does she do then?' asked Jan, trying not to laugh.

The audience never heard what the 'special' was, as not only did I have no idea myself, but Mr Burton had leapt forward and thanked us both, and said that we were ending the show with free movement to music, and we all leapt about expressing ourselves. I could see E.J. was trying not to laugh, and the next day he told me that the headmaster had given him a ticking off and told him he was to stick to plays in future.

In our private lessons E.J. mostly concentrated on my accent, through working on classical speeches with me. After every long summer holiday, as I greeted him on the bus on the first day back, he would put his head in his hands in despair as my accent would have slipped back to its natural rough London (no one in Tottenham used the word 'cockney' – that was the accent of people who lived in the East End).

There are many arguments now about whether RP (received

pronunciation) is necessary or even a good idea. All I know is that I wouldn't have stood a chance of becoming an actress then if I hadn't changed my accent. I've heard some idiot voice-teachers say that you lose your soul if you lose the accent you were born into. Really? Will you lose your soul if you move to another area and have carpet on the floor instead of lino? Your accent will reflect what's spoken around you by the people you mix with, and I think it's somewhat pretentious to hang onto a really broad accent which you've not heard spoken daily around you for years. That must be such an effort. Without that effort most people have a lilt or a trace of their original accent, unless of course they never move. I was only doing what was natural in the school holidays, which was reverting to the accent that was spoken around me. But I understood that if I wanted to play leading parts in Shakespeare, I would have to be able to speak the way Mr Burton was teaching me. The language demanded it.

He was working on a speech of Prince Arthur's from *King John* with me at the end of my second year. It's a wonderful speech where Prince Arthur, who is about ten or twelve years old, begs Hubert, his gaoler, who has been commanded to do so by wicked King John, not to burn out his eyes. '*Must you,*' the boy says in terror and horror, '*with hot irons burn out both mine eyes?*'

There was a production of *King John* on at that time in Regent's Park Open Air Theatre, and Mr Burton said he would take me, with my mother as chaperone, to see it. The outing was approved by everyone (including Miss Cullimore). Me, wildly excited to at last see a play, my mother horrified that she had got to sit through Shakespeare, and very nervous of Mr Burton. But E.J. behaved with exquisite manners, which frightened my mother even more – she was terrified of putting a foot wrong. Robert Atkins ran the company then, and Alec Clunes was playing the Bastard. It seemed to me quite wonderful – but then I had nothing to measure it against. Riding back on the tube that night with my mother, neither of us spoke much. My mind was running over and over the gripping play I'd just seen and the cleverness of the actors, and my mother was probably praying that she never had to sit through anything like that again.

The summer holidays started shortly after this trip, and I had an idea. The only person I hadn't liked in *King John* was the boy playing Prince Arthur. He really was very bad and I thought, Why don't I write to Mr Robert Atkins and tell him that I would be better and that he should see me? I secretly sent off the letter and received a reply, that luckily my mother didn't spot, saying, 'If you think you're so much better, come and audition for me'.

I thought it best not to tell anyone. I dressed in a cotton frock my mother had made me from a *Woman's Own* pattern offer that had buttons all the way down one side and that I thought was chic. I had a pair of white wedge sandals from Bata, a white crocheted hat I pinched for the day from my sister and white crocheted gloves. I also put quite a lot of her make-up on. I thought I looked the bee's knees. I shouted to my mother that I was going out with Jan and managed to slide out of the front door without her seeing me.

I found my way easily to Regent's Park by bus and tube and when I reached the theatre, I saw that there had been a matinee that afternoon – so to arrive in the break between performances seemed a perfect time. The big wooden gates were closed, so I went up to the box office and told them that

Mr Atkins was expecting me. 'You'd better go through then,' the woman said and opened the door for me.

It was a repertory season, and that afternoon's performance had been *A Midsummer Night's Dream* and a large group of actors, including handsome Richard Johnson, were sitting on the grass at the side of the auditorium, still in costume, talking, eating and laughing together. I approached them. 'Could you please tell me where I can find Mr Robert Atkins?' I asked. They all stared at me for a moment, then started laughing again and someone said, 'My God, she can't be more than fourteen or fifteen. What is he thinking of?' Then Richard Johnson stood up and put his arm round me and said, 'He'll be in his dressing room,' and pointed out the way.

I found the door that said 'Mr Robert Atkins' and knocked on it. 'Come in,' boomed a voice. I walked in. Robert Atkins was a corpulent, heavy-featured, rather ugly man. He had been playing Bottom, and was sitting, legs apart, with a dirty linen Elizabethan shirt hanging out of his trousers. He had a mug of tea and was reading the newspaper.

'Who the hell are you?' he barked.

'I wrote to you,' I said. 'You said "come and audition".'

He surveyed me.

'Now look here. I don't give jobs to shop girls.'

I wasn't the least offended. There was nothing wrong with shop girls.

'I'm not a shop girl,' I said. 'I'm a schoolgirl, and I really would be a better Prince Arthur than the one you've got.'

He sat back and stared at me, then finally, with a sigh –

'All right,' he said. 'Come into the tent and show me what you can do.'

The tent was where they played when it rained. I took

centre stage and gave Prince Arthur's speech my all. When I'd finished he heaved himself onto the stage and put his hand on my shoulder.

'Well, you're quite right,' he said. 'You are better than the boy I've got, but I can't change him now, and you're too young to join the company. Finish school, go to drama school, then get in touch with me and I'll give you a job.'

The amazing thing was that he kept his word, and six years later he *did* give me my first job.

That summer, I fell in love. I know that some would say 'I had my first crush', but I promised my almost-thirteen-year-old self that I would never take the emotion I felt then lightly – to always remember that I had genuinely fallen in love – and that feeling lasted four years.

Of course, Nature had set my hormones up for it, as I had started menstruating, and then chance led me to meet the best-looking boy in the school – so although I know now that chemistry, not Cupid, is the culprit who makes idiots of us all, nevertheless there will never be anything quite like the magic of falling in love.

I met him at a party at Gladys's house (she also lived on a council estate), and he must have been a friend of one of her brothers. I thought that my legs were going to give way when I first clapped eyes on him, and Gladys said, 'And, oh yeah, this is Ray Lambert – he's in 3C, Burton's form.' Ray smiled and I thought I was going to pass out. I was so dazzled. There was a silly kissing game where a girl had to go outside the room and the boys drew lots as to who should go and kiss her. I sat crouched on the bare stairs, staring at the peeling wallpaper, promising God anything if only he would send Ray Lambert through the door. He did. It was my first kiss, and it couldn't have been more perfect. Soon after that the party broke up, and I went my way and Ray on his sexy blue racing bike went his. But I knew it was true love and that we would be together for ever. What I hadn't thought of was that at fourteen he might have someone else. And he did. He was already attached to a girl in his class called Patricia Brandon – and for life.

I found out some forty or fifty years later that their mothers were best friends, and had had their two babies within weeks of one another and that they had determined they should marry. The children had known each other from birth and had played together, holidayed together and gone to the same schools together, so at fourteen they were as good as married. I knew none of this then. I just couldn't understand why, after that kiss, he wasn't asking me out. He winked at me as he flew by me on his blue steed, and smiled at me at assembly, but that was all.

As he was in Mr Burton's class, I foolishly questioned him about Ray. 'Don't even think about that,' he said swiftly. 'He's with Patricia, and that's that.' I also knew that I'd made him angry but didn't want to think why.

My obsession with Ray became all-consuming. Already not known for my concentration, I gazed out of the window during lessons and imagined romantic scenes with him. I came bottom of the class for the third time running.

Then in my fourth year, when the plan was that I should play Rosalind in *As You Like It* and E.J. said, 'Art room after school today', I said no, I couldn't. It was the first time I had ever made an excuse and refused to meet for our lesson.

I knew that there was going to be a gathering of boys with bikes after school outside the fish and chip shop on the North

Circular, and I thought there was a good chance Ray might be there. Jan said she would come with me and we would casually hang around. It had now been two years since that kiss, and I was getting desperate – if only I could get him on his own again outside school, he would break up with Patricia and see that he had to be with me. Jan and I stood bantering until there was clearly no hope that Ray would arrive. I cycled sadly home.

The next morning as I took my seat next to Mr Burton on the bus I knew immediately that he was in a fury. 'So you would rather spend your time flirting inanely with a group of boys than work with me?' I started to protest, but it was no good. 'I saw you. I saw you. I looked down from the top of the bus and there you were.' The tirade went on all the way to school. 'Is that what you want? To marry a local boy as soon as you leave school and have two or three children, and that's good enough for you? Then you don't need me any more.' And we had reached where we had to split and that was the end of it.

I thought he would get over it after a few days. I was wrong. Weeks went by and he didn't speak to me. He was no longer taking us for divinity, and if I passed him in the corridor he looked the other way. I was bereft without his company and felt that I had been very stupid. The only person I had to blame was myself. I was very unhappy, so I threw myself into athletics instead, the only other thing I was any good at, and won some sort of inter-school prize for the high jump doing the Western roll, but it didn't give me the thrill I got from acting.

Then a notice went up to say that the next play would be Sheridan's *The Rivals*. If any students wanted to, they could audition. Mr Burton just stared at me for a long time when I went into the room where he was seeing people, then finally said, 'So you still want to act?' 'Yes please,' I said – and then, 'I'm sorry.'

'You realise that if you hadn't been so silly the play would now be *As You Like It* and you would be playing Rosalind?'

'Yes,' I said miserably.

'You must understand that there is no point in my giving all this time I've been giving to you if you're not serious about being an actress. It's a very hard life, and you really have to want it more than anything else. You have to be passionate about it.'

I said I was passionate about it – and I was – it was just that I was also passionate about Ray Lambert.

'Well, I've cast most of *The Rivals*, but you can have Lucy the maid.'

'Thank you very much. I would like that very much.'

There was another pause.

'Do you *really want* to be an actress?'

'Yes. Yes please.'

'Then you and I had better start working again.'

So it was back to the art room sessions as well as rehearsals, and I was happy again. Having been sad at first that I was just to play 'the maid', I was thrilled to find that although small, the part was a good one and I could have fun with it. The rest of the cast were sixth-formers, but they always treated me as one of them and they made me feel grown up, and rehearsals were great fun.

It was a successful production, and I was particularly excited because at the last performance E.J. had told me he had invited an ex-student called Aubrey Woods, who had made a hit quite recently playing Smike in a film of *Nicholas Nickleby*. I would be seen by a real professional. We used the science labs with screens scattered around as dressing rooms, and on the last night the show had gone well and there had been a lot of banter and playing about afterwards when we were changing, and somehow – I suppose because I was longing for it not to end – I was very late getting out of my costume and everyone had gone. I was just putting on my socks behind a screen when I heard Mr Burton's voice. He was saying, 'You understand my worry. I think she's very talented, but I'm not sure about her looks. I can see that she's not conventionally pretty, so I wonder if I'm wrong to encourage her? You know how much looks matter in the profession.'

There was a longish pause. 'No,' came the velvety, strong tones of the actor. 'No, she's not exactly pretty or classically beautiful.' Another long pause. 'But you know what . . . ? She's sexy.' 'Yes,' said E.J. 'I think so too.' And then the subject was changed. They went on and on, and I thought I would never get out from behind the screen, but at last they went. So, I wasn't pretty but I was sexy – well, that would do me just fine – and I happily raced home.

The next time I was alone with E.J., I was full of confidence. It had never entered my head that there was a question in E.J.'s mind, but now I knew there had been but that it was sorted, and I would definitely be going to drama school when I left Latymer's. I presumed that he would fix it with my parents.

'I've come across a problem,' he said, 'about your going to drama school. Your parents of course won't be able to pay the fees, scholarships are rare and I've always known that we would have to get you a council grant, but to get a grant you have to pass your School Certificate, and the talk in the staffroom when I asked about your academic abilities was that it was highly unlikely that you would pass, and if you don't, then of course that would be the end of everything.'

I was dumbfounded. I had never thought that I would have to be academically bright to be an actress.

'Now when I talk to you,' E.J. continued, 'you seem to be quite intelligent – so what's going on?'

'Well,' I mumbled, 'I'm bored in all my classes except English literature, so I just imagine I'm somewhere else and don't listen.'

'Well, you're bloody well going to have to listen, or kiss goodbye to ever becoming an actress. Put your coat back on and meet me at the bus stop.'

He took me to a building that had a big typing pool on one floor. There was a gallery round it and we stood looking down at dozens of girls with their heads bent, clattering away at their machines.

'That,' said E.J., 'is where you'll end up if you don't get your School Certificate.'

I was horrified at this sudden possible reality. The fourth-year exams would be in a few weeks, then I would be in the fifth year and there would be Mock Matric (the School Certificate was also called Matriculation), and then in a few more months there would be the real thing. The teachers in the staffroom were right. I would fail.

Could I somehow pull myself together and not be so stupid?

So I tried not to drift off in lessons, and started to really pay attention to my homework. To everyone's amazement – including mine – at the end of the fourth year I wasn't bottom of the class, I had moved up eight places. But poor Jan, with no one to make her see the error of her ways, was suddenly in an awful pickle. She was now fifteen and could be legally taken from school, and as she wasn't doing much work there her parents sought our form teacher's advice as to whether it wouldn't be better for her to leave school and start work. The teacher agreed – they were encouraged to take her away. Jan was desperately unhappy and I was distraught. I went to Miss Cullimore and asked her to change Jan's parents' minds. She said, 'Janet Bryan is the kind of pretty little feather-headed thing only interested in boys who will marry very quickly and have a big family, and for her to stay at school is pointless.' I wanted to hit her for being so dismissive.

Jan did marry at nineteen because she had met the love of her life. She had one child, Martin, whose birth nearly killed her, and the doctors forbade any more children. She became a librarian – she loved her work and was one of the best-read, wittiest and sharpest of my friends.

I had a lonely fifth year at school without Jan, in which I worked as hard as I could. Ray Lambert and his wife-to-be, Patricia Brandon, had both done brilliantly in their School Certificate the last year, and had sailed into the sixth form. And then Patricia disappeared. I unguardedly asked E.J. where she was. 'She's spending some time in France. Her French is excellent. She's a clever girl, she'll do well.' My face must have prompted his next remark. 'Don't even think about it, Eileen. He will never look at anyone else.'

A few weeks later I was ambling back home along Church Street, missing Jan, when a bike drew up beside me and there was Ray Lambert. Without any preamble he said, 'Would you like to come out with me on Saturday night?' I don't know how I managed to speak.

'Yes,' I said. 'Yes, I would.'

'All right. We'll meet at Enfield Station at six thirty. See you then.' And he turned and cycled off.

I had to go and sit down on a wall, I was in such a state of ecstasy. I'd met him and kissed him when I was twelve and now suddenly, after three years of yearning, at fifteen he was asking me out. I couldn't believe it.

By the time Saturday came I was almost surprised to see him at Enfield Station. I'd begun to think I'd imagined the whole encounter.

We went to the pictures at a cinema called The Florida, and I have no idea what movie we saw because after about half an hour he held my hand and I was so transported with joy that I think the screen could have caught fire and I wouldn't have noticed. We kissed again at the end of the evening and then he said, 'You go to the tuck shop in Church Street, don't you? I'll see you there next week.' He did meet me there and suggested that we go on a cycle ride together at the weekend. We went all the way up to Cheshunt and I loved every moment. Then all went quiet again and he didn't turn up at the tuck shop and I thought he was avoiding me. So I did a brave thing. I left a note in his desk asking him if he would like to come to my brother's twenty-first birthday party, and he left me a note saying yes. My brother Ron was organising the whole thing himself and I knew it wouldn't be the drearily depressing affair that we usually had.

It was to be in a church hall. There would be proper food — quiches instead of sausage rolls (or 'kweeches', as we couldn't stop my sister calling them) and rice dishes and bowls of salad, and I think there was Black Forest gateau for his cake. Ron was going to put quiz-like questions on the walls and there would be a prize for whoever won the quiz. And there was a friend who was going to attempt to be a disc jockey and play records for us to dance to. I felt it would be pretty sophisticated.

My mother, of course, hadn't known I'd been going out with

anyone, but I just said in a very offhand way, 'Jan can't come, so I'm bringing one of the boys from school,' and she didn't question it.

I could tell that Ray was nervous – I thought that was because he'd committed himself to a family affair, but he enjoyed doing the questions that were on the wall, and I finally got to dance with him. We were good ballroom dancers and we floated around that church hall for about half an hour with me in a state of bliss that I hoped would go unnoticed by my family. Then suddenly he said, 'Come outside. I want to talk to you.' We sat on a wooden bench among the gravestones, holding hands. Then he said:

'Look, the thing is, I mustn't see you any more.'

'Is it because of Pat?'

'That' – he paused – 'and something else. There's another reason. I'm really sorry.'

Then he hugged me and left.

I was broken-hearted. What was the 'other reason'?

Now I was altogether bereft. In a few weeks Patricia was back at school, and I could tell Ray was avoiding me and there was no Jan to talk me through it.

There wasn't even a good play to take my mind off my misery. I thought Mr Burton would do *As You Like It* for me but at the last minute, with no excuse as to why, he changed the school play to *The Blue Bird* by Maeterlinck, which I thought was a very silly play indeed. There was a line I had to say in it that caused the whole school to titter. I played the Queen of Light and had to tell Mytyl and Tyltyl how children were born and say, '*When the mothers and fathers want children, the great doors at the back open and the Little Ones go down*'. Each time I said that line I all but winked at the audience. Throughout my last year it was agreed that I shouldn't do a play, to allow me to totally concentrate on work, and in that year Mr Burton finally did *As You Like It* with a girl a year younger than me playing Rosalind. I was deeply hurt.

At Mock Matric I'd moved up another eight places, and so was roughly halfway down the class. I was now really determined, and I worked hard. To get your School Certificate, you had to pass at least five out of eight subjects including English grammar and maths. My last few weeks at Latymer's after sitting the exam were dreary. I was convinced I hadn't passed, and Ray never looked my way. I would have to leave at the end of the fifth form when I was sixteen whatever the results were as there was no way my parents would let me stay. I was spoilt as it was. My sister Peggy had been taken away at fourteen, my brother at fifteen and I was lucky to be kept at home not bringing in money till I was sixteen. 'What did the exam matter!' my mother said. At sixteen I could go straight into a show.

On that last day in school I sat in the cloakroom and wept. I was still there when the school caretaker came in with his buckets. 'What's up with you?' he said.

'I'll never see the boy I love again,' I said.

'Plenty more fish in the sea. Now clear off, I've got to clean.'

I went miserably home.

A few weeks later, the results were in and we all had to go back to school to be given them by the headmaster. I made that journey with great trepidation.

I had passed in seven out of eight subjects and got a credit in English literature and grammar. The only subject I had failed was geography. As he handed me my result, Mr Davis was beaming. He said, 'I'm so very happy with this result, Eileen.' I couldn't believe it. I'd done it. Now I could go to drama school.

*

I was wrong about never seeing Ray again. Twenty-six years later, like Dorothy Margaret Hall, he came with his wife, Patricia, to see *Saint Joan*. He was going bald but was still handsome. He stood smiling, saying very little. It was Pat who told me that they had seen every single play that I had ever done. 'And,' she said, 'God forbid that he would miss you in anything you did on TV.' He had become a bank manager and she was the headmistress of Tottenham High School for Girls. They had no children. My new husband was in the dressing room and they stayed and talked, and I thought what a very good couple they were.

Twenty years after this visit, in 1996, I saw in the school magazine that Pat had died, and after giving it some consideration I decided to write a note of condolence to Ray. After all, she was only sixty-three and they had no children – he must have felt utterly bereft.

I got a sweet, sad letter back from him saying how he had looked after her in her long illness and how he would obviously miss her. He then told me about their mothers' close friendship and how they had been destined for one another. He went on, 'You must have thought my behaviour odd that time when Pat was in France. As it must have been obvious I was very attracted to you, but Mr Burton found out that we had been out together and told me that I mustn't have anything to do with you. I must leave you alone, as you were destined for a very different life. He made me promise not to see you again. I disobeyed and came to your brother's party, and then you know what happened.'

So forty-seven years later all was explained, and of course I had to be grateful to E.J. for being so interfering. It had been the right kind of protection. Ray Lambert was a lovely man but for everyone's sake, including mine, it was better that he'd married Pat.

There was one last postscript to our story. In 2002 Graham Norton was interviewing me on the radio to promote the Samuel Beckett play that I was doing with Michael Gambon, *All That Fall*.

'I hope you don't mind,' Graham said, 'but we're asking listeners to call in with questions.'

'That's fine,' I said.

After some chat he said, 'Right, now we have the first caller on the line. Hello, what would you like to ask Eileen?'

A woman's voice said, 'I'm calling for a relative who is too shy to call himself. Do you remember Ray Lambert?'

'My God,' I said, 'he was the first love of my life.'

7

When I had left Parkside I was still very much my mother's girl. As soon as I came home from school I would yell 'Muuum?' as I came through the back door, and she would say, 'Oh, you're back', and my world was safe. Everything was okay. I have always felt that that was a great gift she gave me – she was always there, at home. It gave me huge confidence to have that security. Although words of love were rarely, if ever, spoken, there was a close bond. But the atmosphere at home had changed throughout my years at Latymer's. She must have felt that she was losing me. I was rebellious, which is natural in one's teens but I was also unpleasantly contemptuous.

I had questioned my mother's decisions from an early age. Now I began to realise the damage that had been done and to challenge everything. With feet now so deformed and painful that I had to wear sandals all year round, I knew that my mother had been wrong not to follow the chiropodist's advice and take away my block-toed ballet shoes and stop all toe-tapping. And while at Latymer's I found out that she had probably ruined my teeth as well.

Because the war was over and a Labour government was now

in power, for the first time in our lives children of my age were being given health checks. One of these checks meant that I was sent to the dentist. I had only been once before when I was three years old, when I was taken to the Eastman Clinic to have a baby tooth yanked out for some reason. They had given me gas and it was a horrible experience so I went to the dentist, which the school had sent me to in Edmonton, with great trepidation.

A girl about my age was just leaving the surgery with her mother. They had upper-class accents and the dentist just indicated to me to get in the chair while he ushered the pair out. There were gushing 'thank you's from the mother and child and oozing obsequiousness from the dentist. As he finally shut the door on them he said to his assistant, 'What a charming woman that was'; then to me, in quite a different tone: 'Have you been sent by the school?'

'Yeah,' I said.

'Open your mouth.' I obeyed. He poked about inside my mouth for a few seconds, then exploded, 'What am I supposed to do with teeth like this? They are a disgrace. Too many sweets. Not cleaned properly. I can't imagine she's ever been to a dentist. It just shows you,' he went on with his angry grumble to his assistant without addressing me at all, 'that when you don't have educated parents, like the woman we've just seen, it affects *everything*. This kid's parents are so ignorant they've just let her teeth rot – so that will be another thing against her when she grows up.'

I was humiliated, but when he took his fingers out of my mouth for a second, I managed to say with some venom, 'I can't have eaten too many sweets 'cos they were rationed.'

'Well, you've eaten enough to decay your teeth with sugar. You'll be lucky if you don't lose them all.'

I wanted to beat him with my fists and run from the chair, but as I lay there open-mouthed and helpless while he continued his gruesome work, I thought, This isn't fair. I wasn't one of those kids who rushed to get her sweet ration. I wasn't even that keen on sweets, and then I remembered I *did* like chocolate though, and my mother always put a piece of chocolate on my pillow at night to try to encourage me to go to sleep, and of course it melted in my mouth *after* I had cleaned my teeth. All those sugar sandwiches can't have helped either.

She herself had had all her teeth extracted when she was eighteen (I believe it was a common way of saving money) and had always had false teeth. I suppose she thought I could do the same thing. The British are notorious for having bad teeth anyway, but there is nothing that screams 'poor working class' as loudly as an unfortunate smile.

I've spent a fortune on mine, and I'm still nervous of smiling.

And then there were the arguments about the plan that Mr Burton had talked my parents into agreeing to. I was to try for a scholarship to RADA (the Royal Academy of Dramatic Art), and if I got it that would pay for my fees and keep. If I failed to win, he suggested that I do a teaching course at the Guildhall School of Music and Drama, where I would get a grant from the government for fees and *some* support. I didn't even listen to this idea. I knew I would get a scholarship. My mother and father agreed uneasily to these suggestions, still hoping that I would tap my way to fame instead. 'You don't need to go to drama school to be in a show,' my father would say. 'I don't want to be in a "show",' I would spit contemptuously. 'I'm going to be a *serious* actress.'

Over three hundred young people applied for the scholarship. I was called back twice to audition and got down to the last three. The news came on the day that my sister was married to a good-looking man who mended traffic lights. Unfortunately he failed to tell my sister that his first marriage had been annulled because he was impotent. They did not live happily ever after.

We were well into the wedding breakfast set on trestle tables in the cramped living room when a neighbour who was helping out came waltzing in waving a telegram in her hand. 'A telegram for Eileen,' she announced with great satisfaction. Now the war was over, a telegram could only mean good news, surely, for a young woman who everyone in the street knew was 'going to drama school'. I ripped it open and read, 'Sorry to inform you that you have not won a scholarship to the Royal Academy of Dramatic Art.' I gasped and tried to push back the tears. Everyone was looking at me. 'I didn't get it,' I said, 'I didn't get the scholarship,' and squeezed my way out of the room as quickly as possible. As I was going I heard my sister say with some fury, 'It's always the same. It's always about her. She's spoilt my day.'

I think my parents were quite relieved that I was going to train to be a teacher. It was a highly respected profession. They could say it with pride, and everyone in Courtman Road would be impressed. Though my mother would *rather* I became a 'Bluebell' (a crack troupe of world-famous chorus girls), I think she had reasoned with herself that this way I would have a teaching degree in my back pocket and, knowing how insecure stage work was, that might be handy. The good thing was that I would have to forget 'this acting business'.

There was nothing to be done about it. I was to train to be a teacher at the Guildhall School of Music and Drama. No one ever told me exactly how much the government's maintenance grant was but my mother always said it scarcely covered my fares, let alone clothed me, and I *did* have to have some new clothes. She bought me a pair of dark brown slacks, and I begged for a sky-blue car coat that was in the window of the Bon Marché in Wood Green High Street. It had a big pleat at the back and was called a jigger jacket, and although it wasn't a *useful* colour, I wanted it. It cost seven pounds, which was an enormous amount for her to shell out, but she bought it. My sister gave me two of her old jumpers (we never used the word 'sweater'), and a pair of flat ballet pumps were also bought to accommodate my now permanently bent toes and huge bunions. That was my outfit for the next three years.

It was to be a longish journey each day. A bus to Turnpike Lane, then the tube to Holborn where I changed for the Aldwych, then a fifteen-minute walk along Fleet Street to John Carpenter Street. When I first started at the college (as people called it), I thought it would be lovely to walk every day through Temple Gardens, but I soon got too tired to do anything but the shortest route along Fleet Street.

I sat on the tube on my first day trying to feel confident and cheerful. I really didn't want to be a drama teacher, I only wanted to act. But I had no alternative other than to pretend I wanted to teach hoping I would get a chance to act as well. I took some comfort in my smart new outfit – I thought I looked stylish and sophisticated.

At the Aldwych tube station, you all had to squeeze into a lift to get up to ground level, and as I stepped into it on that first day a bitter-looking man in his sixties, wearing a wing collar and holding a briefcase, spat at me, hissing furiously, 'It's disgusting – you're disgusting. It's unnatural. Women in trousers shouldn't be tolerated.' Being British, everyone crammed into the lift looked into the middle distance as if no one had spoken. I was very shaken. Trousers for women were quite normal in Tottenham. Was it not the done thing, then, in the West End? When I shakily reached the Guildhall I lost all confidence in my ensemble as hardly any other female was wearing trousers. I had got it wrong already, but it was too late to do anything about it. That was the outfit. It was all I had, apart from a couple of cotton dresses my mother had made me and my school uniform.

In 1950 the Guildhall was known mainly for its teaching of music and opera. I think that the drama department must have been an afterthought, as we drama students were all squashed down in a dark, dank, airless basement. We only got out of the basement for our private lessons, which were in one of the airy rooms on the upper floors where the musicians and singers worked. These private lessons were the one advantage we had over other drama establishments.

In my first year my tutor was an Irishman called Ambrose Marriott who had dark floppy hair and spaniel eyes, and who immediately made me feel at home, which was a relief, because I didn't feel at all at home in the basement.

E. J. Burton had done wonders with my accent, but I was surrounded at home with Tottenham sounds and I know that I often slipped back into them. I was very aware that all the other students appeared to come from middle- and upper-class homes, and that quite a number of them seemed to be using the college as a finishing school. It infuriated me that their parents were paying for them to have the drama classes (which I wanted) when they had no interest in being actresses at all. It was just 'quite a fun thing to do' till they got married.

Of course your accent doesn't matter a damn today – had it been ten years later, it would have been a badge of honour to be working class – but it was very different in 1950 and at first there seemed to be no one there with a background like mine.

I quickly realised that although we had schedules to follow, those students doing the acting course and those on the teaching course shared the rooms in the basement, and it was quite easy to walk into their lessons as well as going to lectures. I could put my name down to audition to be in a play and no one questioned it. And if you were prepared to be in the building from nine o'clock in the morning till nine at night, you could do both courses.

But I felt terribly out of things at first. My mother gave me my bus and train fare every day and the usual awful sandwiches, as I couldn't afford to have food in the canteen. Luckily a girl who had been a dancing partner at the KY School, Jill Popper, who was a good friend, had got a grant to study piano there and we rather clung together that first term. She was as lacking in cash as I was. Then her mother had the bright idea that her daughter could earn money giving dancing classes every Saturday morning in a hall she hired in King's Cross, and Jill asked me to join her as her assistant. Not to miss out, my mother offered to come as well and collect the money as Mrs Popper would be playing the piano for the class. Jill and I were tired after our week at the Guildhall, but we both longed to have some pocket money and we quite enjoyed teaching the children. Although my mother took the money I was paid to help with my keep, she had to give me something and so I could at last afford an occasional snack with Jill in the canteen, and more importantly a mug of coffee at Nings Coffee House in Fleet Street. This was where everyone who was anyone in the drama department hung out. At last, if anyone was friendly enough to say, 'I'm going to Nings, do you want to come?' I could say yes.

This was the first coffee I had ever tasted and I didn't like it, but I drank it most days over the next three years. I thought that the elite little crowd that went daily to Nings were sophisticated, and I would have been marked down immediately as a 'pleb' if I'd asked for tea. Once I could pay for that mug of coffee, I gradually began to feel accepted and enjoy the camaraderie. There was something dashing about turning your nose up at the college canteen, leaving the stuffy basement and walking up the road into the heady air of Fleet Street to sit crammed into a booth and consume coffee and flapjacks. It eased us out and released our tongues. We talked endlessly and only about acting.

In the early weeks at the Guildhall, I had made the terrible mistake of going to an audition that was offered on the noticeboard for 'anyone who can sing for a musical evening' which was being put together by a Peter Reeves.

There was only Peter and someone playing the piano in the room for the audition. I gave them my music and sang a song that Jeanne Crain sang in *State Fair*. I thought I sang quite nicely. Eighteen students had put their names down for the audition. The next day a notice went up to say that seventeen of them were invited to go to rehearsals. I was the only person not on the list. Well, it made it nice and clear. I really couldn't sing.

I would say that there were about eight or nine women to every man in the drama department, so the men were greatly prized, not just for parts in plays (no one would have dreamed of having a woman play a man's part) but also of course as objects of desire. There was a very handsome, charming

American in our year called Gerry and one day after a rehearsal we had been in together he said to me, 'Shall we go up to the roof and have a breather?' I had never been on the roof as it was vaguely forbidden, but thrilled that he should ask me. We took the lift to the top floor and stepped out into the sunshine. We chatted, he held my hand and then kissed me quite sweetly.

When I got back down to the basement I rather proudly told another girl what had happened. 'Oh, Gerry – yes,' she said blithely, 'he's a darling, isn't he? But of course he's queer.' I knew immediately what she meant, though never to my knowledge had I heard the word used in that way before. It was as if a piece of a jigsaw had suddenly slid into place, and I'm amazed looking back how ordinary the revelation seemed to me.

Luckily one of the men who had arrived at the Guildhall at the same time as I had was a young man called Trevor Martin. He had also been at Latymer Grammar School and was in the sixth form when I was in the first form, and I remembered seeing him in one school play. He had gone straight into National Service for two years, so that by the time he reached drama school he was twenty-one. I was sixteen. He lived in Enfield so we travelled the same way home, and I sometimes saw him on the tube, but he didn't seem to notice me so I didn't speak to him. Then one day I had nipped into a rehearsal room to hear a reading of an unmemorable play that was popular at the time of the type we called a 'French door' play because at some point young people in white with rackets came through the doors and said, 'Anyone for tennis?'

The reading was going along quite nicely, with Trevor giving his best imitation of Noël Coward, but when he had the line: '*Don't think you can seduce me by wheedling your way in here with very little on except Chanel No. 5*', never having heard of the perfume he said 'Channel Number Five', and the whole room shrieked with laughter. Trevor was both mortified and furious and couldn't laugh it off. To my horror he showed his humiliation by losing his temper, throwing his chair aside and trying to leave the room. He was persuaded back to finish the reading, and I hung around till there was an opportunity to speak to him and told him I thought that he had read very well. 'Except that I showed myself up,' he said. 'If you'd just laughed with every-one, they would have thought you were *trying* to be funny,' I replied. 'I've never heard of that perfume either.'

That was the beginning of our liaison. We then started to look out for each other on the tube and the friendship devel-oped into something more, not only because we were young and wanted to be in love, but mostly because we felt com-fortable together. After about eighteen months we ended up engaged to each other. In those days that's what you did. There was no thought of living together – that would have been very shocking. And there was nowhere at all to go to make love – so there was a lot of repressed heavy petting which, looking back at it now, seems terribly sad and a touch sordid, but we were all terrified of getting pregnant. I don't think either of us was in love. The relationship happened because we came from the same background and gave each other security.

Although I got along well enough with most of the students in my year, there was only one other person I became really friendly with. Judith Dawson was one of the students that 'Mummy and Daddy' had paid for, but she too was seriously committed to being an actress and this bonded us. I thought she was very talented. The first play we acted opposite each other in was called *Bonaventure*. I was a nun and Judith played a wayward woman who I saved from some dark fate.

I can never forget this play because it was the first time I ever 'dried' – that is, I completely forgot my lines.

Drying is a horrible experience – the terror of any actor. The brain seems to stop, and you find that sometimes you can't even take a prompter's cue or a cue from anyone else on the stage who is trying to help you. You can be simply too petrified to hear the prompt. It had never happened to me before, and somehow after a second prompt from the wings I went on, but I was mortified. At the end of the play I refused to go on the stage for a curtain call and ran down the stairs and hid in a crevice under the stage known as 'the cubbyhole' and wept. It was all over; I could never be an actress now. What if I ever did it again? No, I was a disastrous failure. Somehow my professor, Ambrose Marriott, who had been in the audience spied out where I'd hidden and came and squeezed his portly person under the stage with me. 'I'm giving up,' I said to him. 'I'm giving up all thoughts of being an actress.' 'Of course you're not,' he said. 'This occasionally happens. It's a danger that you have to live with. You must learn not to panic if it happens. You must stay calm.'

If there are any actors who have never dried, I don't know them. Indeed, I know two actresses who have fainted on stage, considering it preferable they should be thought ill rather than be exposed for forgetting their lines.

I've had quite a few dries in my career, the worst being some forty years later when I was in *A Delicate Balance* by Edward Albee at the Haymarket Theatre with Maggie Smith, where it is possible I went too far with Professor Marriott's advice. I was playing Agnes, who has a very long complicated speech that opens the play and that is only interrupted by a word or two from her husband Tobias. It is known to be torturous to learn.

It was towards the end of the run and I was rehearsing a two-handed play by Yasmina Reza called *The Unexpected Man* with Michael Gambon, so was trying to din the words of that into my head, and then I had the bad luck to have to do some reshooting for the film of *The Avengers* on Sundays. This was quite a load to be carrying. One evening, when I was in my dressing room preparing for the performance, I had a phone call from my agent explaining that for some contractual reason I wouldn't be getting any money for the reshoot of the film. I was tired and I went into a fury. As I put the phone down, shaking, I realised they were calling Beginners. I had to rush to get dressed and get myself on stage where the stage management and John Standing, who was playing Tobias, were waiting for me.

'Are you okay, Eileen?' the stage manager asked. 'Yes, yes,' I said. 'I'm fine. I'm sorry I'm late. Take it up.' They took the curtain up and Johnny poured a drink for me as usual and, as he handed it to me – that was my cue to start speaking – I had no idea what to say.

There was a horribly long pause and then the prompter gave me the line, which my brain refused to take in. I kept telling myself not to panic and then with great calm I found myself addressing the audience: 'I'm so sorry,' I said, 'but I don't know what I say or what play it is or even what theatre I'm in. They will have to bring the curtain down so that I can look at the book.' And I nodded to the prompt corner, who brought the curtain down in stunned amazement. With a kind of serenity I walked to the corner and looked at the script. I could hear Maggie at the back of the stage, waiting for her entrance, say, 'What *is* she doing?' I took a few deep breaths, apologised to a shaking Johnny and said, 'Okay, take it up again.' Immediately there was a round of applause, and I went through to play as well as I had done any night – if not better.

I was of course ashamed, and one or two others in the cast were furious with me, quite rightly saying that I shouldn't have taken on so much work. It was also my bad luck that the American producer, Gerry Schoenfeld, who owned half of Broadway, was in that night, as was Matthew Warchus, the director of *The Unexpected Man*, who looked rather pale when he came into my dressing room, but it didn't stop either of them employing me. Even as I write this now I find my mouth has gone dry with terror at the thought of that moment. Apparently Maggie Smith told the tale recently, ending up by saying, 'That took some balls'. I gratefully thank her for that.

Not long after Judith and I had done *Bonaventure*, my sister and my cousin Gladys, who had a car, asked me if I wanted to drive to Stratford-upon-Avon with them. 'And bring a friend with you from drama school.' This was a really big deal in our family. We had no car, and it was considered a massive treat, and the theatre at Stratford-upon-Avon was Mecca to a drama student. So I took a deep breath and asked Judith if she would like to come on the trip and she accepted.

It wasn't until we reached Stratford-upon-Avon and my cousin dumped us outside the theatre saying, 'Well, there it is. Enjoy yourselves. We'll pick you up here in a couple of hours', that I realised it was somehow foolish to drive to a theatre and just look at it, and not go inside and see a play, but we wandered about happily enough gazing at the ugly reddish building that I would one day learn to love, wondering then if we would ever work there. It was called simply the Shakespeare Memorial Theatre then, and there was no big gift shop as there is now nor

The Other Place. We went to the church to see Shakespeare's grave and then went to see his birthplace and, apart from the feeling that where we should have been was inside the theatre watching the matinee of *Much Ado About Nothing*, we had an enjoyable couple of hours. My cousin picked us up and we drove home, me with some relief that they hadn't 'shown me up' in any way.

A few days later my mother said to me, 'When do you think your friend is going to give us the petrol money? I've paid Gladys yours, but apparently Judith didn't pay her share.' 'But she wouldn't expect to pay anything,' I said, aghast. 'She was asked. It was an invitation.' 'Well, she owes Gladys seven and six, so you'd better ask her for it.' 'I can't,' I said miserably. 'You just don't do that.' 'Well, Gladys wants that money and we certainly can't pay for her as well as you, so you're going to *have* to do that.'

I was mortified. How could I ask Judith for petrol money? My mother nagged me all week, and I could think of no other way of finding seven and sixpence, so in utter misery I asked Judith for the money. She was, of course, completely taken aback. 'But you invited me,' she said. 'I didn't know I was to pay something.'

'I'm sorry,' was all I could say, stiff with embarrassment.

'Well, I can't give it because I don't have it,' she blurted.

It never entered my head that she didn't have seven and six to spare – after all, her parents were paying the fees. I told my mother that Judith wasn't going to give me the money and there was an enormous row. My cousin *had* to be paid, and where were we going to find the money? For the next few weeks everyone at home was angry with me, and at the Guildhall Judith avoided me. We simply couldn't get over the awkwardness of what had happened, and I hated my family for humiliating me.

Although we had lessons in fencing, period dancing, make-up, voice production and our private tutoring (in which for some unknown reason we only studied and recited poetry), the only time we ever really learned anything about acting was when we were rehearsing and performing plays.

At the end of my second year I had a big juicy part in a play called *Leading Lady* by James Reach, playing opposite my fiancé Trevor, and we both had our first little success. We played a famous theatrical couple, but the man was envious of his wife because she was thought to be the better actor and it infuriated him – an all too common real-life scenario. I loved our first entrance together, with a few friends after a first night, when I had to exclaim: '*It was wonderful, wonderful, wonderful, wonderful*', and Trevor said, '*That was one wonderful too many, my darling*', with an edge that made you know immediately that he was jealous of her. I felt confident playing that part until I saw the photographs afterwards and realised that one of my two front teeth was going dark. I'd had to have a nerve taken out of it, and the dentist in Tottenham had failed to tell me that it would inevitably go black. Where would I get the money to pay to have a cap put on that? I still hadn't got the money when, a few years later, I married someone other than Trevor and the wedding photographs showed that dark, unflattering tooth.

Another good part I was given to play was Mary of Bethany in a play called *The Acts of St Peter*. Again, looking at the photographs afterwards, I was upset to see the enormous dark circles under my eyes. I knew I was exhausted and didn't sleep much, but simply hadn't taken in how much it had affected my looks.

This lack of knowledge about my appearance should have been made clear to me long before a notice went up on our board saying that students were invited to audition for work as models for various food products at an advertising ball at The Dorchester. We would be paid twenty pounds. All you needed to have was a similarity to the picture of the person depicted on their packets or jars. They would supply the costume and all you had to do was walk slowly across the ballroom at the appointed moment. There was a list of characters that they needed.

I walked into the room at the Guildhall where they were auditioning and there were four or five men seated at a table. 'So who do you think you could represent?' one of them asked me. 'Oh,' I said with great confidence, 'the Ovaltine Girl.'

The Ovaltine Girl, if you're old enough to remember, was a smiling young woman in a pink gown and bonnet with pink cheeks, radiant with health and thrusting an Ovaltine tin joyously in the air with her right arm. They looked at me wonderingly, then one said, none too tentatively, 'Nooo, we don't think you're quite right for that.'

I was desolate. I wanted twenty pounds. I wanted to have a night at The Dorchester with free food and drink. 'Isn't there something else I could be?' There was some conferring, then one of them suddenly burst out and said, 'Nell Gwyn. With those bedroom eyes she could do a Nell Gwyn.' I was thrilled, of course. Nell Gwyn was the marmalade. Yes, I could do that. And bedroom eyes sounded so much better than tired eyes.

On the night, I sauntered across the ballroom at The Dorchester with a basket of oranges on my arm, swaying, I thought, sexily and looking flirtatiously among the crowd seated at tables for my Charles II. I did not show my teeth.

Sheila O'Hanlon marched healthily across with a tin of Ovaltine aloft. Trevor, dressed as Sir Walter Raleigh, walked elegantly, puffing his pipe of Raleigh tobacco. Neil McCallum and Anne Lewis were the Bisto Kids, and our blond American rocked across the floor in striped pyjamas on a big bottle of Bovril. We all had a wonderful night out, even though it was one of the nights Trevor and I had to walk home because we had missed the bus and tube.

It wasn't the first time we'd walked those eight miles. We had also had to walk from Guildhall to Tottenham in the great fog in 1952, and again in 1953 for the Coronation – we had gone with a gang from the Guildhall to sleep in The Mall to be sure of a good view and then got bored and tired and walked home. My mother did not welcome Trevor at 4 a.m., and made him continue on to Enfield. I was too tired to go with my parents to my sister's flat to watch the ceremony on television. I was fast asleep as Princess Elizabeth was crowned Queen. Luckily, over sixty years later when it was re-enacted for the filming of *The Crown*, I had an excellent view of the proceedings as I was playing Queen Mary.

I loved being able to do so many plays at the Guildhall, but was vaguely disappointed with the drama lessons. E. J. Burton had been far more advanced with the exercises we had done at Latymer's. As well as teaching us method acting long before it became fashionable, he had taught me everything I needed to know about breathing and voice production. I had a naturally big voice and could easily throw it to the back of the stalls, and it came as a shock to me some years later when I found out from voice doctors that my equipment was somewhat faulty and I must certainly avoid catching a cold.

In my thirties I was in T. S. Eliot's play *The Cocktail Party* with Alec Guinness. It was a big success, and we played it at the Haymarket Theatre and then the Wyndham's. By then I knew how careful I had to be with my voice and would always check with my favourite voice doctor, a Mr Punt, the minute I felt a postnasal drip on my vocal cords. Alec, who had become a friend, though fond of me was slightly irritated with me. I was out a lot after the show, having too good a time one way and another, and was no longer the adoring young acolyte I had been when we played in *Exit the King* together. One evening on my way to my dressing room I knocked on his door and told him that I was worried about my voice, but that Mr Punt was seeing me before the show and I was sure he would get my voice back to full volume. He immediately attacked me, saying that I was doing too much and was out too late at night with all the wrong people. So it wasn't surprising my voice was ragged. Mr Punt arrived, and soon had me upside down in an armchair pouring obnoxious liquids up (or rather down) my nose and injecting me with some concoction which was probably illegal but always did the trick, and I told him how annoyed Alec had been. 'Don't worry,' he said, 'I'll speak to him.'

What he did was to leave a note in Alec's dressing room saying, 'Dear Sir Alec, you must not be cross with Miss Atkins – all her passages are narrow.' That evening at the point in the play where Alec as Riley had to write down the name of the convent I was to go to, he just wrote on the card, 'ALL your passages?'

I feel I must mention that Mr Punt wore a lamp on his head like a miner's lamp to look down your throat, which left his hands free, and every female patient accepted the fact that at some point he would put his hand on your breast for a few seconds. We all agreed that we cheerfully put up with this, as he was the only throat doctor who would definitely get you back on stage.

At the end of my second year at the Guildhall I had an enormous piece of luck. For the eight weeks of the summer holidays I was offered the chance to be part of a small repertory company in Bangor, County Down in Northern Ireland. This was almost certainly because Trevor had asked the couple who ran it to consider me. He had spent our summer holidays at the end of our first year with them and when asked to go back, had clearly begged them to employ his fiancée as well. So they came to see *Leading Lady* and made me the offer.

John and Grace Whitehorn were a charming couple who did a summer season of seven plays over eight weeks. Our opening play was *Harvey* (which later became a film with James Stewart), and I made my professional debut as the Young Nurse – at just eighteen – at the Dufferin Hall, Bangor. It was a jolly company. We were all in the same digs together where we ate together, learned lines together, but definitely didn't sleep together as the landlady was a strict Protestant.

There was a very good leading lady in her mid-thirties called Cynthia Bowles, who would occasionally offer me tips. One quirky piece of advice was to always have your sleeves made a little short to show the wrist bone if you wanted the audience to feel sorry for you. I can see that it makes you a touch Oliver Twist-ish, maybe a little vulnerable, but I can't say that I've ever proved it works. But I knew from my love of Nat Mills and Bobbie in music hall, where Nat always wore an oversized tailcoat with sleeves dangling, that if you did the reverse you would certainly get a laugh.

Weekly repertory is very hard work indeed. While playing

one part every night six times a week plus two matinees, during the day you rehearse and learn the play that you will be playing the next week. If you are playing a big part, you will be learning it till one or two in the morning. In this company the rules were that everyone helped with stage management, and on Saturday nights when we changed the set for the next week, we had to pitch in and put the new set up and clean the dressing rooms as well.

Of course, putting a play on in a week means that there is no time to find much depth in the part. You tend to play the first idea about the character that comes into your head; there is very little time to experiment as the most important thing is to know your lines. The general public always ask actors how they learn their lines. The answer is, 'The same way as you do. There is no trick – it is by endless repetition.'

I learned one very good lesson about stagecraft in Bangor. I think the play was called *The Happy Family*. It was a light comedy, as most of the plays we did were, and Cynthia as the Mother had a long speech at the end of Act II (there were always three acts in plays in those days) where she had to be very angry. When she finally finished this rant I, as her Daughter, had to say, '*Mum, I feel sick*'.

On the first night, remembering my method work with Mr B., I started to show that I was feeling sick and I immediately got a titter from the audience, and as my nausea grew so the audience laughter grew and when I finally said, '*Mum, I feel sick*' I brought the house down. The minute the curtain came down Cynthia said very sharply to me, 'That's it, then. I won't bother to say that speech tomorrow night.'

I was genuinely at a loss as to why she was so angry with me. Then John took me to a corner of the wings and said, 'You must never, ever pull those faces again while Cynthia is speaking.' 'But the play is supposed to be funny,' I said. 'Yes, but the focus must be on her in that speech, and then you get the laugh at the end with your one line. You mustn't steal laughs like that. Now go and apologise to Cynthia.' You would be surprised to know how many actors haven't learned this lesson.

Trevor and I had a wonderful summer, and finally hoping to at last consummate our relationship, we decided to give ourselves a weekend at the end of the season in a charming old hotel in a pretty place called Crawfordsburn. We had been paid five pounds a week for the season, our digs cost us three pounds ten shillings and we'd managed to save ten shillings a week as well, so we had enough money for this treat. We arrived very late on the Saturday night at this romantic inn and the woman at the desk, as she handed us the key to our room, leered knowingly, 'Oh yes, we've given you the Bridal Suite.' I felt that she was licking her lips at the thought of us copulating and I immediately hated her, and to poor Trevor's amazement I snapped back, 'Oh no, that's not right. We're not married. We want two separate rooms.' At the time I thought I had blurted this out because she had somehow sullied the romance of it all, but later I thought I was probably just terrified at the idea of actually 'doing it'. She gave us rooms as far apart as possible. I went to Trevor's room as soon as I'd heard her go downstairs, saying, 'I'm sorry, I'm sorry. I don't know why I did that.' 'I'll sort myself out,' Trevor said, 'and then I'll come to your room. Your bed is bigger.' I washed, cleaned my teeth and lay in my bed waiting for him. After about ten minutes there was the sound of a massive crash, which meant that lights were put on in rooms and doors were opened. There was Trevor, in his pyjamas, sprawled halfway down the Jacobean staircase with a suit of armour in bits all around him. Apparently, trying to make his way to my room in the dark, he had crashed into the suit of armour at the top of the staircase, lost his footing and fallen down the stairs. He had cracked a rib and we both fled the place in shame early the next morning.

By the time we left drama school we had agreed that we should probably have been just good friends, and affectionately broke off our engagement.

Back at the Guildhall for the last year, things were getting serious. I now had to teach drama one day a week to earn my grant. The first term I taught four- to six-year-olds in Plaistow, which was bearable because the children were mostly adorable. The second term it was seven- to eleven-year-olds in Deptford, and that was upsetting as you saw what had been open-minded, curious babies now aping what their mostly ignorant, angry parents said; and in the third term in Bermondsey I was teaching eleven- to eighteen-year-olds, which, as I was not yet nineteen myself, was very frightening. After a couple of weeks I was in a class with a mixed group of thirteen- and fourteen-year-olds when one boy put his hand up and said, 'Miss – is it true you really wanna be an actress?' 'Who gave you that information?' I asked. 'Old Bonkers,' he said.

'Well, Mr Baker should stick to teaching history,' I said. But he went on, 'It's jus' that if you do fink of bein' a actress, Miss, you'd better grow some tits.' The shrieks of laughter went on for some while as various other suggestions were thrown across the classroom.

Towards the end of my term with this class I had finally caught their interest with the idea that they write a script for a film or play, and I had several lessons of peace where they scratched away at their exercise books with their pens and were genuinely keen on the project. When they handed in their efforts at the end of the term, they were pleased and proud of themselves and I promised I would let them know which one I thought was the best.

When I read them I was so depressed that I'm ashamed to say I never got in touch with the school again. Every single script – if it was legible – was about murder, rape and violence in any and every form, described in graphically ugly ways. It was probably wrong of me not to have encouraged these efforts. After all, these subjects are the basis of 75 per cent of all film scripts anyway. Did I expect a class of fourteen-year-olds in Bermondsey to come up with *Look Back in Anger* or *The History Boys*?

At some time in my last term the principal of the Guildhall asked to see me. 'Eileen, I don't understand, I've just had Professor Warner in here saying that you are going to play Eliza Doolittle in *Pygmalion*.'

'Yes,' I said.

'But you're a teaching student,' he said. 'I'm afraid I'm going to have to say no, or you will never pass your LGSM' (Licentiate of the Guildhall School of Music).

So I missed out on Eliza, and still failed my LGSM. However I was given the chance to take it again a few weeks later and just managed to get the required marks. I was now a fully qualified drama teacher, and eligible to receive wages on the Burnham scale.

But none of that mattered now because my old friend Robert Atkins (from the Regent's Park Open Air Theatre) had come to the school to judge the Shakespeare Prize. I had chosen to do Phoebe's speech from *As You Like It*, which ends with the line '*Whoever loved that loved not at first sight*'. Robert Atkins not only gave me the prize, he also gave me the part of Jaquenetta in *Love's Labour's Lost* at his theatre in Regent's Park, where I would start work immediately. There need be no more talk about being a teacher. With a repertory season behind me and a London engagement in front of me, I was without doubt now a professional actress.

8

Regent's Park Open Air Theatre has had many improvements made to it since 1953, but the experience of watching a play back then when there were no buildings to be seen, just the natural setting of the park and a tent, was very special. There were four layers of seating, with armchairs in the front rows, deckchairs in the middle rows and armless folding chairs in the back rows – or you could sit on the grassy banks at the sides. To watch a play on a warm summer's evening as the sun sets, the moon and stars begin to appear and the birds warble their way to bed as you listen to the words of Shakespeare could be truly magical.

If it rained we did the show in the tent (a marquee it would be called now, but we always called it the Tent), and naturally not many people would turn up. There was a rule that if the number of customers in the audience was smaller than the number of actors in the cast, then you didn't perform the play. I think it was a general rule for performances anywhere, but I only saw it in action one afternoon when, with rain sheeting down, our audience was just one fifteen-year-old boy. He was very upset when he was told that the performance was cancelled as he was studying *Love's Labour's Lost* for a school exam, and not understanding much of the text was hoping to be enlightened. I thought we should have done the play for him anyway.

It was a great pleasure to arrive for work having walked through the park and made one's way to the backstage area which was shrouded with bushes and where there were two long, low dressing rooms – one for men and one for women – with a separate room behind a curtain for Mr Robert Atkins CBE, who never did get the knighthood he so longed for. Robert Atkins was an actor very much of the old school, before the Oliviers and Gielguds. Albert Finney personified his type brilliantly in Ronald Harwood's film *The Dresser* (though that character was based on Donald Wolfit).

Of course, today without question he would be in trouble with the #MeToo movement, as he couldn't keep his hands to himself where young actresses were concerned.

He only bothered me once. After he had given me the Shakespeare Prize, he told me to telephone him to discuss what I would be playing when I joined the company. When I made the call I knew that it was clearly him who answered the telephone as he had an amazingly deep, resonant voice which involved a lot of smacking of lips. Nevertheless I said, 'May I speak to Mr Atkins, please?' 'One moment, please,' and I heard him put the telephone down, walk away three or four steps, then return, pick up the phone and in precisely the same voice say, 'Robert Atkins speaking.' He evidently did this to everyone – presumably he thought he ought to make it appear as though he had staff. He asked me to come to his flat just off Baker Street. When I arrived at the block of flats the address had led me to I was very excited and nervous as I rang the bell.

He opened the door and pulled me inside immediately and in as hushed a voice as he could manage said, 'Ethel's in the bath, me dear, quick, give me a little kissy,' and planted his full, wettish lips on mine. I squeezed my lips together tightly and hoped it would be over quickly, and as he heard the plug being pulled out in the bathroom it *was* over quickly.

My frozen response to him was enough. He never approached me in any sexual way again. I was going to say 'inappropriate' way again, but in those days men had no idea that they *were* being inappropriate – it was just par for the course in the theatre. He approached all the girls in the company that year, but he didn't get anywhere with anyone and we all just laughed about it.

He told me that I would be a walk-on in *Twelfth Night* (that is, I'd have no lines) and understudy the part of Maria in the first production of the season, and then play Jaquenetta in *Love's Labour's Lost*, which is a small but delicious little part, in the second production. As for the third, *A Midsummer Night's Dream*, there were a couple of parts still not cast, and if I was lucky I might get one of them. I couldn't have been more thrilled.

Rehearsals were held in the theatre. Mr Atkins would have no truck with rehearsal rooms. We had to get used to that big, open space immediately and I soon realised that you had to give a big performance; there would be no mumbling or trying to find your way into your character. You learned it, the director (in this case Robert Atkins) gave you your moves and then you simply kept repeating it as he moved further and further back in the auditorium, often shouting in a fury, 'I can't hear a fucking word. I can hear the ducks but I can't hear a quack from you.'

Oddly enough, endless repetition isn't such a terrible way

to work, as some actors seem to believe, as you can often find your way to the heart of a part simply by saying it so many times with your fellow actors that you instinctively ease into the role. Of course, no one would dream of directing that way today, and sadly sometimes the director has done so much theorising and talking himself, and there has been so much time spent on improvisation and what an actor *thinks* about his part, that you find not *enough* time has been spent repeating. You have to open the play probably steeped in your character's backstory but none too sure of your lines and cues, and if you're worrying about that, then you can't 'be' the part. There is no perfect method of working, but I'm happiest when there's plenty of repetition, with the director nudging you again and again in the right direction and opening up paths that you hadn't thought of, until the whole cast find that they have arrived at a point when they are telling the story of the play in the best possible way.

There were three other actresses playing small parts: Mary Law, Amanda Fox and Julie Foot. They were all from professional families. Amanda was the daughter of a good actor called William Fox, and Julie was the daughter of a well-known journalist called Jill Craigie, and her stepfather was the MP Michael Foot. I can't remember Mary's links, but she was very attractive and extremely confident. They all, as they say, had connections.

Our first parts were as ladies-in-waiting to Olivia in *Twelfth Night*, except for Julie who was a pageboy. Because of some business that had been put in, Julie had to stand throughout one scene holding a cushion with an ornate piece of jewellery on it. One evening we hadn't got far into the scene when Julie simply put the cushion on the ground and walked off stage. Amanda, Mary and I looked at each other and looked at the cushion and didn't know what to do as the scene between Viola and Olivia carried on. Then suddenly Julie appeared again and picked up the cushion as though nothing had happened. 'Why did you walk off stage like that?' we asked the minute we had exited. 'Well, I needed to pee,' Julie said in an explanatory way as if it was a perfectly normal thing to do. The others laughed, but I was also outraged. 'You just can't walk off the stage like that,' I said. 'You just can't.' Although I deeply disapproved of her attitude, I couldn't help liking her because she made me laugh. She was never given any lines to say, and one day I asked her if she minded. 'No,' she said, 'I don't understand half of what is being said anyway.'

It was very exciting for me when *Twelfth Night* ended and I got to play Jaquenetta in *Love's Labour's Lost* and had my first review in a newspaper. The *Evening Standard* said ' . . . and Eileen Atkins as Jaquenetta was as rollicking a rantipole as ever missed a ducking in a horse pond'. It is the only notice I can remember and quote. I had to look up what the word 'rantipole' meant (a wild or misbehaved person). I think the critic was as pleased with this sentence as I was.

One evening I was sitting alone in the dressing room waiting for my cue to go on for the last scene (all the other women were already on stage) when I heard Robert Atkins' voice booming from behind the curtain at one end of the long room. I could hear that he was speaking with our designer and they were discussing the casting for the final play *A Midsummer Night's Dream*. I had already done a reading for First Fairy but I was afraid that I wouldn't get it. I was too tall for a fairy, and besides I had mistakenly said '*And hang a cow in every pearlslips ear*' and made myself laugh, and Robert Atkins hadn't laughed. So my ears perked up when I heard him boom, 'Now what are we

going to do about Hippolyta? There is Amanda and Eileen.'
(He paused.) 'Amanda has the body . . . but no voice (another
pause), and Eileen has the voice . . . but no body.' At that point
my cue came and I had to leave the dressing room to make my
entrance. As we all came off stage Robert said to me, 'I want
a word with you,' and took me aside among the bushes. Then,
putting his hand on my shoulder, he said very solemnly, 'I'm
going to entrust you with the role of Hippolyta.' 'What are
you going to do about my body?' I immediately blurted. 'Well
now, we're going to build you out to here.' He indicated the
enormous breasts they would build. 'And you'll wear a tiger
skin which will come to here' – he indicated a point way up
my thigh – 'and you can show those lovely long legs.' I went
home thrilled. I'd got another part, and Hippolyta was a much
bigger part than First Fairy.

Sadly, however, my breasts never did get built up because
'rain stopped play'. We had had such persistently wet weather
that business was bad and Robert had to close the season early.

By the end of August I was what is still sometimes called by
anyone who is not an actor, 'resting'. And as far as my mother
was concerned I certainly *wouldn't* be resting. I must get a job,
any job, as we needed the money, and if she ever heard that I
was in the 'dole queue' (in other words, drawing benefits) she
would disown me. I had to find a job quickly.

These days, most students leaving drama school will already
have an agent. The school will have asked agents to come and
take their pick at the end of term shows. But the Guildhall
didn't do this, probably because most of us were meant to be
teachers. From my small amount of experience I knew that if
you didn't have an agent, the thing to do was to walk the length

of Charing Cross Road and climb up the stairs of every building that had a sign saying 'Theatrical Agency' and ask if there was any work. There were dozens of these offices perched above the second-hand bookshops and tobacconists that dominated this bohemian thoroughfare on the edge of seedy Soho. I did this for several weeks. No one appeared to be faintly interested in me, but the kinder ones would say, 'Call by again. There might be something I can put you up for next week.' I got to know many of the dozens of other actors tramping up and down Charing Cross Road, and sometimes splashed out and sat for hours over one coffee with a few of them and felt comforted that I wasn't alone. They told me that I had to buy *The Stage* newspaper each week as this would tell me when open auditions were being held, and there would be advertisements for certain parts, though these jobs had usually been filled by the time you got to a telephone. At last we *had* a telephone now, at home. There was also a very uncomfortable atmosphere as I wasn't contributing to my rent or food. It was made very clear to me that no matter how I made the money, I must earn my keep. My father would bring a newspaper in every evening, and I think it was him who pointed out to me that there was an advert for a cinema usherette. So I made enquiries. It turned out to be for the Classic Cinema in Baker Street. So, ironically, I would be doing the same journey every day that I had been doing to Regent's Park Theatre. The film that was playing was *The Glass Mountain* with Michael Denison and Dulcie Gray, and after seeing it four or five times a day, mostly slumped at the back of the auditorium clutching my torch, I found it difficult to make my way to work and don the hideous beige and dark brown uniform with any kind of enthusiasm.

One afternoon I was on door duty in the foyer tearing tickets

when in came Robert Atkins with a small group of people. He
stopped in his tracks, clearly horrified to see me there. He ushered his group into the cinema, then stepped back to speak to
me. 'I know that you probably have to earn a living but never,
ever take work where your face is exposed to the public. An
actor should never do that, it's humiliating.' I was miserable.
I couldn't think of a job that I could do where I *wouldn't* have
to meet the public, as ushers and shop assistants were the only
jobs that were available to actors – unless, of course, you had
been bright enough to learn shorthand and typing. That was the
only other work that you could pick up on a temporary basis.

I gave in my notice at the Classic Cinema, afraid that Robert
might turn up again, and got myself a job at Gamages department store in Holborn. I was an assistant on the counter for
men's socks and ties. I was a lousy shop assistant. I just couldn't
understand why we had to stand smiling all the time even if
there were no customers. Why couldn't we be allowed to sit
and read a book until someone turned up? I was tremendously
relieved when, after a few weeks, I was sacked. A female
customer had reported me for being rude and sullen, which
I probably was. The manager of our department called me
in to discuss the incident. He said, 'Even though it's nearly
Christmas and we'll soon be packed, I think it would be better
if I let you go. I don't think you're cut out for this job.' I was
happy to agree with him.

It was indeed nearly Christmas – the pantomime season –
but it never entered my head that I might try to get work in one.
I was no longer a dancer, and I certainly couldn't sing. What
part could I possibly play?

As it happened the well-known entertainer Cyril Fletcher,
who was producing and performing in *Mother Goose*, always

chose his Demon Kings and Fairy Queens, which were looked upon as the serious roles, from students at the Guildhall. To my relief I had a phone call from the principal of the drama school telling me that Mr Fletcher would like to see me with a view to playing the Fairy Queen. I thought I would go all prepared with Titania's famous speech from *A Midsummer Night's Dream*, and went out to Croydon where he was already in rehearsal to meet him. In the wings someone took my name and handed me a tired piece of paper with a badly typed speech of mundane rubbish on it such as is spouted by Fairy Queens in pantomime, and I thought it best to forget '*These are the forgeries of jealousy*'. I had scarcely read it through when the person who gave it to me said, 'Okay, he's ready. Out you go. Just do the speech and leave, all right?'

I did my best and left the theatre. By the time I had reached home there had been a phone call to say that I'd got the part and could I be there for rehearsal the next day. I can only think that someone had let Mr Fletcher down and I was cast in a last-minute panic.

The relief at home was palpable. Not only was it work, but it was the kind of work that they would love coming to see. Light entertainment.

My mother worked out that it would be too far for me to do the journey back and forth to Croydon, so she arranged for me to stay with Aunt Lil and Uncle Alf, who lived there. I would have to give them something towards my keep but it would be cheaper than digs.

I was nervous going to the first rehearsal, but luckily when I arrived I found that I knew the Demon King already. His name was Michael Griffiths, and he was a very good actor and one I knew would be easy to work with. Everyone else was from the world of light entertainment. I found Mr Cyril Fletcher slightly frightening. He was very famous in the 1940s and '50s for his comic act, which always ended with him doing one of his 'Odd Odes'. You couldn't call them poems – they were dozens of rhyming couplets strung together to tell an amusing story rather in the style of cautionary tales.

He put on a faux-serious voice for reciting them, and as a child with my family I had found them quite funny, but now that I was a superior nineteen-year-old they didn't make me laugh.

Nevertheless I was intrigued by the way he worked in rehearsals. He would direct you very precisely, and would impress upon you that you must stand exactly on your marks as we were always in a spotlight, and he would give us every intonation that he wanted. His wife, Betty Astell, wrote the couplets for the Demon King and Fairy Queen, and Cyril made it plain to us that he regarded her trite lines as fine dramatic poetry and that we must never treat it as anything else. Neither Michael nor I intended to send it up – that wouldn't be right and would spoil it for the children – but off stage we used to go through the lines with different inflections, rolling our eyes and making the others laugh. There was a very shrewd, clever comedienne in my dressing room, a lovely woman called Pat Coombs, and she used to warn us, 'Don't you ever let Cyril hear you sending it up.'

When he rehearsed his own scene as the Dame, the other actors would say their lines but he seemed to just say '*biz*' all the time. Sometimes he would say '*sausage biz*' or '*washing biz*'. I couldn't see how he could be funny at all, but of course when he finally put in the business with an audience it *was* funny.

I hated staying with my Aunt Lil (who was Aunt Edie's sister-in-law) in her nasty little house which made 17 Courtman

Road look quite roomy. Uncle Alf was an unpleasant man who aggressively gave his opinions about everything, and I fiercely disagreed with every word he said. Then after about my fifth day there, when I'd come back from a dress rehearsal and we were eating some dismal meal before I had to go back to work, he asked me if there were any 'nancy boys' in the panto. 'If you mean homosexuals,' I said tartly, 'I haven't actually asked but I expect so, yes.' 'It's disgusting,' he spat. 'They should all be stood up against a wall and shot.'

I was suddenly full of such rage that I shouted at him many horrible things that I'm sure included that he was stupid, ignorant and a disgrace to the human race. Then I packed my case and after the evening's rehearsal I went back to Tottenham. The journey back and forth for the run of the panto was tedious and tiring, but at least at home no one said things like that. My father would sometimes say someone was 'a bit of a nancy boy', but it was said with benevolent amusement and an appreciation of 'camp'. He didn't find it offensive.

The cast were a friendly, jolly crowd and things swung along until our very last matinee. There was a very amusing short, fat woman who played the Goose – that is, she just had to don the costume and waddle about the stage. When I arrived for the afternoon show several of the company said to me, 'Watch Frankie this afternoon. She's had a boozy lunch and she's quite drunk.' So I went down to the wings and she was doing all kinds of things behind Cyril's back and I was helpless with laughter. I was still laughing a bit when we took our curtain call, and when Cyril Fletcher stepped forward to give the very pompous speech he always gave at the end of the show, Frankie, who was next to me in the line-up, turned round and waggled her goose backside at the audience and I exploded. Cyril turned

sharply and saw me shaking with laughter and Frankie now
obediently back in line with her beak to the front.

He demanded that I went with him to his dressing room the
minute the curtain came down. He was absolutely furious,
which I admit was understandable. He said that my behaviour
was unforgivable, and that if it wasn't for the fact that there
was only one more performance to give he would sack me. I
left the room very chastened and angry with myself for being
so out of control. I myself have always hated actors messing
about, even at a curtain call. It's amateurish and shows lack of
respect to the audience.

But actors do, of course, sometimes get near-hysterical fits of
laughter if something goes wrong in the action of the play, but
that is a very different thing. In Britain we call it 'corpsing' – I
suppose because once you start to laugh you are out of character and therefore dead. If I'm in the audience and I see it happen
I'm as annoyed as anyone else who has paid for their seat, but
if I'm on the stage when it happens I find it an exquisite agony,
very hard to explain to anyone who is not an actor. You are on
a knife edge when you are playing – particularly in a serious
play. There are your nerves, and the incredible concentration
it takes to will yourself to believe that you *are* the person that
you are playing. So for example, if you're playing Elizabeth
I, as I once was, and you realise that other characters on the
stage are smirking and you glance down and notice that your
own modern lacy bra has somehow become attached to the
panniers of your farthingale, the whole belief is shattered and
your immediate reaction is to laugh, but you absolutely *mustn't*.
It's the absolutely mustn't, coupled with trying desperately not
to give in to the hysteria bubbling up inside you that makes
it almost orgasmic. It spoils the play for the audience, it's

shameful and you could get sacked, but sometimes you just can't help it.

In 1973 I was on stage for one glorious corpse in which the audience finally joined in. It was the last act of *Heartbreak House* at the National Theatre when it was at the Old Vic, and nearly all the characters were sitting on chairs of some kind in the garden of the house and most of us were already seated. There was Colin Blakely as Captain Shotover, Kate Nelligan, Paul Rogers, Anna Massey and me playing Hesione Hushabye. Graham Crowden, a very tall, well-padded actor playing my husband Hector Hushabye finally had to take his seat, which was a deckchair. As he sat down we all heard the canvas of the chair begin to split and saw his somewhat large bottom begin to lower to the ground, and we started to laugh through our lines. We soon became almost incapable of carrying on at all, as what made it worse was that Graham didn't find it remotely funny and remained tremendously on his dignity with his knees nearly up to his chin and a deranged look of fear as to how, having sunk so low, he was going to be able to stand up when his cue came. When he finally managed to get to his feet, the deckchair fitted so snugly to his large frame that it stuck to him and he couldn't remove it, and Paul Rogers playing Boss Mangan had to help him. By then of course the audience were well in on the joke and roaring with laughter. When the deckchair and actor were finally parted they gave a round of applause, and somehow we got through to the end of the play.

Most good actors are bound to have 'broken up' (which is another name for this phenomenon) quite a few times, but I only corpse if it is a genuine accident, never, ever if someone tries deliberately to make me laugh, as many actors do if they are bored in a long run.

After the panto I was back tramping up and down Charing Cross Road, where I met an actor who told me that he was working in market research. All you had to do was go from house to house in a designated area and ask the inhabitants questions about products that they used. You could do it in your own time, and if you worked out of London it was well paid. I applied immediately. Although it was lonely to take a train to some Midland or Northern town and stay in a grim B and B overnight, it was a relief to get out of the house for a few days as there was now talk of my taking a shorthand and typing course.

It wasn't an easy job, as people were mostly suspicious and unwilling to answer questionnaires. On one trip I had to go to Chesterfield and from there had taken a bus to a nearby village. I had to make sure that I questioned a certain number of households from each class.

It was one of those very cold April days, and I was freezing. I had done my quota of working- and middle-class households but simply couldn't find any obviously upper-class residences, when I spied through some trees a driveway that looked promising. It certainly lived up to its promise. The house was enormous but looked dark and unloved and I didn't envy anyone who lived there. It was with some trepidation that I approached the Gothic-looking entrance surrounded by little turrets, and rang the bell.

The door was opened by a very tall woman hung about with many necklaces worn over exotic layers of clothing that reached the ground, and topped by a brilliant-coloured turban twisted high above her very long, pale face. I couldn't speak I was so taken aback.

'What do you want?' she demanded imperiously, looking down her very long nose.

'I just wondered how much flour you used each week?'

'Flour?' It was like Lady Bracknell saying, 'A handbag?'

'Yes,' I said, tremblingly.

'Go round to the tradesmen's entrance and ask the cook,' she said grandly. And shut the door.

Of course when I asked the cook (who was very kind to me) the name of the owner of the house, she said, 'You mean you didn't *know* that was Dame Edith Sitwell?'

I was, of course, at Renishaw Hall, the Sitwells' family home.

While doing this work, I was able to make renewed attacks on the agencies and scour *The Stage*, and one day I saw an advertisement saying that a Mr Frank Fortescue would be holding auditions for actors and actresses for seasons at his various repertory companies. I asked the actors I met about him. His companies were considered to be of a very low standard (though not as low as those of someone called Harry Hanson), as they not only played weekly but twice nightly, which meant, with two matinees, that you did fourteen shows a week. I imagined that there would be very little depth in any performance you could give under those circumstances – you would be lucky if you managed to learn your lines. Well, there was no way I could worry about the standard of acting. I wrote to Mr Fortescue and he replied. I auditioned and, mercy of mercies, I got the job. I would be 'the female juvenile' at his Hazel Grove theatre near Stockport in Cheshire. What's more, he told me that he was sending me to his best company where they only played eight times a week. I would be paid five pounds every Saturday for a twelve-week season, and would have to provide all my own clothes unless they did a period play, which he said was unlikely. I set out with high hopes.

I was the only newcomer. They had all been working together for several seasons and I think that it was the only time I have felt uncomfortable with my fellow players. There was something so dispirited and seedy about them. They were all middle-aged, and had spent most of their acting lives working for Frank Fortescue, playing the trite light comedies and sentimental melodramas that tended to be the fare dished out in weekly rep, and they seemed to have no interest in anything else.

The leading lady held court in her dressing room every night before the show, telling dismally filthy jokes, and although even at nineteen I was quite bawdy, when someone says 'Have you heard the one about . . . ?' I want to leave the room.

There was no one else anywhere near my age – even the juvenile male was nearly forty, and I found them depressing and made little attempt to get to know anyone, and I'm sure they must have found me annoyingly snobbish with my talk of Shakespeare and Ibsen, and wodges of high-flown advice quoted from Stanislavski's tome *An Actor Prepares*. I expect they saw that I was treating my time there as simply treading water until I got to do the real thing, and although I wasn't aware of it, I probably conveyed a contempt for the standard of acting all around me. That said, it didn't stop me from picking up some really bad habits from Hazel Grove. When plays aren't very good, you tend to overact to make up for the lack of talent of the author, and overacting is very catching.

Because we had to provide our own wardrobe, I had a hard time with clothes. In the French's edition (which gives you the clothes, props and moves of the original production) of a play we were doing, it said, 'She enters in evening dress with an opera cloak over her shoulders'. I had no idea what an opera cloak was and spent ten shillings hiring one in Stockport. It was a long black heavy affair with a hood, which I thought looked very romantic over the childish evening dress that my mother had made for me. When I appeared at the dress rehearsal the leading lady shrieked, 'My God, it's the Wicked Fairy Godmother. I didn't know we were doing panto.' I was told that an opera cloak was a tiny velvet cloak that just sat on your shoulders, and the leading lady was asked by the director, who was her husband, if she would be gracious enough to lend me one of hers.

The one thing that cheered me up was that I had had difficulty finding digs in Hazel Grove and someone advised me to take a bedsit in Stockport, a town that I found quite jolly. This was the first time I had ever lived alone. I found a big bare room rather like the lofts that are so trendy now, and all it contained was a bed, a table and two chairs, a battered armchair with the stuffing protruding and a double gas ring.

I had never shopped or tried to cook for myself before, and for the first time experienced the enormous thrill of shutting the door and knowing that you really were on your own. I was so intoxicated by this feeling that I wrote a letter to Mr Burton about it. And he wrote back: 'You've learned the great pleasure of solitude.' I also told him that I was unhappy in the company, but he made me promise to stick out the contract. I was often in touch with him after I had left school, and he made it clear that he was always available for advice. But he never came to see me act professionally.

I was counting the days to my release when to my amazement I was offered a further six months, as the management were very happy with me. Oh, but I was so unhappy with them! I didn't know what to do. Going home and looking for work again would be awful, but I kept holding off confirming the offer.

Then I got a phone call from my ex-fiancé, Trevor, who had won the broadcasting prize at Guildhall, which meant he had become a member of the BBC Repertory Company. Although our engagement had filtered away, we were still good friends and I often phoned him from Stockport, fiddling with piles of change in a public telephone box.

He called the theatre in the half hour before curtain-up one evening, knowing I would be there, and I had to take the call in the manager's office with everyone listening. Trevor said, 'You haven't accepted that extra six months, have you?' 'No,' I answered. 'Well, Anne Lewis is going to try to run a sort of cooperative company in Cornwall for the summer with some of the others from the Guildhall. She wants both of us to be in it. What do you think?'

9

Anne Lewis was short with long dark hair and beautiful blue-grey eyes, and always seemed to be dressed in a pinafore as if she was about to play Alice in *Alice in Wonderland*.

In Perranporth while on holiday with her family she spotted a village hall that seemed only to be used by the Women's Institute. Being an easy chatterer, she questioned the locals to see whether anyone else used it. Oh yes, she was told, there was a very keen amateur dramatic society that put on a play or two in the winter, and before the war they had had the great excitement of a regular professional summer repertory company with Robert Morley, Peter Bull and Pamela Brown. But now it lay empty. Couldn't she, Anne thought, get some of the students she had known at the Guildhall and put a summer season together?

She talked to Trevor, and then they got in touch with Peter Bull, a very well-known character actor who hadn't yet given the performance which playgoers would know him for of Pozzo in the very first production in Britain of *Waiting for Godot*. He told Anne and Trevor that he had had great fun running a few summer seasons down in Cornwall, and encouraged them to

EILEEN ATKINS

give it a try. Anne then forced Trevor down to Perranporth to meet the locals; she knew they would never think her capable of running a company, as not only was she a woman but she looked about fifteen. It did the trick.

I don't know how many others she had got together by the time Trevor called me, but she had done well and gathered a very talented little crew, although we were all terribly young. Only the Greek director, George Theodossiades, and the scenic designer he had brought with him, Valarious, were maybe thirty. Then Trevor had the brilliant idea of asking our leading lady from Bangor, Cynthia Bowles, to join us, and that gave us some ballast.

The idea was that it would be a kind of cooperative company, and we would all take turns at the box office or help paint the scenery or whatever was needed. There could be no assurance of money for anyone, as we would just share out the takings at the end of the week. We would have to pay our own fare down to Cornwall and have enough money for our food for the rehearsal period, but there would be no other expenses as Anne had arranged that we would all sleep in the two class-rooms in the village school – one bedroom for men and one for women. We would use the children's two small lavatories (fit for seven- and eight-year-old bottoms) that were in the playground, and would have to make do with the cold tap and sink in each lavatory.

I missed all the talks about what plays we would do and some rehearsals, as I had to complete my contract at Hazel Grove. We knew that to fill the theatre with people who were on holiday as well as locals we had to do mostly light comedies and farces, but we wanted to do the best light comedies and farces and try to throw in at least one good drama and maybe a thriller. We managed to work it quite quickly that we changed plays on a Thursday, as that way people on holiday for only one week could see two plays. We also intended to try to share the parts out so that everyone had a leading part in one play or another.

In our first season our list of plays was:

See How They Run
Claudia
Hay Fever
The Happiest Days of Your Life
Love's a Luxury
The Deep Blue Sea
Dial M for Murder
Little Lambs Eat Ivy

Perranporth isn't the most picturesque village on the North Cornish coast, but in comparison to Hazel Grove it was paradise. It had expanded more than most of the villages probably because of its mile-long beach, where surfing had just become popular. There were proper shops as well as holiday knick-knackery and there was a thriving, lively community, of whom many were more than willing to give us a hand.

I was somewhat dazed when I arrived, as I had come on the night train and had to pitch straight into rehearsing Penelope, the vicar's wife in *See How They Run* which was quite a big part, and get used to our fiery-tempered but brilliant director (who eventually became director of the National Theatre of Greece) with his outrageously blunt remarks that were somehow acceptable because of his comic accent. 'Why is your breast so low?' he shouted to me from the small auditorium on the first day as I rehearsed on the stage. 'I don't know,' I shouted back, 'no one has mentioned it before.' 'It needs pulling up, your understructure isn't good enough.' He was quite right about this, as I so hated the two hard cones that bras were in the 1940s and '50s that long before we 'burnt our bras' in the 1960s I often didn't wear one.

Another thing I had to get used to was our accommodation. Although I was hardly spoilt for comfort at home, I did at least have a bed in my own room now that my sister was married. Here it was an uncomfortable camp bed in a bald classroom with not just Anne, Sheila and Cynthia but strange girlfriends of Anne's who came down from 'varsity' to 'help'. There was no privacy whatsoever, and I found the tiny loo and single cold tap really punishing. I had never been one of those envied 'girls of Nature' – the girls who could sleep anywhere and wake up looking divine; the girls who slid seamlessly out of their clothes and dived into water and whose hair dried perfectly in the sun. The girls who could eat anything and not have to sit quietly till it went down. No: I wanted a comfy bed, toothbrush and pyjamas, absolute blackness and a lot of quiet before I could think of sleeping. On my own in Stockport I had at last been able to be a 'bath once a day person', and I didn't want to go back to being a 'bath once a week person' in somebody's house in the village.

But even if it turned out that we made enough money to pay for digs, I knew I would look a spoilsport and somehow ruin the infectious jollity of us all being in this together if I went off and lived on my own.

And there was a surprise for me. Trevor had a new fiancée, and I had to get used to that. Yes, sure, our engagement had ended amicably and we had agreed to be friends, but he wasn't supposed to move on quite so quickly. She was a friend of Anne's. Her name was Janet and she was a tall, striking-looking girl with great bone structure and yes, could step out of her dress on the beach ready-wrapped in the skimpiest costume, stride into the sea with her surfboard, ride the waves like a water nymph, shake out her wet hair and sleep on the beach in the sun. I hated her.

The Women's Institute hall, as it was called, had a tiny foyer with a box office that could just about squeeze in two people at a pinch. Then there was the main body of the hall which could hold just under a hundred people, and along the side of that was a long, narrow room where Valarious, our designer, painted flats for our scenery and did miracles with whatever he could beg, borrow or find for furniture. That room also had a large sink and a couple of gas rings and a kettle where we made tea. Valarious was a big, shambling man with a huge smile and a refusal to get into a state about anything – except very occasionally when George would drive him crazy, and then there would be a monumental Greek screaming match.

The stage was small and Valarious wanted every inch of it for his decor, so we incorporated the two side doors of the stage into the set. Unfortunately these doors opened straight on to the path that ran round the back of the theatre, so if it was raining during the performance you would have to make your way from the dressing room, which was immediately behind the stage, to down left or down right under an umbrella and drop it sharply before you made your entrance. There were quite a few times when an actor would forget to drop it and walk into what was supposed to be a sunny sitting room holding a dripping umbrella.

There was only one dressing room, and no one ever spoke about putting up a curtain.

See How They Run is a terrific farce, a trifle dated now but perfect to play in 1954. George directed us to play it absolutely straight, which of course is how you have to play farce. He also begged us to remember what the great farceur Robertson Hare had said about it. That you must take the first act very fast, hardly giving the audience the chance to laugh at all, ease out in the second act and then in the third, when all the set-ups should be paying off, you can at last let the audience laugh, and then they should be roaring.

It was a hit. The empty sheets of paper for the seating plans piled up in the box office started to be filled up with crosses as people booked to see more plays. We were all thrilled and excited, and soon settled into the routine of playing one play while rehearsing the next. Even with shifts in the box office and helping Valarious paint flats and running around the town with adverts, there was time to go to the beach and swim or surf. If the weather was gorgeous we knew that holidaymakers would be loath to go into a stuffy hall, certainly for matinees. So we would get a long strip of material and paint the name of the play and the venue on it, stick it between two poles and whoever was on the beach would run back and forth in pairs weaving their way between prone bodies sunbathing, picnickers and waddling children.

We were a surprisingly amicable company considering that we were so young and all living together, and I don't remember any problems between the actors, just the odd Greek explosion. There are sometimes jealousies among actors about who is getting what parts, or there can be personality clashes when you have actors living on nervous energy, which most actors do. I had even managed to become fond of Janet, who I realised was a perfect partner for Trevor; indeed, reader, she married him.

The only people I sometimes seemed to have trouble with were Anne's friends, who came down in their summer vacation from Oxford University (they *all* seemed to be at Oxford) to help in the box office for 'a bit of fun'; for us it was our bread and butter. I tended to think automatically that they were clever upper-class snobs.

One afternoon we were doing a dress rehearsal before the opening of *Hay Fever* that night. I was playing Myra, the sophisticated sex siren. It is unlikely, with my wardrobe, that as I made my entrance I looked in any way as Noël Coward had imagined. When one of our 'helpers', a strident young woman called Ann Harrop, watching the performance from the back row barked in a loud, commanding way, 'Oh, my God. What *is* she wearing? You can't dress like that and play Myra', I came right out of character and addressed her from the stage in my strongest Tottenham accent: 'Would you mind keeping your big fucking trap shut and getting back into the bloody box office, which is what you were asked to do?' I had learned to swear at drama school and enjoyed it much too much.

As things fell out, Anne Lewis played all the very juvenile parts that both clever Sheila Leonard and I were also the right age for, but neither of us minded as I had some really good older leading women's parts and Sheila became our character actress. Cynthia settled happily to playing matriarchs. I only had a slight feeling of jealousy when Sheila was cast as Miss Gossage ('call me sausage') in *The Happiest Days of Your Life*, which I had wanted to play. But when I saw her play the part she was so funny that my envy disappeared. I find that this has happened throughout my career. I have of course been jealous of an actress sometimes who got to play a part that I'd wanted, but the resentment and fury completely dissipate if it is then played beautifully. I am only left with a residual grudge if the actress is no good. Then it rankles.

One really wonderful part I got to play that season was Hester Collyer in Terence Rattigan's *The Deep Blue Sea*. Hester is a very upper-class woman in her forties who is married to a judge, but she has fallen passionately in love with a young man half her age, Freddie, who has been a fighter pilot in the war. It is clearly a deeply unsuitable match – indeed, the play begins with Hester trying to commit suicide.

I had only just had my twentieth birthday and Peter Mander, playing Freddie, was two years *older* than me. Undaunted, I threw myself into the role, and maybe because it was the only drama we did and it *is* a very good play, it attracted more attention than the other productions. I was confident that I had played it really well, which I couldn't possibly have done at that age. About forty years later I received a cassette recording of the performance. Someone in Perranporth found it when cleaning out her father's house after he had died, and thought that I might like to have it. It took me ages to pluck up the courage to listen to it as I didn't want the image of my success in it to be shattered, as I was sure it would be. When I finally played it I found that I had done an almost perfect imitation of Celia Johnson, one of the great actresses who had played it originally in the West End, which wasn't the worst thing I could have done and was actually quite touching. But I find it hard to listen to or watch my own performances, and try to avoid it. You are always disappointed.

It was soon after I played Hester that my very unreliable digestive system (never sorted out since my mother's dismissal of the hospital's advice that I shouldn't eat the white of eggs) went crazy and I had bad stomach cramps and couldn't stop throwing up. This wasn't a sign that I was bulimic – it was simply because we tended to live on all-day breakfasts, sandwiches and buns and I was always tense with our living conditions and was nearly crazy with lack of sleep. I gave in and went to the local GP and asked for 'something for my stomach'. He was straight from central casting – elderly, white-haired and kindly-looking. He got up from his chair and put his arm round my shoulders. 'My dear young lady,' he said, 'you look absolutely exhausted.' I burst into tears and said that I never *did* sleep well, but could hardly sleep at all in the conditions at the village school. Within a couple of hours my bag was packed and I was in a very pretty bedroom in one of the best houses in the village with a view of the sea, but best of all it had a big comfortable bed and a bathroom next door. My prescription from the doctor was to stay there for at least two weeks, if not the rest of the season and to eat what I was given. A rather glamorous couple had been kind enough to take me in (I think it was their second home) and they had a cook, so as I ate at different hours from them I mostly ate with her, and didn't feel a nuisance.

I was glad that I only had to eat once or twice with the owners of the house as I felt uncomfortable with such cultured, classy people. It made me horribly aware of how unsophisticated I was. They talked of the opera and the ballet as well as the theatre and I had absolutely nothing to say, not even about the latter, as I had only seen plays when the Guildhall had got free tickets for the students, so even my theatre knowledge was thin. I suppose that as they had seen me play Hester Collyer with my Celia Johnson accent they thought I would be from the same background as them, and were kind enough to want to hear a young woman's opinions. But I had no opinions. I was much happier eating with the cook.

I felt slightly guilty that I hadn't withstood the rigours of the village school. Valarious confessed to me that he couldn't face living at the school either and had simply been sleeping in the theatre on the stage. 'That is why there is always a comfortable sofa on my sets,' he said. It's as well for him that there were no 'kitchen sink' plays being performed yet.

I was doing a stint at the box office when into our tiny foyer stepped a tall, tanned, very attractive young man. I knew immediately that he wasn't a local or a holidaymaker.

'Can I help you?' I asked.

'Well, I'm here to help *you*, actually.' He smiled tentatively. 'Anne told me to come down here and take over from you.'

Oh God, I thought, another of her 'varsity' friends. I put on a silly, posh, drawling voice and said disdainfully, 'Another of Anne's friends deown from Awksford in the vac to have a "bit of fun"?'

'Goodness,' he said, still smiling. 'Are we that bad?'

I showed him what he had to do and left the theatre with a distinct sashay, wishing I'd been wearing some mascara and my good shorts.

I was under strict orders to rest as much as possible and certainly not to go out at night after the show when most socialising was done, which I stuck to, so I didn't see much of David Jeayes, as his name turned out to be, during his week with us. I was leaving the dressing room late one evening when everyone else had gone to a party, and I found him lurking outside. 'I've just heard that you won't be coming to the party,' he said.

'Oh no, I've not been well, so I'm not doing parties at the moment.'

'Yes, they said' (that tentative smile again). 'It's just that I'm leaving tomorrow and I wanted to say goodbye.'

'Back to Oxford then?'

'Yes. My last year.'

He's *really* attractive, I thought.

'I'm so sorry you can't come tonight. I hope we can meet again.'

'Yes. That would be nice,' I said, and thought, and so highly unlikely.

With the air buzzing with sexual attraction I said, 'Bye, then,' and sloped off, knowing I was doing the right thing but wishing I wasn't.

We had been a success, which was a huge accomplishment for such a venture, and there was much talk of doing another season next year, but next year was a long time away and there was an empty-looking nine-month gap to try to fill with work, and the dread of living at home again.

I had written to practically every repertory company in Britain asking for work. Only half a dozen had replied with the usual, 'We are not looking for anyone at the moment but will keep you in mind'. I had now done three repertory seasons, but Bangor, Hazel Grove and Perranporth were of course not impressive enough for me to be considered for any of the first-class companies that gave the actors two, three or even four weeks to rehearse.

I'd gone back to live at the school for the final two productions, as I was feeling better and missed the camaraderie. Then suddenly it was all over. The last performance, the party, the packing and the misery as I sat on the train going back to London. The only thing to be looked forward to was my own bed in my own room.

In the first week I was back in September, an agent I dropped in on said that there was a production of a play at Lichfield Cathedral and they wanted a female assistant stage manager who would also understudy the leading lady. I said 'no thank you' in the office. I didn't want to accept a job where I wasn't doing any acting – just being the dogsbody who swept the stage, made the tea and went begging for props. But after an evening at home with my mother pointedly telling me how well Shani Wallis was doing, my father buried uncomfortably behind his newspaper, knowing she was provoking me and nervously waiting for me to retaliate, I changed my mind. I rang the agency the next morning. Anything was better than sitting at home, and it was only for two weeks – one week's rehearsal and one week playing. I took the train to Lichfield that day.

The play was called *St Chad of the Seven Wells*. St Chad had a link with the cathedral, and the burghers of Lichfield were celebrating some momentous anniversary. I had lovely digs in a close near the cathedral and I liked the director, Warren Jenkins, and Hugh Goldie who seemed to be the producer. Part of the cathedral had been hung with huge drapes and a platform had been built for the stage. There was a cast of about ten men and one woman, who was Warren's wife. She had just had a baby and looked none too well. Even though it was only a week I might have to go on, I thought hopefully, and rapidly learned the part.

On the whole the actors treated me affectionately and I didn't mind all the fetching and carrying I had to do. If you were a young female ASM you became a sort of company pet and got patted on the head, patted on the bottom and often thought fair game to try it on with.

One day I was toiling over a huge copper of boiling shirts that I had to wash, dry and iron before the show when a very handsome actor called Patrick Horgan wandered in, probably out of boredom, and stood leaning against the wall watching me. I felt horribly unattractive with the steam making my face sweat and my hair plastered to my skull, stirring the bubbling cauldron with a stick. Suddenly he bent forward, took the stick out of my hand and kissed me. Remembering the image today I see it as a Hogarthian drawing: 'The Handsome Gentleman Pauses to Kiss the Lowly Laundry Maid'. But of course I'd never heard of Hogarth then; I was just flustered and quite thrilled.

That evening after the show there was a reception at which there would be dancing, so I made a terrific effort to look as good as possible as surely Mr Horgan would ask me to dance. I had only one skirt with me. It had once been a pretty blue linen dirndl with a wide band at the waist that my mother had made for me. Unfortunately frequent washings had faded the material and made the hem fall out of shape. I did my best trying to straighten it with an iron but it was a lost cause; it was still very uneven. I washed my hair and put some make-up on and was quite excited at the thought of dancing with what would undoubtedly be the best-looking man in the room. I'd heard in the dressing room that he was engaged, but that didn't bother me – I was just looking forward to dancing with him.

He took me onto the floor as soon as he saw me and I twirled happily round the room with him.

'You've washed your hair,' he said.

'Yes,' I answered.

'And I love the dippy hemline,' he went on. 'It's quite sexy.'

I thought, He's laughing at me. He knows that this skirt looks pathetically wrong and he's laughing at me, and as soon as the dance was over I walked away from him, out of the reception and went miserably back to my digs. Of course he *was* laughing at me in a way, but he was only flirting. I'm sure he didn't mean to be cruel in any way. The remark had just pointed up my inadequacy. I never had the right clothes or the right look or the right background. I would always be a peasant.

On the very last day that we were in Lichfield there was a concert in the cathedral in the early evening. The cast were told that as long as we didn't make a sound, we could listen to it on our set behind the curtains. It was the Hallé Orchestra conducted by Sir John Barbirolli. We all sat round on bits of scenery hidden behind the drapes, listening to the music. It was the first time I had ever heard a live orchestra. At home the minute a note of classical music strayed out of the wireless my father would say, 'Let's give it a rest,' and it was switched off sharply. I was enchanted. When it was over the Mayor made a speech of thanks. He was obviously originally from Birmingham and he had a strong accent. 'Well,' he said, 'I'm sure we would all like to thank Mr John Barrybolly and his Alleyband . . . '

The cast were all shaking with laughter. I just hope that Sir John saw the joke as well. I had laughed, but at the same time I felt a hot, protective kinship with the Mayor. His background had 'let him down' and he would be mocked.

I was packing the next day when I got a message to say would I speak to Mr Goldie before I left for my train.

'Warren and I are taking over the Oxford Playhouse, and wondered if you would like to come with us and be our ASM there.'

'Only if you will definitely give me parts as well. I won't be an ASM only.'

'Oh yes, you'll have a contract saying "ASM and small parts", and I promise there will be some good little roles you'll be able to play. Warren was very taken with the way you read in for his wife at rehearsal.'

The Oxford Playhouse Repertory Theatre was twice weekly and had an excellent reputation. The city also harboured at least one attractive man. I didn't really have to think about it.

I loved Oxford immediately. I was enchanted by the ancient colleges with their peaceful quadrangles, and the students seemed so romantic sailing by on their bikes or swishing down the streets, gowns flying, clutching books. They seemed so carelessly confident it made me slightly envious of them. But that envy disappeared as soon as I walked through the stage door into the untidy green room of the Playhouse Theatre.

The actors in this company were of a much higher standard than anywhere else I had worked, and as long as I had that important phrase 'and small parts' in my contract, I wouldn't mind the drudgery of stage management. Also there were three ASMs, and the other two were really friendly young men, one called Michael and the other the very aristocratic-sounding Charles de Houghton, who was amusing and witty and livened up many an all-night dress rehearsal where he made us laugh so much we had to be called to order by a tiny dragon of a stage manager called June Dandridge.

In the first few days I was there I was sent with Michael to get drinks for the company from the pub whose entrance backed on to our stage door. My eyes were immediately drawn to a young woman sitting alone with a beer in front of her, looking vulnerable and very determined *not* to look vulnerable. She had a delicate auburn beauty and I was intrigued by her, and I suppose that I was staring and she seemed to stare straight back as if to say, 'So? What?' 'That girl you're looking at,' said Michael as he gave her a nervous nod, 'was the last girl we had as ASM.'

'Oh, why did she leave then?'

'I think they sacked her,' said Michael. 'I've only been here a couple of weeks myself.' I thought she was very brave if she had been sacked to be boldly sitting in the pub.

Only a few years ago Maggie Smith explained to me that she hadn't been sacked at all. She was a student at the Oxford School of Drama and part of their training was to spend a certain number of weeks ASM-ing at the Playhouse. So when her time was up she had just left, as was expected, and as she lived in Oxford was still around.

Warren Jenkins and Hugh Goldie gave me a tiny part on their first production. I had one line at the end of the last act, '*I'm pleased to meet you, Madame*', that I had to address to an actress called Lally Bowers. I had the enormous excitement of having a dress made for me for the first time by a theatre designer. He dressed me in a beautiful full mid-calf red velvet skirt with a wide, high waistband over which sat a dear little white broderie anglaise bodice. Feeling very confident, I walked on stage at the dress rehearsal to say my line, but as I was presented to Miss Bowers, she paused and looked me up and down. Then stepped forward and said to Warren and Hugh, who were in the stalls, 'Surely she shouldn't be wearing this bright red. It totally clashes with my dress.' She herself was wearing a lovely terracotta-coloured evening dress. Please, please don't let them take away my beautiful clothes, I thought. 'It really looks fine, Lally, and you look lovely in that burnt orange.' Lally gave in, but I knew that she was cross. They gave me my costume when the play was over and I wore it for years.

Then Warren and Hugh suddenly disappeared, and they

were replaced by a director called Lionel Harris. I had a non-speaking role in the play he directed. I played a waitress, and all I had to do was walk on stage to the set of a café with a tray of drinks, serve them and walk off again. Mr Harris wasn't in a good mood as he gave notes at the end of the dress rehearsal to the cast huddled together in the stalls. 'Where is the idiot who plays the waitress?' I nervously put up my hand. 'Well, I don't know what the fuck you think you're doing, but you look ludicrous.' I was devastated. I had practised very hard to be able to carry the drinks on the tray on the flat of my hand held high above my head and sashay across the stage. A lovely clever actor called Ronald Barker came up to me immediately we had been dismissed. 'Don't get upset – just think about it. Have you ever really seen a waitress hold a tray of glasses above her head like that?'

'No, I suppose not,' I said dismally.

'Well, no, because they don't,' he said kindly. 'Just do it as simply as possible with no fuss, as a real waitress would. Always try to make it real.'

After that, Ronnie would sometimes take me to the local café for sausage and chips, and once did a funny drawing of me sitting on my high stool as prompter with the script dangling from my lap, looking utterly fed up. I wish I still had it. Years later I did a BBC TV of *A Midsummer Night's Dream* with him, and I played Titania and he played Bottom (he was famous by then from *The Two Ronnies*). We were all booked into a very upmarket boutique hotel somewhere in Kent where we were shooting, and Ronnie knocked on my door as soon as I arrived, saying, 'So where do you think we'll find sausage and chips?'

Then Lionel Harris also disappeared, and we were told we were getting some whizz-kid director called Peter Hall.

Apparently he had made a name for himself at Cambridge University and was coming to us straight from the Worthing Repertory Company.

But before he arrived someone else turned up at the stage door looking for me.

10

There, one day, was David Jeayes, saying apologetically, 'I've only just found out that you're here.' Well, I suppose my name wasn't exactly in lights outside the Playhouse. 'When do you get free time? When do you eat?' I had to eat at the somewhat unglamorous hour of around four or five after the day's rehearsal finished, as it was too late to eat in the cafés I frequented after the show. 'High tea it is then,' he said. 'Why don't you come to my place as soon as you finish tomorrow afternoon?' He wasn't staying in college and didn't live far from the theatre. I dressed as well as my skimpy wardrobe allowed, washed my hair overnight and was horribly, deliciously, anxiously overexcited.

He had a large pleasant room with a table in the big bay window covered in books and papers, a fireplace and a double bed with two oars fixed on the wall above it, which I learned later were the oars from a race his boat had won in Eights Week. After greeting me he said, 'Look, I'm really sorry but I've just got to finish some work I have to hand in. I won't be long. Why don't you amuse yourself with this while you're waiting?' And he handed me what looked like – and was – an exam paper.

I was slightly taken aback, but he so naturally pulled a chair up to the table and made a space for me I just thought, Well, I suppose this is the way students entertain themselves, so you had better try it. It entered my head later that it might have been a test to see if my brain was good enough for him to bother with me. But I don't think that was the idea. The first question was about T. S. Eliot which, thanks to all that poetry at Guildhall, I found easy. So for ten or fifteen minutes we both scratched away with our pens at the table. Then he said, 'Right, okay. Let's go.' And over Welsh rarebit and scones and tea we talked and talked, and he walked me back to the theatre and he said, 'Can we meet for a drink after the show?'

And we met the same way every day for the rest of the week, and then it was Sunday and we had all day, and it was heavenly; he had put together a picnic and borrowed a bicycle for me, and we cycled to some idyllic spot and picnicked and rambled and talked and kissed and, heady with the sun and desire, we cycled back to his room. He said, 'Shall we go to bed?' and I said, 'Yes, but I'm sorry, I'm a virgin.' He was taken aback. 'Well, if you don't want to, that's fine.' 'No, but I *do* want to,' I said. 'If you're absolutely sure?' 'Yes. I'm absolutely sure.'

So we went to bed, and I couldn't have been happier or luckier. He was a very experienced lover, but then he was two years older than me and had done his National Service before going to Oxford. I never asked about other girls. He was with me now, and that was all that mattered. I did understand at this very early stage in our relationship, though, that he was terrified of being tied down in any way. When he had cycled back with me to my digs in the early hours of that Monday morning, he held both my hands as he said goodbye outside the front door and said, 'This morning, right now, at this moment, I think it may be possible that I love you very much.' And I walked inside

the house almost laughing at his terror of commitment. I was
ready to say 'Yes, yes, yes, for ever and ever, amen'.

One of the first poems he left for me, which he always said
was written by a friend of his, but I think was his own because
I've never found it in any anthology anywhere, was:

Do not ask me for a year
A day perhaps I'll hold you dear
If you tie love
It will die love
Time enough when age is here
All we know is how to greet
Love that comes with summer heat
Do not fear love
While it's here love
Hold me close and kiss me sweet.

That was his creed then, and I was perfectly happy with
that because I knew I didn't have to tie him down – he was
mine anyway.

He boldly asked my landlady if he could have the other
room on the top floor with me as it had become vacant, and he
moved in and we were delirious with love. Every hour apart
seemed wasted.

Actually I was beginning to think my long hours spent at the
theatre *were* wasted, as Mr Peter Hall just wouldn't give me a
part at all. I had thought that because he was so young he would
be friendly and easy to talk to. But he wasn't. We had done
The Corn is Green, and he had brought Billie Whitelaw into the
company to play Bessie Watty and I was just one of the children

in the class. Our teacher was played by Tony Church, who had joined the company when Peter took over, and he was very sweet and encouraging to me and said, 'You could have played Bessie,' and I thought, Yes, I could. Although, thinking back, I wouldn't have been nearly as good as Billie, who was perfect. Then we did a music hall evening, and Peter Hall brought Maggie Smith into the company and she sang 'The Boy I Love Is Up In The Gallery' with such engaging charm and a pretty voice that, as I couldn't sing a note anyway, I couldn't really complain that all I was asked to do was turn the pages of music while Peter played the piano for each number.

A new musical was next called *Listen to the Wind*, known in the company as 'Hark the Fart'. Maggie Smith stayed on to play West Wind, and Peter brought two or three more young women into the company and was still disinclined to give me even a line. One evening the pretty, innocent-looking sixteen-year-old who was playing Sunshine (yes, this musical *was* as twee as it sounds) was unwell and couldn't play and our stage manager, June, told me to get myself into Sunshine's costume, which was a gold lamé tunic with a sort of halo of glittery rays sticking out round my head, and be prepared to say her one line. It was a scene that was supposed to be on a beach, and there were a few rocks on the set, and the two young children who were the main characters were being invited to enjoy all the elements. I think Maggie's line was something about being playful with the West Wind, and then the last character to speak was Sunshine and all I had to say was, 'Or you can just lie on the rocks and enjoy me'. I couldn't resist it. I said it in a deliberately risqué way and brought the house down. June was furious with me. 'You know very well this is a play for children. I don't know what Peter will think.' I didn't care what

Peter thought. I was completely fed up with never being given a chance, and my private happiness made me more and more resentful of going to work. One night when a dress rehearsal for a new play had gone on well into the early hours and I was longing to be in bed with my lover, I suddenly flipped.

Peter Hall had just requested that we rehearse the scene change that we had just done again, and we were laboriously putting the scenery, furniture and lighting back into position when he thought we were taking too long and shouted tetchily from the stalls: 'What's the matter with you all? I asked for this scene change ages ago. Why are you being so slow?'

I walked out onto the stage and down to the footlights, and shading my eyes to peer over them into the auditorium I shouted back at him, 'If you knew anything about the theatre you would know that it takes a little while to reset the lighting board back. Perhaps you'd like to come up and learn how it works, as they obviously didn't teach you at Cambridge University.' I walked back into the wings to be faced with a fuming stage manager. 'Go down to the stalls IMMEDIATELY,' said June, 'and apologise. You've behaved disgracefully.' Of course, I had.

I went slowly up the aisle to where Peter was sitting. 'I'm told I've been very rude to you,' I said, 'and that I should apologise.' Peter was tired and exasperated. 'You know you're a very sullen girl?' 'So would you be if you came here to play small parts and no one ever gave you a line,' I snapped back.

'Don't you think it would be better if you left then?'

'If you're never going to give me a part, yes.'

'Well, I'm certainly not after that outburst. I really think it's better that you leave.'

So I was sacked.

*

There was no question of going home to Tottenham. The problem was, how could I keep myself in Oxford? David wasn't a rich student who could pay for me as well. His father was a vicar, now retired, and his mother a teacher. He had won a chorister's scholarship to Magdalen College School, and from there he got to Pembroke College, Oxford.

His first idea as to what work I should do really upset me. He suggested that I become a bus conductress. I was horrified at the thought of doing such an obviously working-class job. 'But you'll earn much more than you would in a shop. What's the difference?' he asked. I couldn't explain the difference, I just knew that I couldn't shout 'fares, please' and 'move along there, please' in the accent I had acquired, and I would have to be jolly and wear a horrible uniform. I couldn't bear it. So I found myself a part-time job in a launderette. That wasn't too bad as I could sit down when I wanted to chat to customers, and as most of my customers were students I really enjoyed talking to them. The boys would give me a tip if I did their washing for them and flirt a bit and it was quite fun. But being part-time it wasn't enough for rent and food, so I bravely went to the manager of the Playhouse, who I knew quite liked me, and asked if I could be a front-of-house usher. He was a dear who knew why I wanted to stay in Oxford, and so he said he would make up my money if I just came and tore tickets in the foyer before the show each night. I needn't stay for the interval and do ice creams.

David's college was doing a production of a play called *Under the Sycamore Tree*, and he suggested that I audition for the leading role, which was the Queen Ant, and I got it. So life was suddenly perfect. I would do four hours at the launderette in the morning while David worked (he had to take his finals that summer), then we would have the afternoon together, except when I had rehearsals, which were very easy-going and spread over several weeks, while he would get out on the river and row or work again. Then I would do forty-five minutes' work front of house at the Playhouse and we would spend the evening together. It was an idyllic time.

Autumn, winter and spring had passed and now it was a wonderful early summer, and I had had quite a success playing in *Under the Sycamore Tree* in the Fellows' Garden at Pembroke College, and we had even gone to a ball.

David was determined that we should go to the May Ball and I longed to go, but had no idea how to find a dress. Then my mother, in one of my rare phone calls, said, 'Since it's your twenty-first birthday in June and you are refusing to have a party here at home, why don't I make an evening dress for you for this ball as your twenty-first birthday present?' I was quite worried that she wouldn't have any idea how to make the kind of dress I had in mind, but it was so good of her not to be angry with me for doing them all out of a party, I said thank you nicely and hoped for the best. Indeed my mother did do her best making that ball gown. She even came to Oxford for the day to do a fitting. I had to make sure that David wouldn't be in the house that day and that the landlady would be discreet. My mother mustn't know that I was sleeping with David. I whipped her out of the house as soon as possible and took her to the Kardomah for tea. I had no clue as to what a smart student's idea of a dress for a ball would be in 1955, and neither did she.

I had agreed to the yards of pale blue organdie. I had agreed to the puff sleeves and the sweetheart neckline and the full skirt that simply wasn't full *enough* and the sash with a bow at the back. I wasn't thrilled with it, but I thought I looked quite nice, and David seemed happy enough when he saw me in it, so I thought it was acceptable.

It was a beautiful evening, and I was very excited to be going on David's arm among all these students who, since I had done a play now with some of them, I was no longer so in awe of. I knew as soon as we walked into the grounds of the college that I'd got it wrong. My dress was far too unsophisticated and screamed home-made. Unfortunately one of the first people to greet us was Ann Harrop, who had so disapproved of my dress as Myra in *Hay Fever*. She was now on the arm of Anthony Thwaite, who she was shortly to marry, and she was dressed in a very chic black number that had cost a *lot*. After the pleasantries she turned to me, surveyed me with distaste and said, with a raised eyebrow, 'Pale blue organdie?' She stressed the *org*, whereas my mother always stressed the *gan*, and for a moment I didn't know what she was referring to. 'God, I haven't seen anyone in that for years,' and went back to sipping her drink. I refused to let the remark spoil the whole evening, but the glitter had gone from it. Years later, when she had become a well-known biographer and Anthony was a well-known poet, they came to see me in the theatre and managed to say complimentary things about my performance, and I hope I responded graciously. But I still have two faint scars from her two sharp cuts.

David and I would have both been truly depressed if we had had to go back to our homes at the end of June, but all was set for us to return to Perranporth. I always knew that I would be going for our second summer season as I'd been in touch with Anne Lewis all this time, but the joy was that David was coming for the whole season as well, as he was going to run the box office.

Anne had made other changes as well. We would no longer sleep in the village school as she had rented a large house for everyone in St Agnes, which was one train stop from Perranporth, and we were to have the luxury of a live-in cook. To top it all I had some good parts to look forward to.

All we had to do was say a fond farewell to our love nest in Oxford, go to our homes for only a few days and then go down to Cornwall. There was no way David would spend money on rail tickets, so we were to hitch-hike down there. I would have been very nervous if he hadn't been so determined.

We took the tube to Osterley and then he stood in the road trying to thumb lifts while I stood well back, looking embarrassed. But it was all a lot easier than I had imagined. People were much more willing to give lifts then than they are today, and most people were really friendly. We started from Osterley at 9 a.m. and we ended up rolling into St Agnes in a horse and cart, our lift from a farmer for the last few miles, just as it was getting dark. It had already been agreed that we would be sharing, and there we were in a charming room with garden views and a large bed.

The cast was pretty much as it had been the year before, with a couple of additions, and I can scarcely remember anything that season because I was on such a high of sheer happiness. St Agnes was a very attractive village to live in, the house and garden were roomy and comfortable, the cook was terrific – even the train ride to Perranporth was pretty. I can recall only one play from that season. It was *The Living Room*. Anne was the young girl and I was the neurotic wife. We played it the one week that David had to go up to London, which is why I remember it. All the other plays have got lost behind a mist of sun, beach, surfing and sex. All too soon that summer season, which had again been a success, had to end and be slotted in the memory as a golden time.

Going back to London and living at home after being with David for nearly a year was awful. We never talked about the future. There was no question about what I would do. I would press on trying to make a living in the theatre, but now a big question hung over what he would do. He had no craving to do anything in particular, and it turned out that he had only got a third-class degree in his finals, for which his mother blamed me, and she might have been right.

It was autumn and we met as often as we could, but it was difficult without money, and in the early 1950s you had to be a bold spirit to live with anyone outside marriage, and neither of our families would let us live together under their roof. That was totally out of the question. My mother would have wanted to die of shame if she had known that we had been living together. It was back to tramping up and down Charing Cross Road again. I saw in *The Stage* that the Shakespeare Memorial Theatre was holding open auditions and I went and did my best with Lady Percy from *Henry VI*, was thanked very nicely and heard no more because, I found out later, the women for the season had already been cast, but Equity had a rule then that they *had* to hold open auditions.

I was in very low spirits when I had a telephone call from Hugh Goldie. He made no mention of why they had left Oxford and came straight to the point. 'Eileen, how tall are you?' 'Five foot seven,' I replied. 'Oh dear. We feared you might be too tall but thought it was worth a try.' 'Why, what are you doing?' 'Well, Warren is about to shoot a television of *Pinocchio*, and the boy who was playing the dog has broken his leg and we need someone his size to get into the skin that's been made, and he was only five foot three.' 'Five foot three?' I whipped back. 'I'm scarcely five foot four. I don't know why I said five foot seven. I promise you that I can get into that skin, Hugh.' They knew that I was lying, but I insisted they let me come to the studios and try on the skin. Trying to wriggle and shrink myself into that five-foot-three-inch dog suit was possibly the nadir of all my humiliations, and only their kind hearts must have stopped Warren and Hugh from shaking with laughter at the various desperate contortions I got into in the attempt – all the time assuring them desperately, 'No, honestly, I *can* get into it.'

David suggested that we could earn money sorting letters at the GPO as they took extra people on over the Christmas rush, which started in November. So we both applied, and found ourselves at some ungodly hour being instructed at the sorting office. You had to reach a certain speed or they wouldn't take you on. David got accepted quickly, and after about another half hour I was taken on as well. It was shift work and it was back-breaking and boring, but it was only for the six weeks before Christmas and it was well paid. So we gritted our teeth and did it.

Then a few days before Christmas, on the morning of a day when we were doing the late shift, I got a telephone call from one of the agencies I used to frequent saying could I get myself on a train as soon as possible. A girl had dropped out of a show in Norwich. 'What kind of show?' I asked. 'Is it a panto?' 'You'll find out when you get there. You'll be met at the station and there's no need to worry about digs. That's all fixed. You'll get four pounds ten shillings a week, less our ten per cent,' and the agent hung up. I rang David immediately. 'I've got a job in

Norwich, so tell them I won't be coming in any more, and I'll ring you as soon as I can.'

I arrived at the station in the dark feeling apprehensive but having told myself on the cold, dusky journey that I would soon be with a jolly company and would probably have a lot of fun playing in a Christmas show of some kind.

There didn't appear to be anyone to meet me at the station. I'd expected an efficient-looking stage manager who had probably checked my picture in *Spotlight* – the publication that every actor had to pay to have their photograph in. No, there was no one promising-looking. Then, when the platform was practically empty, a small, exhausted-looking woman carrying a baby approached me. 'Are you Eileen Atkins?' 'Yes.' 'Oh, thank God,' she said. 'Come on, we have to take the bus.' I thought it was a very odd company that sent a woman with a baby to meet me, but followed her meekly to a bus stop. As the bus swung along what appeared to be the High Street, all Christmassed up, it stopped at one point right outside a theatre where none other than Cyril Fletcher was appearing in *Mother Goose*, and among the other names, I noticed that the Demon King was now being played by Peter Johnson. Peter had been at the Guildhall with me, and apart from being an actor was a brilliant fencer. Good for him, he's working, I thought, and rued the day I had laughed at Cyril Fletcher two Christmases ago. I could have been playing the Fairy Queen if I hadn't been so silly. Well, I suppose I'm being taken to a smaller theatre somewhere, I mused to myself as the bus started off again. I had questioned the woman whose name was Carla as to the name of the play or show and which theatre was it in, but she just smiled nervously and said, 'You'll see. My husband will explain everything.'

We were now leaving behind all the lights of the city and seemed to be heading into the countryside when Carla indicated that we would get off at the next stop. We alighted at what looked to me like a common where there appeared to be a fair, but all was dark except for a few lights from the caravans. I was so taken aback I couldn't speak, and followed Carla with great trepidation. There was no way I was going to work at a fair in any capacity, but I was here now and would have to talk my way out of it.

At last we stopped at a caravan and the door was opened by a tall, broad, frightening-looking man with slicked-back black hair and a Dalí moustache, and I found myself inside a stuffy, smelly space with not only Carla, her husband and baby, but two more toddlers and two huge Alsatians. Apparently they were a knife-throwing act, 'Carla and Conchetti – Her Life in His Hands'. They had to have a girl outside their booth to dance enticingly to get people in to see the show. I said it wasn't something I could do. I was a serious actress. 'You're perfect,' the man said, 'and because I like you I'm going to let you choose any costume you like out of this box of beautiful clothes.' He pulled a large cardboard box out from under some rubbish and fished out a grimy sequined bra and see-through Turkish trousers and dangled them in front of me. 'No, I really couldn't do it,' I repeated. 'It's an easy job,' Carla said. 'Not like me, practically stark naked having knives thrown at me.' 'You've given a verbal contract,' the man said threateningly. 'The fair opens tomorrow night and our girl has been taken ill.' I'm not surprised, I thought, if she's been dancing in clothes like that in this freezing weather. I picked up my suitcase and tried to make for the door, but he took it firmly from me. I thought that the only thing to do was to play along with him, so I said, 'Well, all right, but I'll need to go and find my digs first. I'm told they've been booked.' 'Digs,' he said. 'You don't need digs. You stay here, all cosy with us in the caravan.'

'No,' I said sharply, 'I have to have my own digs.' I racked my brain desperately to think of something and blurted out, 'I'm allergic to dogs and will come out in a rash from head to toe if I stay here any longer. I'm going to look for digs,' and picked up my suitcase again.

After more arguing he said he would let me go and look for digs but that he would keep my suitcase, and when I found somewhere to stay, I could come back and he would be a gentleman and carry my suitcase to my digs and make sure that I was all right.

There was nothing for it but to leave without my suitcase. I found the bus stop we'd arrived at and walked across the road and waited for a bus going back into town. I had no idea what to do. By now it was about nine or ten o'clock and I could maybe get a train back to London still, but I really couldn't afford to lose everything I had in my suitcase.

As we approached the city and I saw the lights, I had an idea. I got off the bus outside the theatre and went to the stage door and asked the doorman, 'Could I please speak to Peter Johnson?' 'No,' he said, 'they are having a dress rehearsal.' 'Please,' I said, 'it's an emergency.' The man kindly put out a call for him. Peter came down the stairs to the stage door in full Demon King drag. The green leotard with a balaclava-type helmet with horns. His face painted green with a wicked red slash that was his mouth, and over it all a huge black cloak lined with red satin. I tumbled out my predicament to him. He said, 'Hold on a moment,' and went to check where they had got to in rehearsal, then said to the doorman, 'They're going very slowly. I'll be back before my next entrance. Come on,' he said to me, and walked straight out of the door and to the amazement of passers-by, hailed a taxi and told the driver to take us to the fairground as quickly as possible and wait there while he dealt with something.

Thank God I roughly remembered where the caravan was. Peter banged on the door. The minute the door opened he said to the man, 'I'm sorry, but this young woman isn't suitable for the job you want her to do. Could I have her suitcase please?' The man gave the Demon King my suitcase without a word and we rushed back to the waiting taxi, which returned us to the stage door. As Peter jumped out, he paid the taxi and told him to take me to the station. I couldn't thank him enough. He had been Superman in a black cloak. I had just missed the last train to London. I would have to take the milk train up at 3 a.m. I was so relieved not to be in a packed, smelly caravan with the horrible prospect of having to dance sexily with hardly anything on outside a booth in freezing weather that I didn't care that I had to spend a few hours in a cold waiting room.

I hadn't of course been able to telephone David at all, and he couldn't have helped anyway, but jolting home on the train that stopped at every station, I blearily noted that we were drawing into East Dulwich where he lived, and I was so miserable I decided that I had to see him and jumped out of the carriage instead of continuing to Euston and going home. His mother was not pleased to see me and said that David was still asleep as, of course, he had been on the late shift the night before. But she gave me some breakfast and left us alone when he came downstairs. It was wonderful to have his arms around me, but a tremendous feeling of helplessness settled on me like a straitjacket and I felt I couldn't move. But I had to go home and he had to go to work.

When I arrived at Courtman Road later that day, I had to tell my mother the sad tale and disappoint her once again. For some reason my brother was at home and, apparently full of concern for me at what I'd been through, said to her, 'How can you let her do things like this? Anything could have happened. Isn't it clear that she's never going to get anywhere and she should forget about being an actress altogether?'

He may have meant well but my heart froze. 'Don't say that!' I yelled. 'Don't say that!' and ran upstairs to cry and try to sleep off the misery of it all.

11

Christmas was even more dismal than usual, with absolutely nothing to look forward to except another summer season in Perranporth, this time without David as he would be working.

When we at last managed to meet again after the holiday, his career had been settled. It sounded so boring to me that I never listened properly to what it actually was, and I can still only describe it as an insurance salesman, but of course coming from an educated family and having got a degree from Oxford – even if it was only a third – this didn't mean that he was going to be travelling with a little suitcase. He wouldn't be 'The Man from the Pru'. No, he would work in pleasant offices in London and later, starting with Zambia, all over Africa.

The first time we talked about it we had our only quarrel. We had just seen the first production of *The Boyfriend* in the West End, which we had both loved, and we had gone backstage because David knew someone in the cast, and coming out of the stage door I tripped and fell. As David picked me up he saw that the paving hadn't been laid properly and an edge was sticking up and that was why I had fallen, but I hadn't been hurt at all. 'You could sue for that,' he said. 'What?' I snapped, horrified that such a thought should spring to his mind. 'There's money to be made from accidents like that,' he assured me confidently. 'And then some poor sod who put the paving in is tracked down and loses his job,' I argued. It blew into a big row because I realised that dealing with this kind of thing was going to be part of the work he would be doing, and I found it a pathetic job and couldn't bear that he should be doing something so dull.

Our unsatisfactory meetings – the odd uncomfortable visits to his house, a horribly awkward one at mine, and sad, desperate good-night kisses in an alleyway near Leicester Square tube station – went on throughout January and February, and I was once again trudging up and down Charing Cross Road, 'doing the agents' and getting nowhere.

One evening at home my parents were discussing which holiday camp they would go to that summer, and my father was trying to persuade my mother to 'give Butlin's a go'. 'No, I will not go to Butlin's, Arthur,' my mother said firmly, 'because Butlin's is common.' 'Well,' said my father, still trying, 'it can't be *that* common because they have a repertory company at their camp!' He said the word 'repertory' reverently, making sure that all four syllables counted and glancing at me triumphantly. But my mother wouldn't budge. She knew that if you said you'd gone to Butlin's for your holidays you would be dubbed working class. But if you said 'We go to a very nice holiday camp on the East Coast – not Butlin's, of course', people would think that you went somewhere much classier. 'How do you know that Butlin's has a repertory, Dad?' I asked. 'They've got a showroom in Oxford Street and I had a good look in me lunch hour.' My father had reached retirement age and had been forced to leave his job as a meter reader, and was now addressing envelopes in his beautiful italic writing for some animal charity. He had lost some of his chirpiness since having to give up his uniform, and no longer talked about retiring to the countryside. Throughout my life I had watched him every so often stand gazing out of our living room windows in a reverie and then say, 'Just a small place in the country, a bit of a smallholding – chickens, ducks, maybe a few pigs . . . and I'd be happy as a sandboy.' My mother would give him a count of three to enjoy the mirage, then she would say very sharply, 'Well, I hope you know you'll be living there on your own.'

I decided to take a walk down Oxford Street the next day and find the Butlin's showroom. There it was, with two huge window displays including, among the many pleasures you would enjoy at the camp, 'Our repertory company with two plays for your entertainment with first class actors'. I went in and asked the girl at the counter if I could see the person who ran the repertory company. 'Oh, they're not here. I'll give you their number.' As soon as I got home I rang them and was given a date for an interview – they didn't say audition – the next week. And indeed it *was* just an interview. Nobody asked to see my acting. My CV was at last acceptable – at least, it was good enough for Butlin's. I was booked for their Skegness camp.

To start with we would be performing the two plays that we would put on at the camp, with another play that we *weren't* taking to Skegness, at what used to be the Palace Pier Theatre in Brighton. We would open there at the end of March, and on 22 April we would go to Skegness where we would rehearse and add a science fiction play to perform for the children at the camps on Saturday mornings. We would play twice nightly, and the contract was from the third week in March through to the beginning of September – almost six months. I would have to kiss goodbye to going back to Perranporth again, but I couldn't be upset about that as I would be earning more money and it would be for so much longer.

I never understood why we did the one extra play in Brighton that never went anywhere. It was a farce called *The Honey Pot* and had a comedian in it called Leonard Henry, and I think he must have just wanted to try it out somewhere. The two plays we were taking to the East Coast where *Tell-Tale Murder*, obviously a thriller, and once again *Love's a Luxury*, obviously a comedy.

I met David the evening before I had to go down to Brighton, and all kinds of promises were made to see each other as often as we could, but I didn't hold out much hope as there was already talk of him going away on courses, and worse, of him going abroad. We were both sad. The joy in each other had just got washed out. We both actually looked bleached. I remember turning to look at him again when we had parted and he was walking down the street and I thought, He's defeated. I can see it in his shoulders. And I think I am too.

I arrived in Brighton on a wet Sunday evening and found my way to the bedsit I had rented in a block of flats near the pier, where we would be rehearsing. It was the most depressing room that you could possibly imagine. Oddly enough, six years later, I was filming in that very same room for the film of John Osborne's play *Inadmissible Evidence*. As the crew walked in the director said, 'God, what an awful place. Was it advertised as suitable for suicides?' I never confessed that I had stayed there.

I bought some fish and chips and ate them at a covered bus stop along the front, and then went to bed praying that the cast I would meet in the morning and have to live with for six months wouldn't be as bad as the company at Hazel Grove, but I honestly wasn't expecting much.

It was sunny the next day and Brighton looked better, and as I swung along the pier I was humming, 'Oh I do like to be beside the seaside'.

The actors and stage management were gathered on the dark stage of the Palace Pier Theatre when I arrived, and there were mugs of coffee and introductions. I noted a quite pretty blonde girl who looked even younger than me, and a middle-aged man who looked rather jolly and had a very loud but seemingly genuine laugh, and the rest were a blur of nondescript faces. Then suddenly a young man joined us and he was a bit of a dazzler. He was tall, broad-shouldered, almost handsome and definitely attractive, with a smile that said, 'Isn't life fabulous?' It was as if he had brought the sunshine in with him. I cheered up and the other young woman immediately fished for her powder compact.

When we broke for lunch, having read through the play, Julian, as I now knew the young man was called, invited Penny (the blonde) and me to go and find something to eat with him, and the jolly man whose name was Charles joined us as well. I was immensely relieved to find that at least three members of the company were friendly and talkative. Julian Glover, who had just finished his National Service and was thrilled to be working, was determined that we should have a good time doing what we all agreed were really dreadful plays. He clearly found Penny attractive, and I could see that she was quiveringly thrilled at his attentions, and I had a faint twinge of jealousy that I rapidly reprimanded myself for. The good thing was that I wasn't going to be with a gloomy bunch of has-beens, and at the end of that first day the four of us walked cheerfully back down the pier more than happy to say 'cheese' as we were snapped by the pier photographer.

We whizzed through our weeks in Brighton and then took the train to Skegness. Julian drove up in style and dashingly arrived in an Austin Twelve. The first man I actually knew who owned a car. I thought he might have driven Penny up, but no. Things hadn't gone that far, apparently.

Although I'd been to holiday camps with my parents, I wasn't quite prepared for Butlin's. It was massive, and run on very strict lines. Most amusements were timed to last an hour and then a clanging bell would ring and everyone would obediently go to the next thing that had been arranged for their delight, whether the current entertainment had finished or not. So our two plays had to be cut to one hour each, which I can't say ruined either of them, and it was a wonderfully strict lesson for us actors never to let the pace slacken because if you did, the bell would ring and the whole audience would rise as one and file neatly out of the auditorium whether you had finished the play or not, to whatever it told them on their timetable they were to go to next – bingo, clock golf, a beauty contest or quiz, or whatever the numerous entertainments were that they provided to take your mind off your worries. And you didn't even have to think about the kids, because you knew for once where they were, what they were doing and that they were all right because they were being looked after by a Butlin's Redcoat.

These Redcoats really worked for their money. Their hours were long and the first rule was that they must never leave their chalet without a smile on their face and it must remain there all day, as they could be sacked for not having a cheerful expression. They were expected to be professional entertainers as well as knowing how to call bingo, set up a treasure hunt or do 'Incy Wincy Spider' with the young ones. Most of them were either just starting out in show business, trying to get a foothold, or performers who had had careers and were now slipping down the ladder. Butlin's also had quite big names as guest stars but they, of course, were not Redcoats.

Once we were in Skegness our schedule wasn't so bad. We just had to do the one-hour play twice a night and the science fiction play, which we had rehearsed immediately we had got there, on Saturday mornings. I had to wear something absurd on my head and walk about in the audience and the children would pinch me and blow raspberries in my face.

The whole company were in digs and, thank God, *didn't* have to stay in a chalet and come out smiling each day. I was in a room in a fairly deadly bungalow, but it was comfortable enough, and there is something about staying in a seaside town in England in spring or summer that is tattily cheerful. Quite soon after we arrived I noticed that Julian seemed to prefer my company to Penny's or anyone else's, although he was very sociable with everyone.

I think probably we were drawn together – aside from sexual attraction – because we both had the same sense of humour. At the beginning of the thriller *Tell-Tale Murder*, for example, the curtain rose on our middle-aged leading lady and our older character actress, both dressed from head to foot in black bombazine, gazing down on the flagstones of a Hammer Horror-type house. Then the old woman lifted her head and in sepulchral tones, and some really bad acting, had to say, '*Flies again? You'll never get rid of them now*'. It always made Julian and me, waiting in the wings for our cue, laugh and we had to pull ourselves together to make our entrance.

I soon discovered that Julian came from a very literary

family, so I could be at home talking 'books' with him. His godfather was Robert Graves, whose *Goodbye to All That* I'd read, and he introduced me to James Baldwin's passionate books about Black America. His father wrote and performed regularly a radio programme for the BBC called *By My Cottage Door*, and his mother was a journalist, Honor Wyatt, and had been the editress of *Woman's Hour*. They were divorced but still amicable, his father now married to a children's writer and his stepfather a psychologist. Oh, how glamorous all this sounded to me. I must sound so dull, I thought. My dad is a retired meter reader and my mum's a dressmaker. He was the first actor I had met who was as eaten up by the theatre as I was and could talk about it for hours and was as passionate to play in the classics as I was, and we talked theatre night and day. He asked me to his place to listen to some Shostakovich (who I had never heard of) – he'd brought records and a gramophone with him – and you can guess the rest. It would have been perverse of us if we *hadn't* gone to bed together.

I didn't feel guilty about David because he hadn't made an effort to get down to Brighton, which hurt me, and his letters now were all about his first trip to Zambia, and I thought that there was some kind of agreement between us, that we had fallen apart and there was nothing to be done about it. It's hard for young people today to understand how this could happen when it's so much easier to deal with things now, but you have to remember that even a phone call was quite difficult. You had to make sure that the person you were calling would be by their phone, you had to collect enough change to make the call, then you had to find a public phone box that you often had to queue for. So it was difficult to make a call on time, and then just as you started to relax and speak naturally the operator would say, 'One more minute, caller', and 'beep, beep, beep' and that was it.

One of the surprising things about Julian was that he seemed to be almost as poor as I was. The car was a second-hand gift from a godfather. There had, of course, been money on both sides of his family once, so his parents were brought up and educated grandly, but *their* parents had gone through the money. They were now, certainly in his mother's case, having to live on their journalism, and that has always been a dicey way to make your living. So Julian, with his mother and stepfather, and two – sometimes three – siblings lived a somewhat hand-to-mouth existence. From Alleyn's School in Dulwich he had done one year at drama school and then had to do his National Service. He was already quite political, influenced by his mother and stepfather leaning very much to the left. He was the first person to make me *think* about politics. My parents voted Conservative because my mother thought she was middle class and only the lower classes voted Labour, and my father genuinely loved the aristocracy and 'didn't want no revolutions 'ere'. So we were the only house in Courtman Road displaying blue posters at elections. I had formed no opinion of my own.

We both knew we needed to earn as much money as we could and Julian suggested that since we had the weekends off, apart from having to do the kids' play on Saturday mornings at 10 a.m., we could probably get jobs as waiters, and we were quickly taken on at the Palace Pier Restaurant in Skegness. We then discovered that they were short of help in the kitchens at Butlin's, so on Sunday nights we were washing up in the camp. It was horrible work with no dishwashers, but it meant we could save a bit.

I was a lousy waitress. I have a very short fuse. I wish I didn't, and now that I'm in my eighties I try very hard not to be so quick-tempered, but it's in my genes. Both of my parents died in sudden rages. It's not a bad way to go, and I do warn companies now that if they want the play to open – or not to have to reshoot the movie – it would be a good idea not to annoy me.

One day at the restaurant I was serving high tea to a table of eight: one middle-aged man with seven teenagers, who kept changing their minds and then saying when the dishes were brought to the table that they weren't what they had ordered. They were altogether a nightmare. I had smiled and kept smiling as they messed the order up yet again, and borne the oozing, paternalistic jollity of the older man with gritted teeth, sure that I would get a big tip. I know I was expecting that a crisp pound note would be left under a saucer for me. I gave the man the bill, which was paid at a cash desk near the door, and was fishing under the crockery left on the table for my tip, when the man called out to me to come to him at the cash desk. I thought, Well, if he's making a thing of it, it definitely can't be less than a pound note. He took my hand and with a broad, benevolent smile, ceremoniously pressed a threepenny bit into my palm. I couldn't believe it, and in a sudden fury threw it straight back at him. The manager was called and I thought I would be sacked, but after placating the odious man, the minute the door was shut the manager just told me to 'watch it', but he was laughing.

I had obviously had to let Anne Lewis know that I couldn't do Perranporth that summer, and she had suggested that if I could get myself down to Cornwall immediately after my

Butlin's stint was over I could just make it for their last play of the season. I told her about Julian, and she said, 'Bring him with you.'

So after our last performance in Skegness, with the Austin Twelve already packed with our suitcases, we set off at about eleven to drive through the night, hoping to arrive in time to rehearse the next morning.

The drive was fun at first, but we broke down at about 3 or 4 a.m. in the middle of Bodmin Moor in a thick fog, and I began to realise why the Cornish believed in 'ghoulies and ghosties and long-leggedy beasties'. Someone came to our rescue and we made it to the St Agnes house in time for breakfast, before going into Perranporth to rehearse *Who Goes There!*, which Anne had chosen as it had lovely parts for the three of us. It was a relief to do, not a wonderful but a decent play, and we had a highly successful couple of weeks. Finally we had to go home, but in good spirits this time as Julian had made it clear it wouldn't mean separation.

His family lived in Kent, so he had to find himself a room in London. He found one overlooking the railway near Olympia and immediately got another job as a waiter in a rather awful restaurant nearby. At weekends he went back to Kent, and soon asked me to go down with him and meet his family.

They lived in a crumbling Georgian house standing well back from the road in Lydden, just outside Dover. I will never forget the first time I went to Wellington House.

I was first introduced to his mother, Honor, who was cooking in the kitchen. There were pies, cakes and savouries spread on every surface. I had never seen a kitchen anything like it. She was a short, plain, but joyously lively woman who gave me a wonderfully warm welcome, saying blithely, 'You're in the room next to Julian, and there's a connecting door. Just don't make it obvious to the younger ones.'

Then in the study, surrounded with books, there was George, his stepfather, reading and smoking a pipe, who took my hand, rather than shaking it, in both his hands and said with such a warm smile, 'Julian has told us so much about you – it's lovely that you've come.'

There were books in every nook and cranny of the house, and someone was playing notes on an organ in another room who turned out to be Julian's twelve-year-old brother (who became the famous musician Robert Wyatt). And then down the stairs came his teenage sister Prue, saying, 'I've put make-up on because you're an actress. Does it look all right?' Just before supper, as I learned to call it, George's son by his previous wife turned up and we all sat round a table laden with food. In our house you just ate the really badly cooked plate of food that was put in front of you, and I couldn't wait to leave the table and get back to my book. Here there was a lot of talk, and everyone pitched in, and each person was listened to and there was a lot of laughter, and I couldn't believe how mouth-wateringly good the food was. To be invited into the kitchen to take a bite or two of anchovy toast to give myself an appetite (what were *anchovies*?); to be offered fish flan or risotto, neither of which I had ever heard of, and be helped to an enormous salad with all kinds of herbs in it that I never knew existed and a dressing to die for, followed by orange mousse, was an amazing culinary experience for me. There wasn't a mouthful that I'd ever tasted before and there wasn't a mouthful that wasn't delicious. I suddenly realised why people enjoyed eating. I would always like fish and chips, and my mother's Spam fritters weren't too bad if you put OK Sauce on them, but this was something else.

And I was made so welcome. I was overwhelmed by the sense of what a family was, and I wanted to belong. This was, of course, unfair of me and snobbish. I had a family. I just preferred this one.

Julian heard from a friend that the Arts Council were sending out a school's tour of *Twelfth Night*, and he had an audition for it and got the part of Malvolio. He found that they hadn't yet cast Maria and asked if they would see me. They did, and I got the part.

We were based in Nottingham and rented a rather dark and depressing bedsit together. The weather was freezing, and the room had a very small gas fire which I spent a lot of time crouched over trying to get warm.

We played at the schools in the mornings and afternoons, mostly in their gymnasiums if they had one. We did two schools in one day, and my overriding memory is arriving at the school cloakroom just after the children had gone into assembly, to put on our costumes and make-up amid a stench of smelly plimsolls, pee and plasticine. Apart from giving them a break from geography or maths, I don't think the children appreciated us much. Of course, it's wonderful that Shakespeare is always taught in schools, but you need an amazing teacher like my Mr Burton to really convey the brilliance of the writing, and children have to be primed before being given that language. Also, I doubt if our performance of the play was one to astonish and amaze a young audience.

That job saw us through to Christmas, and then Julian heard that he had got into the company at Stratford-upon-Avon. It was the kind of company we had both dreamed of being a member of one day. He was to be a walk-on with the possibility of the odd line and understudying. He was rightly ecstatic, and

I was thrilled for him. He would be away from February until the very end of November.

I have to confess now to a blank in my memory. A blank that makes me think that it's likely I did something I wished to forget. What, you may wonder, happened to David? I must have told him about Julian, as Anne Lewis was one of his friends and she didn't question Julian coming with me to Perranporth. I suppose I must have written him a letter. I know that I didn't see him at all in London when we came back from Cornwall, and I don't remember him trying to see me.

Amid all the excitement of Julian getting into the company there was, of course, much sad talk that we would now be parted, and I was gazing at another stretch of looking for work and possibly going off to some substandard company in some godforsaken part of Britain while my beloved would be living and playing in the actors' Mecca of Stratford-upon-Avon. I do know that, looking back, my next move definitely appears a little calculated, and I hope you'll remember that many of Jane Austen's characters are also a little calculating, and that you really can't always rely on Cupid to give you a happy ending. You have to take matters into your own hands.

So one evening when Julian and I were at his place in London and he was saying how very much he would miss me, I said, 'Well . . . you don't *have* to.'

There was a very long pause while Julian, I'm sure, wondered if my mother *wouldn't* kill me after all and would be very liberal, and I could just go up to Stratford with him until I got a job.

He said, 'You mean . . . ?'

I waited, breathless, for him to get it.

'Get married?'

'Well, yes,' I said.

Darling Julian was thrilled with the idea. I know he was thrilled because I accidentally overheard a conversation he had with his mother a few days later, in which she wondered whether he was maybe rather young at twenty-one for such a momentous decision, but he joyfully said, 'No, no. She's the right girl. Why wait?'

I think it was all done in a matter of weeks. Kensington Registry Office was booked, a ring was bought, my mother ran me up something to be married in – not white, even she accepted that. I designed it and the skirt wasn't full enough – the skirt is *never* full enough when it's home-made – and I think my parents were bemused but relieved. At least I hadn't shamed them by getting pregnant. My old pal Dorothy next door *had* got pregnant and had 'a shotgun wedding', as my mother put it. And I think she was slightly nervous that I was too, as it was all done in such a rush, but she didn't dare ask.

The horror for me about the wedding was that Julian's lovely, classy parents and siblings would have to meet mine. What a snob, you will think. But even today, when people try to say there is no such thing as class, we still all laugh at the TV sketch of John Cleese looking down on Ronnie Barker, and Ronnie Barker looking down on Ronnie Corbett, even though it was first shown so long ago, because there is still some truth there. This was two very different classes meeting, and I knew Julian's family, with all their social graces, would manage and mine would be silent with the fear of saying the wrong thing, and secretly resentful that I had put them in this position by marrying above my station, and hideously embarrassed that Julian's father, Gordon, was paying for everything.

He had booked a very discreetly posh restaurant in Kensington for the reception and was giving us three days' honeymoon in the lovely Queens Hotel in Brighton. This was chosen as it was where Gordon had met Honor and *they* had had *their* honeymoon at the Queens Hotel, and it charmed them both that Julian and I had met in Brighton as well. He would have given us a longer time there but we had to be in Stratford almost immediately.

I spent the weeks before the wedding worrying about a lot of things. Had I pushed Julian into it? Was I going to look all right? Was my family going to shame me? Why hadn't I somehow saved up enough money to have my front tooth done? Would I throw up at the wedding breakfast?

The night before the wedding, with my anxiety about to peak, the telephone rang. My brother took the call and said to me, 'There's a reverend someone who wants to speak to you.' My first thought was that it was E. J. Burton, my teacher, whom I had written to and told I was getting married. Maybe he had suddenly started calling himself reverend again.

'Hello,' I said.

'Is that Eileen?' I didn't recognise this soft, educated voice.

'Yes.'

'This is David's father, Reverend Jeayes. We have met.'

'Yes.'

'Is it true that you are getting married tomorrow?'

'Yes. Yes, I am.'

There was a sigh of such sadness.

'You've broken my boy's heart,' he said.

I couldn't say anything.

'Are you sure you're doing the right thing? It's never too late to change your mind, you know.'

'No. No. I can't change my mind.' The awful thing was that I was now crying.

'I saw you together,' he went on, 'and you loved each other.'

'Yes. Yes, we did. But I'm getting married. I'm so sorry, Mr Jeayes. I'm so sorry.'

I put the phone down and just stood in our dark, dank hall and cried. I felt that I'd betrayed everyone. Clearly David felt betrayed, and if Julian saw me weeping, he would feel betrayed. I disliked myself intensely. I was a duplicitous person and obviously didn't know what the truth was any more.

I slept very little, and in the morning when my bouquet arrived I went into a sudden fury. I'd ordered a small posy such as bridesmaids usually carry, and the local florist had decided to add lots of trailing fern. I tore at the fern and nearly pulled the whole arrangement to pieces. Then I got into the car that Julian's father had paid for to drive me and my father to Kensington Registry Office. My sister's husband was taking my brother and mother in his car.

I don't remember my father and me speaking at all. I do remember that when we stopped at some lights, I recognised a musical comedy actress who had been in *Listen to the Wind* at Oxford called Christie Humphrey. She had been particularly sweet to me, and I wound down the window and shouted, 'Christie, Christie,' and she turned and came to the car. 'Ooh, look at you,' she said. 'Oh, Christie, I'm going to be married and I've behaved so badly.' The lights changed. 'No, you haven't,' she said, 'it's just stage fright,' and shouted as we moved off, 'Just remember. Tits and teeth.' That's what she always said to give herself courage before going on stage.

'That was a very good-looking woman.'

My father spoke at last. Christie's cleavage had obviously not gone unnoticed.

'Yes. She's lovely,' I said.

There was a brief pause.

'Don't tell your mother, but a tart stopped me yesterday in Regent Street.'

'What did you do?'

My father put on his haughty butler voice.

'I said, "Thank you for the offer but I'm a very busy man and don't have the time today."' Slight pause. 'Well, there's no need to be rude to them, is there?' And we had reached the registry office.

I calmed down when I saw Julian's grin, and suddenly everyone was there and we were being shown into the room where the ceremony was to take place. I saw my mother push hard to get a seat in the circle of chairs where she would get the best view of my face and I thought, Well, that's it. Now I won't show anything. Not one single expression. I don't know why. It was just what I felt. We said the words and it was over, and then we were in a lovely restaurant and I was sitting between Julian and his father, who was charming and made a lovely speech. And I began to feel better, knowing it would all soon be over, and then it *was* over and we were all putting on our coats, and I heard Gordon say to Honor, 'Well, that wasn't too bad, was it? But who were the weird couple who had insects instead of children?' (My brother-in-law collected insects.) And Honor said, 'The sister and her husband.' And I wanted to punch Gordon and say, 'Don't be cruel. They *can't* have children. Don't make fun of MY FAMILY.'

And then it was just me and Julian driving to Brighton and I thought, It's all right, it's going to be all right. The room in the

Queens Hotel was splendid, the bed beckoned us as the bellboy left the room with his tip and Julian and I moved towards each other – and then I stopped. I could see nothing but my mother's face looming at me, and I couldn't go on. 'I'm terribly sorry, Julian,' I said, 'but I can't do this now because my wretched mother is here and won't go away.'

So we went to the pictures and saw John Wayne as Genghis Khan, and when we came back my mother had left the room.

12

The next morning we learned that we had at last got some-where to live in Stratford-upon-Avon, so we had a glass of champagne with our eggs and bacon to celebrate, and in the pale February sunshine almost skipped along the pier to revisit the place where we had met. For the first time since I had proposed to Julian I felt enormously happy. I was Mrs Glover, and it was going to be all right.

By the end of the week we were in our flat in Stratford, the top half of a semi-detached 1930s house on the main road to Warwick. Although I had a secret hope that we might be in one of the period cottages, the fact that we had our very own two rooms, kitchen and bathroom was enough to make me pretty ecstatic, and it was just a ten-minute walk to the theatre where Julian had to report for rehearsals the morning after we arrived.

It cost us four pounds a week, and Julian was to earn six pounds a week. I obviously had to earn some money as well, so I asked immediately at the theatre if they needed usherettes. They did, and we were just wondering if we could scrape by with the small kitty we would have to live on when the actors' union, Equity, amazingly got the lowest-paid actors a rise that would make their pay eight pounds ten shillings a week. So with my small amount we could manage, and I wouldn't have to do another job. So I settled down to being a Stratford wife.

Of course I couldn't cook at all, and we had some very weird meals. Honor had given me a cookery book but it gave me recipes, not basic things like how to cook a cauliflower, and in the first week I put a whole cauliflower, uncut, to cook in the oven. But I persevered and slowly began to try the recipes. I then got totally confused as to what was considered a main course, and having found the recipe for potato salad delicious, and as far as I was concerned very unusual, I served it on its own as a main course at our first supper party without even a lettuce leaf.

The first production was *As You Like It* with Dame Peggy Ashcroft as Rosalind and Julian as a forester. He was loving rehearsals, and very quickly made quite a few friends. I would wave him off to work in the morning and watch from our living room window, which overlooked the main road, as he joined up with the other actors who lived along Welcombe Road and, laughing and talking, they would walk to the theatre together. It was hard to watch and not be part of them. I would then work out what we would eat and do the shopping.

I was aware of other wives of the actors around the town. You could tell by their London accents and different clothes. In the butcher's one day I saw a stunning-looking woman. She was not a beauty, but she was very attractive with marvellous bone structure. She was wearing a simple sweater with a full, mid-calf skirt and had a basket on her arm, a baby on her hip and a toddler clinging to her skirt. She looked perfectly ready to be painted by Augustus John. She noticed me staring and said as she paid the butcher, 'Hello. Are you one of the wives?' I said,

'Yes, Julian Glover's.' 'I'm Patrick Wymark's wife, Olwen. We live out at Avonside. You must come to tea.' She had two other children and a wonderfully welcoming home that she had made and she seemed to me the embodiment of contented domesticity, though years later when she had become a close friend I found this conception to be far from the truth. As much as she loved her children, she was eaten away with the desire to be a playwright, which in middle age she finally became. In 1957 it was presumed that motherhood came first.

After six weeks *As You Like It* opened and I could at last go to work with Julian, though I had to go in at the front entrance as he went to the stage door. This first play was a success, so everyone was happy, but charming, lovely and talented as Dame Peggy was, I thought it outrageous that Rosalind was played by a woman of fifty. It's true that you are often not ready to grapple with Shakespeare's great heroines until you're in your thirties, but I thought she was pushing it a bit.

After a few weeks as an usherette the front-of-house manager told me that they were going to put a table in the foyer and sell postcard photos of the famous actors in roles that they had played at the theatre, and would I like the job of selling them? I would be paid a little more than the usherettes, so I said, 'Yes I would like that, thank you very much.' It meant that I had more engagement with the public and heard more of their chatter sitting still in the foyer. I was also asked some amazingly stupid questions. There was a slit in the wall that said ASHES for people's ash and cigarette ends, and one American, pointing at it, asked me, 'Are those Shakespeare's ashes?' And I was asked twice if he ever came to see his plays. 'Oh, his shade is a pretty regular visitor,' I would say.

The company was now performing *King John* with Robert

Harris playing King John, Alec Clunes playing the Bastard and Julian playing Second Executioner – not First Executioner, sadly, who had one line. The members of the company were advertised on a large board in front of the theatre. At the top in big letters were the stars of the season; in the middle in a smaller size were the supporting players, and at the bottom the largest number of actors in small print were all the walk-ons and small parts. And the company pretty well stuck to these three groups outside the theatre, so our social circle was made up of spear carriers.

I loved the supper parties (even when I nervously had to provide food myself), as I lapped up all the talk of rehearsals and what had gone wrong in performances, and how the stars were behaving, and of course who was a good actor and who was useless. I felt wistful that I couldn't join in, but actors like nothing more than a captive audience listening to their stories so to a certain extent I was embraced into the group, although there is no doubt that actors look upon people who are not in the theatre as 'civilians' and are happiest with their own kind. I had been to a couple of coffee mornings with the wives of the actors and found them utterly arse-achingly boring. Olwen Wymark was an exotic exception and didn't appear at these gatherings, and after a couple of meetings of an hour or so of 'who was the best butcher to go to' and 'which schools in the area were good' and 'well, actually, I find Shakespeare a bit boring', I didn't go either.

With so much time on my hands I decided to write a play. This kept me happy for a few weeks. It contained murder, incest and sodomy, and I was sure that the Royal Court Theatre would snap it up. Then came the ceremonial moment when I thought I would read all three acts straight through and solemnly time them. My play lasted seventeen minutes. I was clearly way ahead of Harold Pinter, as the play I did for him thirty-five years later called *Mountain Language* was exactly seventeen minutes in length and was taken very seriously. Luckily I realised I was no Pinter and threw the script away.

I was bored. I was beginning to whine. I knew it but I just couldn't stop it. I was working in the wrong part of the building and I was beginning to be jealous of Julian.

Julius Caesar had now opened, with Caesar played by Cyril Luckham and Antony played by Richard Johnson and Varro played by Julian with two lines and a '*My Lord*'. Hurrah!

But there was a problem in the company. Brian Bedford, a promising young actor, had had a motorbike accident and wouldn't be playing in anything for a while. They just hoped that he would heal before the last play, *The Tempest*, as he was to play Ariel to John Gielgud's Prospero. Then another actor got an American film contract and left the company, and three other actors left for various reasons and Glen Byam Shaw, who was director of the company, began to see that the crowd scenes, particularly in *Julius Caesar*, were beginning to look a little thin on the ground. He happened to mention this to someone one day in Julian's hearing. The next day, without telling me, Julian did a very brave thing. He bearded Glen in his office and asked him to take me into the company. Glen Byam Shaw had a very quick temper and wasn't the easiest man for a young actor to approach, and was somewhat affronted and said tetchily, 'We can't just give jobs to wives.' But Julian begged him to give me an audition. He didn't seem to be bothered, but finally in exasperation said, 'All right. She can come and fill up the stage but that is *all*. She won't get any lines or understudying.'

When Julian told me I was over the moon. When I told the front-of-house manager that I was joining the company, he seemed quite put out and said, 'Oh, I was hoping you would join us in the box office one day.' The actors were slightly put out that they had to rehearse the three crowd scenes so that I could be put into them, and the wardrobe mistress was *very* put out that she had to find me a hempen homespun dress and shawl and sandals for my bunioned feet. I would not be required to fill up the stage in *As You Like It* or *King John*. I was put in a dressing room with the three female walk-ons, Pamela Taylor, Liz Evans and a tiny, middle-aged woman called Mavis Edwards who I think didn't approve of my joining the company in this fashion, but I didn't care. Within thirty-six hours of Julian's meeting with Glen I was on the stage and couldn't have been happier.

I had only been a member of the company for two or three weeks when one night Julian and I were woken at about 1 a.m. by John Grayson, Liz's boyfriend, banging on our door. He told us that Liz couldn't breathe properly, and as they lived close by and Julian had a car, he wanted him to take them to the hospital. Julian threw on some clothes and went back with John to pick up Liz. As I was going back to sleep I suddenly remembered that Liz was playing Audrey in *As You Like It* for a week or so because the principal, Stephanie Bidmead, was already in hospital. I sat up again in bed. I bet they don't have a second understudy, I thought – that would be very unusual – and *As You Like It* was playing tomorrow night, so it would do no harm to find Julian's copy of the play and learn Audrey. It was a small part in three short scenes. I learned it and went back to sleep. When Julian came back at about 4 a.m. he said, 'They're keeping Liz in overnight.'

I was at the theatre early the next morning, hanging about by the noticeboard hoping to see someone who would know what was going on. Finally our stage manager, Maurice Daniels, walked by.

'I hear Liz is in hospital,' I said.

'Yes,' said Maurice.

'So who will play Audrey tonight?' I asked.

'Someone will have to go on with the script, I suppose.' He started to move away.

'Well, I played it at drama school,' I lied, 'so I actually know it.'

'You'd better come with me then,' he said. Grabbing my arm, he marched me to the offices. Glen Byam Shaw wasn't in yet, but he was phoned and gave his permission for me to go on that night. Then Patrick Wymark, who was playing Touchstone, was called in to rehearse with me. He was very encouraging and very kind and slapped me on the back after we had done it a few times and said, 'I'll see you on stage tonight – you'll be grand.'

Both Stephanie and Liz had taken no notice of Touchstone's line about Audrey that made it clear that she was plain. He says, when asked who she is, '*A poor virgin, sir, an ill-favoured thing, sir, but mine own*', and she herself says, '*Well, I am not fair, and therefore I pray the gods make me honest*'. And they hadn't seemed to work out that as she was a goatherd she would be rather dirty. They were both pretty girls, and had played the part looking pristine with cute ponytails and an artfully attractive smudge or two on their faces.

I made myself as filthy and as plain as possible. I greased my hair into lumps and gave myself a very unflattering red nose that blunted my face. When Patrick came to the dressing room before our first scene to wish me good luck, he was delighted with the way I looked. We made our way down to the stage together and stood waiting in the wings for our cue. I was utterly terrified.

'Why are you wearing sandals?' he whispered. 'You're supposed to be barefoot.'

'Wardrobe gave them to me 'cos I have bunions,' I whispered back.

'Perfect,' he said. 'Kick 'em off.' And then we were on.

That night I had a small triumph because Patrick got more laughs than he had done before, simply because he had this very unprepossessing girl to play off. At the curtain he kissed my hand and Dame Peggy Ashcroft then took it and pulled me forward for a solo bow. I was utterly thrilled.

Though Liz was released from hospital and back in time for the next show, that performance had done wonders for me. The company now totally accepted me with open arms and Patrick became my sponsor, admirer and friend for the rest of his life.

I was nervous when we went into rehearsal for *Cymbeline*, as to my horror it was being directed by Peter Hall. Would I be sacked immediately he recognised me? It was two years since he had seen me and I had had long hair then, which I had cut when I got married. I would keep my head down and hope for the best.

When we all gathered for the first rehearsal and Peter talked to us about his ideas for *Cymbeline*, I breathed a sigh of relief as I noticed that when he glanced over his company his eyes hadn't shown a flicker of recognition. I was to be one of the Queen's ladies-in-waiting. One of them had to say '*Yes, madam*' in a scene, and at the reading of the play when we got to those two words, nobody spoke. 'Who are playing the ladies-in-waiting?'

Peter asked. I put my hand up along with Pam and Liz. Peter looked straight at me and said, 'You take that "*Yes, madam*".' He can't possibly have recognised me, I thought triumphantly, or he wouldn't have given me those two words. Well, I'm not going to tell him that I'm not supposed to say a word on stage. Although I don't think that that rule applied any more as I knew that Glen Byam Shaw had been very pleased with my Audrey.

When I went to have my first fitting for my lady-in-waiting costume, I was disappointed at first as Lila De Nobili, the wonderful and very eccentric designer, walked slowly round me and then announced that I wouldn't be wearing a pretty silk taffeta dress like the others. 'You will be a nun. An Ancient Briton nun,' she said. But when I saw the ensemble they made me I could make no complaint. I was in yards and yards of thin, gorgeous, pale cream wool with a soft cotton wimple round my face and a huge broad-brimmed straw hat with trailing flowers round the brim, placed over the wimple. A wimple does wonders for a long face. Even Joan Miller, who was playing the Wicked Queen, said 'Goodness. That looks so beautiful', when she first saw me, and I wondered for a moment if she, like Lally Bowers, would complain, as of course it was very eye-catching.

I had another extraordinary costume in *Cymbeline*, as I was also Leader of the Britons when the Romans and the Britons had a very stylised battle. Again I had been picked out by Peter. He said at a rehearsal, 'I suppose the Britons should have a leader,' and pointed at me (probably because I was tall) and said, 'You lead them on. It will be more fun to have a woman leading the army.' Lila dressed us all in blue rags and then we daubed ourselves with blue make-up that was to look like woad, and we had wooden clubs to fight with. On the very first night when I was waiting in the wings to lead my army on,

With Maggie Smith in *A Delicate Balance*

With Michael Griffiths in *Mother Goose*

Actors Julie Foot, Mary Law, Thomas Dance, me and Amanda Fox watching a
rehearsal of *Twelfth Night* at the Open Air Theatre in Regents Park

With Raymond Jago (standing) and
Julian Glover in *Who Goes There?*

On the beach
with David

Top: Cynthia, Janet,
Valarious, Trevor and me
Bottom: In the garden
with David

First day of rehearsal
on Brighton Pier. Left
to right: Julian Glover,
me, Charles Rowley and
Penny Stephens

The wedding. Front row left to right: My father, me, Julian, my mother, my sister

That unflattering dark tooth still not fixed

George Elldige and Honor Wyatt at Wellington House

Playing a nun in *Cymbeline*, Stratford

Top: Vanessa enjoying the sea
Bottom: And me

With Vanessa Redgrave in *Vita and Virginia*

Joan of Arc in *An Age of Kings*

You can just about recognise me standing next to the great Leonard Rossiter in Arnold Wesker's *Roots*

The only photo I have with Jean Marsh

Zoe Caldwell

With Alec Guinness in *Exit the King*

Viola in *Twelfth Night* at the Old Vic

Lady Anne in *Richard III* with Paul Daneman at the Old Vic

Left to right: Me, Laurence Olivier, Mona Washbourne and Patsy Rowlands, with James Bolam on the floor, in rehearsal for *Semi-Detached*

As the girl in *The Square* by
Marguerite Duras

Not quite with Judi Dench, as we descend different staircases in *Hilda Lessways*

In *Fable* by John Hopkins

Peter Hall (second from left) and me with our *Evening Standard* awards

In my dressing room about to play Childie in *The Killing of Sister George*

Arriving in New York with Beryl Reid

Lila suddenly appeared next to me and put a crown of twigs and flowers on my head and wound a long streamer of flowers round me. I thought she was going to come on with me.

I enjoyed playing in *Cymbeline* and came to really appreciate Dame Peggy's enormous talent. She was quite wonderful as Imogen, and her age became immaterial. She was also a very sweet-natured woman. Years later when I was playing Rosalind in a disastrous modern production of *As You Like It* at Stratford, she came to my dressing room and said sympathetically, 'My dear, you can't be expected to play Rosalind without a tree and a hat.'

Our final play of the season was *The Tempest*, where we would be on stage with the great Shakespearean actor Sir John Gielgud. It would be directed by the then wunderkind, Peter Brook. We were all excited. I was *very* excited as I was given the task of understudying Ceres, a goddess in the masque scene, and the actress playing the part was Stephanie Bidmead, the original Audrey who had been in hospital – so with any luck (for me, that is, not Stephanie) I might get to play it. Julian was a sailor in the shipwreck scene and then every walk-on was in the masque.

The Tempest is a wonderful play, but the masque is one of the most difficult things to stage as, just as the audience have got used to the monster Caliban and the spirit Ariel, Prospero conjures up three goddesses, several reapers and some nymphs, and there is a lot of talk about vegetation and it's all some kind of pagan marriage ceremony. At the first rehearsal Peter Brook told us that no scenery would fly in to make it a beautiful mirage. No. *We* were to be the scenery – the '*bosky acres*', as Ceres says. So could we start by improvising what vegetation we might be. Most of the actors began waving their arms about as if they were trees, and Liz Evans tried to be a climbing plant on John Grayson, and all I could think of was *not* to be a tree or a climbing plant and do some different movement. So I got down on my knees and started doing somersaults round the rehearsal room. When Peter stopped us he said to me immediately, 'So what are you?' I'd been vaguely thinking about harvest festivals and said the first word that came into my head: 'A cabbage.' Peter thought about this and then asked a very nervous actor called Norman Henry what he was. At a complete loss, he said, 'I'm a cabbage too.' Nobody giggled because this was Peter Brook. 'Think about it,' he said, 'and come back tomorrow with some more ideas.'

The next day he had decided that four of the men (not Julian, who was to be a tree) would be reapers with scythes and the four women would be stooks of corn, not nymphs, and we would dance together and the men would reap us. That's going to be an interesting costume, I thought – a stook of corn. It was a *hilarious* costume. The men were in brown onesies with a hood and straw hats, and we poor girls were in mustard-coloured onesies (Babygros, I think we called them then) with bits of straw stuck here and there, and hoods with only our eyes, nose and mouth showing which had to be covered with yellow greasepaint. And four more different shapes you couldn't imagine. I was the tallest with very little bosom, Liz was Junoesque (think Kardashian), Pam was hefty and squarish and Mavis only came up to our armpits. We looked distinctly comical, but no one laughed – it was a Peter Brook production. There was a great deal of stamping in the dance and the men had to flourish their scythes a lot, and one night Barry Warren's scythe came loose from its handle and flew out into the auditorium and nearly decapitated someone.

The critics were divided about the production, but not about Sir John Gielgud's performance, so thanks to him at the end of the season at Stratford we did it for several weeks at the Drury Lane Theatre in London.

Before leaving Stratford, Julian and I were both offered one small part and a good understudy each in the next year's season. Julian was to understudy Tybalt in *Romeo and Juliet* and I was to understudy Viola in *Twelfth Night*, which was particularly promising as so far Dorothy Tutin, who was playing the role, was known to have been 'off' in nearly every part she had played. Julian was to play Conrade, one of Don John's accomplices in *Much Ado About Nothing* and I was to play the Goddess Diana in *Pericles*, who has one ten-line speech. We went back to London very pleased with ourselves.

We were staying with Anne Lewis, who had a big flat in Hampstead. She had become Mrs Harvey since the Perranporth season as she had married Alan Harvey, who had been in *Who Goes There!* with us. They had a baby and they had generously offered us a room in return for the odd bit of babysitting.

It should have been exciting, but it was strange playing at Drury Lane. It seemed far too big for a play and only meant for musicals. There were problems with sound. There was no trouble hearing Sir John; it was the young actors who couldn't be heard, and it's even worse today. I know that the acting style has changed, but I'm both sad and ashamed that actors are miked now, even in our smallest theatres. When did drama schools stop teaching students how to throw their voice to the back of the stalls *and* be natural at the same time? It is possible.

After a matinee one day, I came down from our dressing room several minutes after everyone else for some reason, and Julian had already gone out to eat. At the bottom of the stairs outside Sir John Gielgud's dressing room was a small open space which I think must have been for dancers to limber up in before making their entrance, and Mr Gene Kelly was leaning back against a practice barre. I had seen British stars outside Sir John's room, but not Hollywood stars. I just stood gaping at him. He smiled. I said, 'Are you here to see Sir John?' 'Yes,' he said. I was outraged that he should be kept waiting. It was quite a time since the curtain had come down. 'I don't think he can know it's you,' I said. 'I'll tell them.' I meant the ass of a dresser who was keeping this great star waiting, and went to knock on the door. 'No, it's fine. They know I'm here,' he said, and then with immense charm: 'You'll have to tell me what you played.' 'I play a stook of corn,' I said, and we both laughed. Then I told him how much I loved his films and in no time at all (always having been such a blabbermouth), I had told him how I had disappointed my mother by not becoming a tap dancer. 'I bet you can still do it,' he said. 'Come on, do a time step with me.' We had done about three time steps when Sir John threw open his door crying, 'Gene, darling, this is disgraceful. They have only just told me that you are here.' And he shook my hand and went into the dressing room. I couldn't wait to tell everyone I had danced with Gene Kelly.

I phoned my mother.

'He must have thought you looked a right sight in that mustard outfit.'

'I wasn't still in my costume.'

'Thank the Lord for that.'

Before returning to Stratford, Julian and I were going on a skiing holiday with John Davidson and Pam Taylor. We had been saving up for it, and the 'all in' cheque for the holiday for both of us was a hundred pounds, and we nearly fainted with excitement that we could write such an amount.

I thought skiing was a fantastic sport and loved my time on the slopes, but when we came home and I saw the rows of people with broken bones laid out on stretchers at most of the railway stations, I vowed *never* to do it again. What actress can afford to have broken bones?

It was lovely to be back at Stratford. This time we were living in the top half of a very pretty seventeenth-century cottage in Sheep Street above a florist. We even had a garden, and it was a three-minute walk to the theatre. There were several new members of the company, and one young man we became very friendly with was called Ian Holm, and in my dressing room there was an extraordinary young woman from Australia just a year or so older than me called Zoe Caldwell who went on to become a big Broadway star. She was in no way beautiful – she even had an eye that strayed when she was tired – but she had such a totally arresting personality, was so sexy, vital, funny and original that I loved her immediately and she became a very close friend for life.

The first production was *Romeo and Juliet*, in which we all appeared as citizens, Julian had the tiny part of Sampson at the beginning of the play and I was a guest at the ball where Romeo first meets Juliet. The choreographer picked me to dance with our Romeo, who was Richard Johnson, who had been with us the season before. He was good-looking and good fun and rehearsals were very jolly. I had a beautiful medieval dress with one of those wonderful cone-shaped hats, which suited me because I had a high forehead with a widow's peak. It was all going well, and Romeo and Juliet were keeping up theatrical tradition and were obviously falling in love off stage as well as on, and we were just coming up to the opening night when Julian, as understudy, had to go on for Ron Haddrick as Tybalt. Not only was he very good but he had been so diligent that every lunge, parry and riposte of the extremely complicated fight was correct, which was no mean accomplishment.

For *Twelfth Night* we had Peter Hall back again to direct us. I had to go to rehearsals although I wasn't actually in it because I was understudying Dorothy Tutin. There was quite a lot of unease in the company as Peter was directing it in a very different way to the usual take on it. It was a very much younger group of leading players. Olivia had always been played by a stately, almost middle-aged actress and we had the deliciously skittish Geraldine McEwan who looked about sixteen. Also, everyone was bemused by the fact that Lila De Nobili had dressed all of Olivia's retinue in yellow, when it was made clear in the play that the Lady Olivia *hated* yellow. There were mutterings in the company that we were in for a disaster with this production.

Obviously as an understudy you try to keep out of the way as much as you can, but when Peter was giving notes one day, I was sitting as usual on the edge of the group when Dorothy Tutin left the room for some reason and, coming back, sat next to me. Peter drifted over to give her a note and was persuasively suggesting a new move which I had my pencil poised to write down in my script when Peter suddenly broke off and stared at me for a moment, then blurted, 'You're that girl, aren't you?' There was nothing for me to do but nod. Was he going to dismiss me immediately? He didn't, but weirdly and uncomfortably I was told the next day by stage management that Miss Dorothy Tutin found my gaze distracting and wanted me removed from rehearsals. I of course thought that it was Peter who wanted me removed, but a couple of weeks later when I had a call from Wardrobe to come in and try on Dorothy's costume, an obligatory fitting so that they knew what alterations would be necessary if an understudy had to go on, I was told that Dorothy Tutin had refused to give her permission. Wardrobe were very taken aback and very vexed as I was about five inches taller than her, and they were embarrassed because this had never happened before. The wardrobe mistress kept saying, ' . . . and you're one of the cleanest girls in the company.' Finally we went to the dressing room, took the costume and we did the fitting on the understanding that I said nothing about it. So for some reason Dottie, as everyone called her, had taken against me.

I felt very uncomfortable and unhappy at being banned from rehearsals. I couldn't follow the thinking and logic that developed and underpinned Dorothy's performance. All I could do was sit in the audience when the play finally opened as often as possible and practise copying at home. It was very unsatisfactory. An understudy's job is not to do anything so different from the principal that the company would be thrown if you went on, but it's not good to just parrot their performance. I also had my own problem with Dorothy Tutin as an actress, as although she was very much admired when she was young, I found her too fey.

In spite of all the qualms of the company, Peter Hall's autumnal Caroline production of *Twelfth Night* was a huge success and, simply by being so young, Geraldine McEwan changed the playing of Olivia for ever. Although the critics were divided over her witty, adorable performance, they all loved Dottie who for once in her career was never off. I could see that Lila De Nobili had made it *look ravishing*, but I

couldn't at the time appreciate what a game changer the production was. I think it was the production that secured Peter's
takeover of the company, which under him became the Royal
Shakespeare Company. Knowing that he was never likely to
cast me in anything now that he had remembered I was that
bad-tempered girl, I didn't *want* to believe how wonderful the
production was. I didn't *want* to realise what a great director
he was because it made it worse that I'd been silly enough to
be rude to him.

Years later, in my thirties, when I had become quite well
known in the profession, he asked me to come and audition for
Ophelia. Glenda Jackson had said yes, and then I think got a
movie and Peter thought he was going to lose her. I arrived to
read for him at the Aldwych on a very cold morning. I had not
seen him since Stratford. I had been told I would be reading
with David Warner, who was playing Hamlet, but he wasn't
there. There were just two or three people to do with stage
management. Peter was two hours late. None of us were to
know then that he had just had the final huge row with Leslie
Caron that ended their marriage. For the two or three people
waiting with me it was just a boring hold-up. For me, in a
terrible state of nerves because I at last had a chance to make
Peter see that I could act, it was a tense and very stressful wait.
When he finally arrived, looking absolutely dreadful, he just
asked me curtly to do Ophelia's speech which begins: '*O what
a noble mind is here o'erthrown*'. I did it – not well. There was a
pause and I heard Peter say wearily, 'That really wasn't very
good,' and I went potty again and shouted at him, 'Of course it
wasn't good. I've been waiting here terrified for two hours in
a freezing theatre expecting to do the whole scene with David
Warner and then you say, "Just do the speech at the end of the

scene", and with no preparation I'm supposed to just DO it.'
He got up from his seat in the stalls and walked to the edge
of the stage. 'I don't know what it is about you and I,' he said,
'but we seem to spark the wrong thing in each other. I'm sorry
I was late. I should have said that before. Shall we take a deep
breath, and in your own time, try it again.'

So I did and at the end he said, 'That was much better. You
could be really good. If Glenda doesn't do it, the part is yours.'
Glenda did do it, and it was a wonderful production.

He finally employed me in his last season at the National
Theatre. I was in my mid-fifties and played Paulina in *The
Winter's Tale* and the Queen in *Cymbeline*. Working with him
was sheer delight: he cared so much for the text that he didn't
lift his eyes from the script for three weeks. Many actors disliked this, but I loved it, as my holy grail as an actress has always
been to search the text to serve the author. To be a conduit that
brings the writer's imagination to an audience. Peter gave me a
private lesson to explain his method of speaking Shakespeare;
that the sense of the line is written into the rhythm of the pen-
tameter. This was revelatory, and I wish I had been told about
it in 1957. I found him to be a shy man, even more eaten up
and passionate than I was about work; and that I had stupidly
severed myself from such an exceptionally brilliant talent who
did so much for our theatre I deeply regret to this day.

13

Hamlet, directed by Glen Byam Shaw, with the fifty-year-old Michael Redgrave playing the Dane, was our third play that year. All we young members of the company thought he was far too old, but we knew we were lucky to be on stage with him as he was a big star and a truly great actor.

Julian was playing Second Gravedigger and I was just playing a lady-in-waiting. About a week into rehearsals, which so far had been spent plotting the moves, we came to the scene where a gentleman comes to tell Gertrude that apparently Ophelia has lost her mind. Googie Withers, who was playing Gertrude, got up to work on the scene and Glen was suggesting where she might enter the stage from when he said, 'Who's playing the gentleman?' Most of us who were playing courtiers sat through all the rehearsals in case Glen decided that he wanted one or two extra people in a scene, and we all looked around to see who it was. No one moved, and Glen suddenly said, 'Eileen, you come and do it. There's no reason why it shouldn't be a gentlewoman.' I was thrilled.

The gentleman enters with the Queen, who says:

GERTRUDE: I will not speak with her.

THE GENTLEMAN: She is importunate, indeed distract.

   Her mood will needs be pitied.

GERTRUDE: What would she have?

And then the gentleman has a really good ten-line description of poor Ophelia's madness. That Glen had given it to me meant that he really trusted me.

We had reached the day of the public dress rehearsals, one in the morning and one in the afternoon. That day I didn't feel well, but 'not feeling well' is not an excuse for an actor not to go to work.

When it came to the last scene of the play when Gertrude, in the middle of the duel between Hamlet and Laertes, takes the poisoned chalice, drinks and sinks dying to the floor, I as her gentlewoman fainted, fell with a smack on top of her and had to be revived for the curtain call.

'Are you all right?' everyone asked. 'Yes, yes, I'm fine,' I said. 'I'm so sorry, Googie.'

'It probably looked rather good,' she said cheerfully, 'to have my lady-in-waiting faint with shock at my death.'

At the evening's performance I was feeling horribly ill, and as we reached the same point of Gertrude's death and Googie once again sank to the floor, I said to myself, Whatever you do, don't faint, and repeated it like a mantra. Don't faint – don't faint, don't faint. And then suddenly threw up all over Googie. She was amazingly forgiving about this, even though it went all over her jewel-encrusted bodice – because she thought I was pregnant. I wasn't pregnant. I was simply the first person in the company to get Asian Flu. After that, many actors dropped like flies. Julian passed out very dramatically carrying Hamlet up a flight of stairs at the end of the play, and the three actors left nearly dropped the six-foot-five Michael Redgrave.

The production was well received, and we were soon in rehearsals for *Pericles*. The youngest members of the company had looked forward to this tremendously as it was to be directed by Tony Richardson, who was George Devine's assistant at the avant-garde company now at the Royal Court Theatre.

Tony was a breath of very fresh air at Stratford. He seemed to take no notice of billing or stars at all. He made us into one big cohesive egalitarian company, and his ideas for this strange, difficult play thrilled and exhilarated us. One of his ideas caused quite a stir in our dressing room.

It so happens that I have three times in my life pre-dreamed things. I had dreamed that while we were playing *Hamlet*, Glen Byam Shaw had come to our dressing room and suggested that as ladies-in-waiting to Gertrude we should all be in Elizabethan dresses but that the bodices would be cut very low and totally expose our breasts. 'How do you feel about that?' Glen had asked. I had told Zoe, Pam and Mavis of this dream (Liz had left us to have a baby) the next day and they had all laughed at the mere idea of Glen asking us to do such a thing. Then exactly one month later there was Tony at our dressing room door, in his white jeans and trainers (the first we had ever seen) saying to us with his attractive, lisping drawl, 'Now listen, girls, I'd like you all to expose your breasts for the brothel scene. How do you feel about that?'

The main feeling in the dressing room was shock that I had pre-dreamed this request. I had just got the wrong director and the wrong play. So we all looked agape. 'Oh, come on,' he said, 'don't look so shocked.'

'We're a bit stunned because Eileen dreamed about this,' said Zoe, 'but I'm up for it, Tony, if that's what you want.'

'Me too,' I said, though I was none too sure that I really would be brave enough to do it.

Pam and Mavis said, 'No, we absolutely couldn't.'

When we came to the dress parade it was decided by a tight-lipped wardrobe mistress that they would make one costume which would totally expose the breasts and they would put a hold on mine until Zoe's had been passed by everyone concerned. There was of course a lot of interest in the company that Zoe was going to be half-naked, and there were many extra people at the dress parade. Zoe was totally blithe about the whole affair, and couldn't understand what the fuss was about as she sallied across the room in her harlot costume happily swinging her tits. She was a very sexually free soul, and when telling me about her affairs in Australia made me feel naive and unadventurous. I thought she looked wonderfully decadent and correct for the part.

Apparently the board of directors heard about this costume (we thought that the prudes in Wardrobe had leaked it) and were very shocked and sent an edict saying that on no account were any of the actresses to be bare-breasted. Zoe was furious; I was relieved. The next day Tony told the two of us that to get round the problem with the board he was having real-looking rubber breasts made for us which we would wear as massive bras. They would look completely natural from the audience, but it would satisfy the board that none of the actresses were actually naked.

Those rubber bosoms worked wonderfully, and Zoe and I would wander out onto the balcony that led off the green room on matinee days and relax with a cup of tea and watch the people in the rowing boats catch sight of us and sit with open mouths, believing that they were looking at two topless actresses.

I was also playing the Goddess Diana, who had one somewhat boring speech. After the last dress rehearsal Tony took me aside and said, 'Can you sing, Eileen? I think that speech might be more interesting as a song.' (There were many songs in the production, led by the wonderful voice of Edric Connor.)

'Oh, I'm sorry, Tony, but I just can't sing at all.' He looked disappointed. 'I could always wear a totally diaphanous robe. That would liven it up.' He laughed and hugged me. 'I shouldn't have worried you about it. The speech is fine, really – just fine.' I can't imagine any other director at the Memorial Theatre hugging a walk-on to cheer them up, and am truly sorry that today no such harmless non-sexual gesture would be allowed.

While we were playing the last play of the season, a delightful production of *Much Ado About Nothing*, we heard some wonderful news. We were going to take *Romeo and Juliet*, *Twelfth Night* and *Hamlet* to Russia! But before this adventure, we all wanted to know whether we were going to be asked back for another season, which would be Glen Byam Shaw's last. We already knew that Laurence Olivier was going to play Coriolanus, and Charles Laughton was to play Lear, and Peter Hall was going to direct *A Midsummer Night's Dream*. Who *didn't* want to be asked back?

One by one the actors were called in to see Glen and learn their fate. This of course was done in order of billing. Finally it was Julian's turn, and he came home thrilled, with a really good clutch of supporting parts.

Then Glen asked to see me. The minute I went into his office

I knew something was wrong. He was pacing up and down and seemed to be quite angry.

'I want you to know,' he started immediately, 'that if there was anything I could do about this I would do it. But I can't. It's all tied up. There is nothing I can offer you for next season because everything is cast, and you really *mustn't* come back as a walk-on and understudy again because you're much, much better than that.' He slumped into a chair. I was trying very hard not to cry. I knew I had done well that season. When we did the understudy performance of *Twelfth Night* and I had played Viola, the company had been wonderfully complimentary, and why had he picked me out for the speech in *Hamlet* if I was no good?

'The thing is,' Glen continued irritably, 'that every part that you could have played next year I had already promised to other actresses before *this* season even started. I promised Michael' (he meant Redgrave) 'that I would give Vanessa Helena in *A Midsummer Night's Dream* and some other smaller parts, and Zoe Caldwell is here on a special two-year contract because Tyrone Guthrie wants her for Helena in *All's Well* and she has had to be found parts. So as you can see, it was all tied up a year ago and there is nothing left worth playing. It's a damn shame because you don't deserve this . . . ' he petered out.

I started to say that I didn't mind understudying but he stopped me. 'It would be wrong for you to waste another year not playing parts. So I've had a talk with the director of Birmingham Repertory Theatre and asked him to take you into his company. That's the best I can do. I'm so sorry, my dear.'

I said, 'Thank you, Mr Shaw. Thank you very much,' and went home. Julian is always a positive person. 'Birmingham Rep,' he said, 'that would be wonderful for you.'

We both clung to this possible offer. Surely with Glen Byam Shaw's recommendation they would welcome me with open arms. They didn't. I had a very nice letter from the director telling me that sadly, highly praised as I was by Mr Byam Shaw, he could find no room for me in his company.

I had some fleeting anger at Zoe, whom I was now so close to, that she hadn't told me about these parts sitting in her contract. She said she had tried to tell me a couple of times that she had a very specific arrangement with the company because of her link with Tyrone Guthrie, but was embarrassed.

It was a slight cloud over the last few weeks of the season, but the excitement of going to Russia soon overtook us.

In 1958 Britain's relations with Russia were not good. It was the middle of the Cold War, and to set up this trip at all was an artistic triumph. We were given a list of things we could not do. One of the most firm requests was that no one should have a liaison of any kind with anyone they met. If you sleep with a Russian, we were told, it will cause tremendous trouble and you would certainly put that person in a dangerous position. We were not to get involved, just stick to what would be arranged for us socially and not wander off and do our own thing. It was also very possible that our hotel bedrooms would be bugged.

They had either bought or borrowed (the latter, I would imagine) a pile of padded Royal Air Force coats that they issued to anyone who wanted them. Julian took one – it didn't look bad on him, but I looked like a badly lagged piece of piping in mine. I think that they expected the women to turn up in furs. I was very anti-fur, so even if I'd had the money I wouldn't have worn one. My one winter coat would have to do.

Leningrad (now known as St Petersburg) was *freezing*. The

Neva River was chopped frozen waves and Coral Browne, who had taken over from Googie, told us she had put 'spit black' on (mascara that you spat into and put wet on your eyelashes) in the foyer of the theatre and then walked out into the street with them still wet and they had frozen and broken off. We had all loved Googie, but Coral was something else, and she had such an adventure in Moscow that an enchanting film of it was made called *An Englishman Abroad* with Alan Bates playing Guy Burgess.

Burgess, the British diplomat and Soviet agent, had come backstage in the interval of *Hamlet* at our first performance to see Michael Redgrave, who refused to see him. The whole company heard that he was outside the dressing room and we rushed downstairs to catch a glimpse of this flamboyant traitor. He was very drunk and when refused, barged into Coral's dressing room and was sick in her sink. Unknown to anyone in the company Coral struck up a bond with him. How Coral kept the whole thing a secret I shall never know. She finally told what happened to Alan Bennett, who wrote the film script, and John Schlesinger made the movie.

The first night we arrived in Leningrad we were taken to the circus, and when the tickets were handed out there was one odd ticket sitting separately from everyone else's, and I offered to take it and found myself sitting next to a friendly American student who was studying there. He was very excited to be talking to one of the British actors.

He insisted that we really must ignore company rules and meet some Russian people. He would arrange it, but it must be kept absolutely secret and we must stick to instructions. He said he would arrange a dinner, and he suggested that I bring four or five other members of the company. He himself would give me instructions as I left the theatre the next night. He repeated that we mustn't tell anyone.

Of course Julian was one of the group, and I know Ian Holm came, and there were three other actors. We were to leave the hotel and walk two blocks to the left where a taxi would be waiting for us. This taxi would take us to a street where we would then all get into a car. This car would drive us to huge gates that enclosed several blocks of flats. All this we did, giggling nervously at all the secrecy. A man met us at the gates who, with his finger to his lips to ensure our total silence, opened up and led the way as we crept through the snow to an apartment where the door was opened and we all slithered inside. Our hosts were a couple of Russian professors and they had invited several friends of theirs and some students.

The wine flowed and the food was not only generous, it was delicious (in the hotel it was truly disgusting), and within ten minutes it was a riotous party. A lot of vodka went down, balalaikas were played, guitars were strummed and we sang and we danced.

At about 2 or 3 a.m., we decided that we should think about going. 'We'll walk with you,' several of our new friends said. It turned out that actually we were only about a twenty-minute walk from the hotel. The taxi and car had been to put the KGB off the scent.

With all secrecy now forgotten, or so it seemed, our drunken group, with quite a few of our new friends, singing and roaring in both languages, staggered back to the hotel where everyone embraced several times and made even more noise saying goodbye.

I never understood whether they really had to be secretive if they met with Westerners and they were so drunk that they forgot, or that Russians simply love secrecy for its own sake. At least, there were no repercussions that we knew of.

The food in the hotel was so unappetising that I just couldn't keep much down, and when I fainted one morning Julian insisted that they find me a doctor. I was sent with an interpreter to a gloomy surgery.

No sooner had the doctor clapped eyes on me than he wanted me taken to hospital. 'Why?' I asked the interpreter. 'It's your thyroid,' he said, 'you must have test.' Because I had very large, slightly protuberant eyes, this had been guessed at by a couple of medical men in England, who had been proved totally wrong. I had had the tests and my thyroid was perfectly balanced. I protested straight away, 'No, no, I know it's not my thyroid,' but no one would listen to me and I was carted off to a really frightening building looking more like a prison than a hospital, where they insisted on giving me a rather horrid test, of a kind that I had never been through in England. I was strapped to what looked like an execution chair with tubes trailing from it, and they injected me with something and apparently watched its course on a screen in another room. It took quite a while. Then they seemed to get very annoyed. 'What is it? What are they saying?' I asked. 'They are very cross that you have wasted their time because there is nothing wrong with your thyroid.' I knew it was the food that was making me sick, but that was clearly not an acceptable answer. There could be nothing wrong with Soviet food. And when our dressers at the theatre talked to us one day about what it had been like to live through the Siege of Leningrad for over three years, in which thousands had starved to death, and they told us that among many other horrors they had had to kill and eat their own pet dogs, I felt very ashamed that I had complained about the food at all and didn't say another word. But I did lose 16lbs (over a stone) while there.

Leningrad was very beautiful, with the huge Palace Square and the Summer Palace and the Hermitage, where we begged them to show us the Impressionists. We knew they had them there, and finally with tight lips they took us down to a basement where Monets, Cézannes, Sisleys and Pissaros were casually stacked. It was a ravishing city, but in 1958 there was a great feeling of depression, with drunks on every corner, which wasn't surprising knowing what they had been through, but it made the beauty of the city seem desolate and we were all glad to get to Moscow.

I didn't think Moscow was in the least beautiful. There was Red Square with its coloured domes, and that was it! Even their huge shopping emporium, GUM, had nothing in it that you wanted to buy. But we found the atmosphere much more buoyant, and people seemed less secretive and appeared to enjoy life a great deal more than in Leningrad. They *seemed* more open, but we were warned again that our rooms would be bugged.

We were in Moscow for Christmas Eve, and Julian being sentimental had brought with him his recording of carols from King's College Cambridge. He had always listened to it on the afternoon of Christmas Eve at home, and he had borrowed a gramophone from somewhere and to my horror he had put an invitation on the company noticeboard saying that he would be playing it on the afternoon of 24 December and that everyone was welcome to come and listen.

I was very embarrassed. I felt that a mere walk-on shouldn't have such cheek. Also we had a very small double room in the hotel. There simply wasn't room. We were already crammed when he put the record on and we heard the clear, sweet treble of the young chorister start 'Once in Royal David's City'. Soon we overflowed into the corridor as every single member of the company turned up to listen. At the end of the service I found two long arms wrapped round me from behind and I was lifted off my feet. It was Michael Redgrave with tears streaming down his face saying, 'Thank you, thank you.'

It was hard to tell whether our productions in either city were as successful as they seemed from their rapturous receptions. We were aware that our audiences were just thrilled that we were there. I certainly had a feeling that they thought their twenty-seven-year-old charismatic Hamlet was better than ours, but we were certainly a diplomatic success.

On one of the last evenings there was a big dinner for our company and the Russian acting elite in a huge, ornately moulded room. After formal speeches and a great many toasts had occurred, the Russians started to perform. They really do perform at the drop of a fur hat. There were some brilliant soloists, and then they all sang songs of the Motherland and did dances of the Motherland, and finally they were urging us to perform songs and dances from our country.

There were jolly end-of-season shows at Stratford where people got up and made fools of themselves to entertain the rest of the company. At the end of the last one Zoe and I had discovered that we could both tap-dance, and had dressed up in funny chorus girl outfits with frilly short skirts and big red bows tied round our heads and on our tap shoes (I have no idea how we found tap shoes, but we did), and we tapped along to *42nd Street*. It had been a big success.

Suddenly now in this big formal hall, with both me and Zoe in evening dress, the company answered this request for a national dance not by singing 'Jerusalem' and doing some

Morris dancing but by yelling drunkenly and insistently, 'Zoe and Eileen . . . Zoe and Eileen.' They started to clap and stamp and finally we both tucked up our evening dresses, clambered onto a couple of tables they had cleared . . . and did our absurd tap dance. What it must have looked like to the Russians I cannot imagine, but our company were helpless with laughter. The evening ended with a Russian military choir singing in English 'It's A Long Way To Tipperary', which left most of us in tears.

I was very glad to leave Russia. Interesting as the experience had been it was not comfortable living in such a repressive country. And indeed one of our boys did flout the rules and had a fling with an interpreter – and she was 'disappeared'. He was terribly upset and tried to find out where she had gone but was told by the company that he must leave it alone. He had been warned, they said. I went to Russia again in 1988 with the National Theatre when Gorbachev was in power. This time we went to Moscow and Tbilisi in Georgia. Things were much more relaxed but I still felt uncomfortable there, and again was glad as the plane finally lifted us away from Russian soil.

Back in England Julian went straight into rehearsals for the opening production of the 1959 season, which was *Othello*. It so happened that Paul Robeson was unable to join the company for the first two weeks, and as Julian was his understudy he had the great pleasure of rehearsing the title role. When Robeson finally arrived Julian told me how charming he was and how friendly Sam Wanamaker (playing Iago) was, and I was beginning to feel terribly out of things when in the middle of March I had some wonderful news.

Patrick Wymark, who had been quite angry on my behalf that there were no parts for me in the 1959 season, had got in touch with a TV director and pushed him to cast me in a six-part dramatisation he was doing of Arnold Bennett's Clayhanger series called *Hilda Lessways*. Hilda was to be played by Judi Dench, who we had all heard about as she had just had great success playing Ophelia at the Old Vic in London. I was to play Maggie Clayhanger, which was a really good supporting part, and I'm pretty sure that Judi ended up by becoming my sister-in-law – this was remarked on when fifty years later we played sisters in *Cranford*. I couldn't wait to start work in this strange new medium that I knew nothing about, and I don't remember at this point ever having *seen* anything on TV.

Apart from an actress called Violet Carson (who of course became famous in *Coronation Street*), the main parts in the cast were all played by quite young people – even the director, Peter Dews, was only just in his thirties. He was a bluff north-countryman with a wicked sense of humour who I liked very much. He created a wonderful atmosphere, which isn't difficult when you have Judi Dench leading the cast. Even at twenty-four, which we both were then, I could see that Judi was exceptionally talented. She had a great natural gift and she had a sharp, quick brain, but what she was loved for by her fellow actors was the humour that bubbled inside her and burst out at any absurdity.

The only person who didn't always see the joke was Violet Carson, but she tolerated us. It was a very happy little group. The script was good, the work was good and we young ones were able to enjoy the terror of performing live at nine thirty every Friday evening. It *was truly terrifying* to know that if anything went wrong it would be seen by several million people. Often furniture that wouldn't be seen by the camera would have to be moved about while you were doing a scene and didn't always end up where it was supposed to be, and no *way* could you corpse or be seen to laugh by a large percentage of the British Isles. The relief at the end of the live episode each week was highly enjoyable near hysteria.

One Sunday afternoon while we were doing *Hilda Lessways* I was in our cottage in Sheep Street on my own, as Julian was playing cricket – I had long ago given up pretending to like the game and be a good wife and make sandwiches when they played – when Judi turned up on my doorstep. She was in Stratford for some poetry reading, and had a couple of hours free before having to be there in the evening. I said it was a pity she couldn't stay as Julian and I were giving a party that evening. She was immensely impressed. 'A party,' she said, almost in awe. 'I would be terrified, Eileen. I wouldn't know what to do.' 'Oh, it's quite easy, Judi,' I said loftily. 'You just get a few bottles of wine in and ask everyone to bring a bottle, then go to Pargeters and get about two dozen cheese puffs.' I felt very sophisticated.

When the TV ended, June went by, and July, and there was no work in view and I became restless, knowing most of the company but not being part of them.

One day I had gone into the green room to be with Julian between the shows and Vanessa Redgrave was there. She was quite friendly with Julian, and I had played tennis a couple of times with her and her sister Lynn. They were both about six feet tall and made me at five foot seven feel small and fragile, which made a nice change. Vanessa said that she had a week off and wanted to go on holiday but had no one to go with. 'Go with Eileen,' Julian said. 'She's not doing anything.' I was really cross with him. 'I don't know her,' I said when she had gone. 'Well, you soon will. She's good fun, and it will do you good to get away from Stratford.' I had probably been whining a bit.

So I went with Vanessa to the Gower Peninsula in Wales, which was the nearest bit of sea to Stratford-upon-Avon. It was August Bank Holiday but neither of us thought to book anywhere. We took the train to Swansea and then a bus to Mumbles, which was the terminus. The bus conductor asked us, as we were the only people now on the bus, where we were staying. 'We're going to look for somewhere,' we said. 'You won't find anything vacant now,' he retorted. 'You two girls had better come back with me. We've got a spare room.'

'Oh, what a dear little house,' Vanessa said as we arrived. It was a council house. My idea of a holiday is not staying in a council house. Our room had a small double bed.

'I'm not keen on this,' I said.

'Oh, we'll be fine,' Vanessa said gaily.

The bus conductor's wife said she didn't do food.

'Why don't we try and live off the land?' Vanessa said excitedly. 'I've always wanted to try that. It will be fun.'

No, no, it won't be fun, I thought. Delicious food in a hotel would be fun. I shoved a bolster down the middle of the bed and inwardly groaned. None of this was my idea of a holiday.

We ate mostly apples that we'd shaken from people's trees and mushrooms that we'd gathered, from which I expected to die with every mouthful, but Vanessa knew her chestnut from her fairy ring and I survived. The weather was good and we just swam and walked and in the end I did enjoy it, because Vanessa has a nature that I envy that is ready to enjoy everything.

As we talked she made me realise how unsophisticated and working class I still was. I didn't know about anything much, I thought. I didn't even know there was such a thing as Tampax! It was she who told me about this clever innovation.

On the last day she bought some movie magazines. I thought, why is she buying that trash? I lay on the bed reading my book and she sat at the horrid little dressing table flicking through the pages.

'Why aren't we movie stars?' she asked suddenly. I was startled. Why would she want to be such a thing? They weren't real actors. They were just beautiful people.

'Well, because we don't *look* like movie stars,' I said finally.

'I don't see why we shouldn't. I'm going to make myself look like one.' And she fished for her make-up bag. Good luck with that, I thought.

She then tore out pictures of Sophia Loren, Jeanne Moreau and Brigitte Bardot and stuck them on the wall and went to work. I went back to my book. After about half an hour or so she said, 'Eileen, look at me.' She looked quite different. I was taken aback. 'My God, Vanessa, I think you *could* be a movie star.'

She then listed all the things that she was going to work on – starting with losing weight, growing her hair and becoming a blonde. There was no talk of surgery – there was no need – but she did tell me that she knew models who had had their lowest ribs removed so that they could have the really tiny waists necessary for the New Look when it had come in.

A year later I was walking in Shaftesbury Avenue when a woman stopped me. 'It's me, Vanessa.' I hadn't recognised her. She looked utterly beautiful.

We have met many times over the years, and worked together twice: on my own play *Vita and Virginia* in New York, and again in *John Gabriel Borkman* at the National Theatre with

Paul Scofield. I've grown very fond of her. She is an extraordinary actress and a unique human being.

Some time that September I had a panic call from Toby Robertson. He had been an actor in our first season and was now directing *The Winter's Tale* and *Peer Gynt* for an Arts Council tour. Being as ready to use a star name as anyone else, he had cast the youngest Redgrave, Lynn, who was only sixteen and hadn't even been to drama school, to play Perdita. Equity had heard about this, and I think a little out of spite at the star system had made a huge hullabaloo and said that he couldn't use her as she didn't have an Equity card or done any training. Of course, this wouldn't happen today – he could cast a girl he met in the street. He was already into rehearsal. Would I come to London immediately and take over? In a couple of hours I was packed and on my way.

14

I had got to know Toby Robertson a little during our first season at Stratford because I had been bold enough to ask him to lend me some money. I had badly needed a winter coat for our skiing trip to Austria. The hundred-pound cheque for the holiday had left us with nothing to spare, and I had fallen in love with a pale blue duffel-type coat that had fake fur round the hood. It was twenty pounds, which was expensive, but I wanted it. I looked round the company to see who might be willing to lend me the money. *Who* looked as though they might have private money? Who looked posh? I picked on Toby, who had been playing William when I briefly played Audrey in *As You Like It*. He had that casual, laid-back air of self-assurance, an easy smile and the confidence to wear frayed shirt cuffs – all the marks of an aristocrat. Actually he wasn't rich at all. He was the son of a playwright, but I'd certainly picked the right person as Toby was someone who would give you the shirt off his back.

'What do you want the money for?' he asked.

'A winter coat,' I said.

'Oh, all right.'

I went to his dressing room that evening to show him what his money had been spent on.

'Is that it?' he said. 'I thought at that price it would be something glamorous!'

I heard that sentence said to me by men on and off for the rest of my life. I don't like 'glamorous' clothes, I like clothes that are well cut and quietly different and you have to pay for that.

I had always longed to play what were known as the breeches parts, that is, Viola, Rosalind, Imogen and Portia, who all dress up as boys, but I had never thought that I would be right for Shakespeare's innocent young women like Juliet, Miranda and Perdita. For a start I wasn't obviously 'pretty'; I was tall, and I thought that my upbringing had always made me seem a bit too knowing for those parts.

But here I was playing Perdita, and I quickly understood from Toby's direction that what was needed was absolute simplicity and direct honesty. It sounds easier than it is, but I loved playing it and Toby was very happy with me. I worked for him many times throughout my life and he became one of my dearest friends.

The tour was hard work. An opening week in Cambridge, which I loved, where we tried out both plays. (In *Peer Gynt* I played Ingrid, a Cowgirl and a Slave Girl.) Then a six-week tour of mostly one-night stands all over Wales. I quickly palled up with a couple of actors and luckily one of them had a car. I drove with them to every town we went to and the three of us always lodged in the same digs. It used to make me quietly smile that wherever we stayed I would get a severe lecture from the landlady impressing on me that if either of these men was found anywhere near my bedroom, I would be thrown out. Little did she know that she had two men under her roof who were at it every night.

It was tiring playing a show and packing the next morning and moving on, but we saw some wonderful parts of Wales, and I gained confidence that I *could* play Shakespeare's simple, unworldly young women.

The tour finished as the season at Stratford finished, and Julian and I had to pack up Sheep Street and drive to London with no sign of work for either of us and nowhere to live.

We eventually found a flat for four pounds a week – which was a snip in London. The street was opposite Earl's Court tube station and the flat was on the ground floor. Although we had a lovely front room with a high ceiling and a big bay window, at the back we overlooked all the trains coming in and out of the station; I think there were six or eight tracks, and the noise was awful. But we were immensely relieved to have a place of our own, and painted the walls what we thought was a very chic shade that was called 'White Coffee'. My father on his first visit was horrified. 'What on earth made you paint the walls khaki?'

The worry now was how we were going to pay that four pounds every week and eat. A month or so went by and there was no work whatsoever in view. Any savings we had were disappearing, and we began to get desperate. Finally Julian's sister, Prue, who had a cooking job at the London School of Economics, said that the school needed cleaners and we decided to grit our teeth and do it. It was a horrible job but it paid the rent until Julian finally got a part in two episodes of a schools production for TV of *Androcles and the Lion*.

In those days television didn't pay a great deal more than the theatre. My fee for an hour's television remained twelve guineas until I was twenty-seven and finally got an agent. I doubt that Julian earned more than ten pounds an episode, so it was a bit cavalier of me to throw the cleaning job in when he did, but by then I was making and selling the odd brass rubbing.

I had started doing the rubbings just as a hobby. One of the first ones I did, my favourite, was of Sir Robert De Septvans, which is in Chartham in Kent, and I particularly liked it because he has pushed his chain-mail cap off and has glamorous flowing hair. Julian and I hung it between two scrolls on our wall and friends started saying that they would like one and were willing to pay me. Then Julian had the brilliant idea of putting them onto hardwood by painting the wood white and pressing the rubbing onto it, and as the paint dried the rubbing stuck beautifully. They looked very effective and professional as panels and I really enjoyed doing them. There was something childlike in the pleasure of slowly seeing the picture appear, and I found it a peaceful way of spending an afternoon. Through an actress I was to meet that year called Mary Morris, who herself did designs in iron, I got commissioned to do six big rubbings for a hotel in the Bahamas for which they paid me really well.

So one way and another we managed. There was enough food, and when friends came round we could always rustle up a bottle of wine. After three months more we heard the wonderful news that Peter Dews, who had directed *Hilda Lessways*, had had the magnificently daring idea of doing Shakespeare's history plays on television with a company of about twenty actors, with occasional stars, and that he wanted Julian to be part of the company. He also promised to find something for me in it as well.

He cut and shaped the plays into fifteen one-hour episodes and they would play live every two weeks from April to November. Julian would be in all of them. He was to play Edward IV, which was a wonderful part. I was to be a walk-on in the first episode, and then play lady-in-waiting to Richard II's Queen in the second episode, where I had one line: '*I could weep, madam, would it do you good*'. Peter said he would do his best to find me something better later in the series.

In those first two episodes Richard II was played by an actor called David William. David, a thin, fine-boned academic, really wanted to be a director and although in the right part he could be very good (and Richard II *was* the right part), he was already trying his hand at directing.

As we finished the end of the second episode, he told me that he was doing a production of *A Midsummer Night's Dream* in Ludlow Castle in July and he was going to play Oberon – would I like to play Titania? I was very flattered, as he'd only heard me say one line. John Woodvine played Bottom and we had great fun in Ludlow.

David was a temperamental perfectionist, and at one rehearsal when I dared to disagree with him he threw several cream cakes at me that someone had brought for our coffee break. I just laughed, it was so childish. Then he laughed as well and we were friends ever after.

While I was playing Titania, Peter Dews had found something for me. I was to play Joan of Arc in *Henry VI*, where she is called La Pucelle. That performance caused a bit of a stir. The episode was not live, and I had to have my head put in a clamp and not blink for thirty seconds while the camera put two dancing 'devils' in the pupils of my eyes to show that I was a witch (a cheap trick, but people liked it).

It was the first time that I had really been noticed, and in all the round-ups at the end of *An Age of Kings*, as the series was called, I was picked out as memorable – not always for the right reasons. My performance was called 'weird' or 'original' or 'a very different Joan from what we're used to'. Whenever clips of it are shown in programmes I feel slightly ashamed of my performance (though I was very pleased with myself at the time) as I think that I look more like Joan of the Catwalk than Joan of the Battlefield. I was deeply uncomfortable in my battle-dress – they couldn't afford to have new armour made for me, and I had to struggle into what had been made for Jean Seberg (who was five foot two) in the film of *St Joan*, and the only way I could shrink into that armour was to not wear the padding that all the men wore under their chain mail, and the armour dug into my flesh. But I'd managed to make quite a splash with the part in this prestigious Shakespearean television.

It seemed a bit of a comedown to then do two episodes of a TV series called *Emergency Ward 10* and then a rather sweet little TV comedy, directed by Toby, called *A Diabolical Liberty* where, as the newspapers put it, I gave Richard Briers his first screen kiss. *An Age of Kings* had been an exception. TV work in those days wasn't regarded as the serious art form that it is today, and there was a general feeling that it wasn't a good idea to do too much of it if you wanted to be taken seriously. In fact you were positively warned against being in a 'series' as it was considered harmful to your career, and I think to a certain extent that was true. Of course, it's the absolute reverse today, and young people are eager to 'get known' on TV not just for the money but because it will get them better parts in the theatre as well. The way of thinking in the early 1960s, though, was strong enough to make me glad that I wasn't offered a long-running part in *Emergency Ward 10*, and it was why I absolutely refused some years later to appear in my own creation with Jean Marsh of *Upstairs, Downstairs*. I felt that it would ruin my theatre career. Also the thought of playing the same part for what everybody hoped would be several years filled me with dread. I would get very bored.

Jean and I met briefly at this time because Julian and her partner, Kenneth Haigh, were doing a play called *The Condemned of Altona* at the Royal Court together and I often saw her backstage, but we didn't become friends till some years later when the two of us were single again. We had both had a parent in service, which gave us the idea for *Upstairs, Downstairs*, and then we followed that success with *The House of Eliott* and I had (still have, though she's had a stroke) the greatest friendship of my life with Jean. I've probably laughed more with her than with anyone.

There was one more TV play that year called *Poor Sidney* in which I had one line, and that was it, in spite of the splash I'd made with Joan of Arc.

After several months with no work, I was feeling very low when, chatting on the phone to an actor, he said that his girlfriend had gone that morning to audition for the Bristol Old Vic Company.

'How did she get the audition?' I asked (she wasn't a very good actress).

'Her agent fixed it,' he said.

I was suddenly furious. Why, why, why could I not get an agent?

'Where are they holding the auditions?'

'At the Old Vic,' he said.

I ended the conversation as soon as I could, put some make-up on and took the tube to Waterloo. I'll just turn up, I thought, and see if I can wangle my way into an audition. There was a woman in the foyer of the Old Vic with a list. I said I'd come for the auditions.

'You're not on the list,' she said, 'but I'll ask if they'll see you.'

She soon returned. 'Someone hasn't turned up. You're lucky. They'll see you now.'

There were two men in the stalls who introduced themselves as Nat Brenner and Duncan Ross, and I thanked them for seeing me.

'Do you know the play?' they asked.

'What play?' I asked. 'I thought this was a general audition for the company.'

'No,' they said, 'we're doing a production of *Roots* by Arnold Wesker and we just need to cast the girl. Did you see the play at the Royal Court?'

It was one of the working-class plays known as kitchen sink dramas that John Osborne's *Look Back in Anger* had heralded.

'No,' I said, cross with myself for not having scraped the money together to go and see it. It had had wonderful notices and put Joan Plowright firmly on the map.

'Well,' said Mr Nat Brenner, 'why don't we give you a copy of the play and you go away and read it and we'll see you at the end of the day.'

I thanked him and, clutching the script, went to find somewhere where I could read. There was nowhere, so I sat hunched on the stairs. At the end I found myself crying. Beatie Bryant's story was so close to my own.

The play tells how Beatie, a young girl from a working-class farming family in Norfolk, goes to London and meets a young man who shows her a vision of life which opens her mind to a different world. When she goes back home she tries to express how she feels to her determinedly ignorant, complacent family who can't even express their emotions. Everything Beatie said to her family I wanted to say to mine. At one point she has put the radio on. It is Mendelssohn's Fourth Symphony and her mother says:

> MRS BRYANT (*switching off radio*). Turn that squit off!
> BEATIE (*turning on her mother violently*). Mother! I could kill
> you when you do that. No wonder I don't know
> anything about anything. I never heard nothing
> but dance music because you always turned off the
> classics. I never knowed about the news because
> you always switched off after the headlines. I never
> read any good books 'cos there was never any in
> the house.

When they called me in at the end of the day, I said straight away to the two men: 'I've been so moved by this play because, you see, I *am* Beatie Bryant – just from a council house in Tottenham instead of a cottage in Norfolk.' They told me that I could read whichever speech I wanted to. I did the last speech.

> BEATIE. Do you think when the really talented people
> in the country get to work they get to work for
> us? Hell if they do! Do you think they don't know
> we 'ont make the effort? The writers don't write
> thinkin' we can understand, nor the painters don't
> paint expecting us to be interested – that they don't,
> nor don't the composers give out music thinking we
> can appreciate it. 'Blust,' they say, 'the masses is too
> stupid for us to come down to them. Blust,' they say,
> 'if they don't make no effort why should we bother?'
> So you know who come along? The slop singers and
> the pop writers and the film makers and women's

magazines and the Sunday papers and the picture-
strip love stories – that's who come along, and you
don't have to make no effort for them, it come easy.
'We know where the money lie,' they say, 'hell we
do! The workers've got it so let's give them what
they want. If they want slop songs and film idols
we'll give 'em that then. If they want the third rate,
blust! We'll give 'em *that* then. Anything's good
enough for them 'cos they don't ask for no more!'

I wasn't good enough. Of course I wasn't good enough.
To start with it was written in a Norfolk dialect that I wasn't
familiar with, but I gave it my all and they thanked me and I
left the building.

I was still trembling. Not only from the performance I had
just given but from the effect the play had on me, and I did
something that I had never done before and have never done
since. I walked into the first pub I saw and ordered a brandy.
There was an actor at the bar that I recognised. His name was
Edward Judd and he had just had a hit in the West End. He very
sweetly asked me if I was all right, and as he was an actor I said,
'Yes, I'm all right. I'm in a bit of a state because I've just come
from a reading for a part in a play that I know I'm absolutely
right for, and I know I won't get it.'

'Why won't you get it?'

'Because,' I sighed, 'I'm not *known*.'

He knew what I meant. We talked about the theatre – 'The
Bitch', he called it – and not accepting another drink, I left.
As I got to the door he raised his voice and said, 'Don't let it
get you down. I think you'll get home and find they've called
you.' The amazing thing was, he was right. I had got the job

and would have three weeks of rehearsal and three weeks playing in Bristol. I couldn't believe I was actually going to play that part.

My landlady in Bristol, now in her early seventies, had been in the Folies Bergère in Paris and never let you forget it. Every breakfast or evening meal that she put on the table was accompanied by a high kick or an attempt at a pirouette, and she sang French songs and talked as though Josephine Baker had been her best friend. She also, at one point, to my horror, dressed herself in one of her old costumes from the Folies – it was not a pretty sight.

The company was not so forthcoming. I didn't notice at first, as I was so excited to be in that beautiful old theatre with such a wonderful play to perform, and I could tell from the first reading that I had some superb actors to work with. They just weren't very friendly.

We had been rehearsing about ten days when surprisingly, the most surly actor, who was playing my father, the brilliant Leonard Rossiter, asked me to have supper at home with him and his wife, Josephine Tewson, who was also in the play. They then explained why everyone had been so cool with me. Annette Crosbie, who had been in the company for some time, was all set to play Beatie, and then she had had some disagreement with the management. She evidently made a stand in which she was supported by most of the company, never believing that they would sack her – and they had. So loyalty to Annette had made them slightly awkward with me. But they now accepted me, and I had a marvellous time working on that play. It made me search deeply my relationship with my family.

In the three years Julian and I were there, my parents hadn't attempted to get to Stratford-upon-Avon, and it wasn't just because of the expense. 'People like them' just didn't go to Shakespeare any more than 'people like them' listened to classical music or went to art galleries, although the art galleries were free, and thanks to Lord Reith there was classical music on the wireless as well as some very good plays and discussions. But in our house we had only been allowed to listen to the headlines, comedy shows or *Mrs Dale's Diary*.

I wasn't as angry as Beatie because I'd got away – out of that atmosphere.

But although I did my best not to seem different when I visited, they were now very uncomfortable with me. One actress friend that I had taken home said to me, 'Your mother looks at you as if she'd accidentally hatched a snake.' That had made me feel guilty and sad. Wesker's play took some of my guilt away, although rereading the play today I think Wesker was a little hard on working-class families. It wasn't *all* their fault.

Because it had already played at the Royal Court, no critics came down from London to see it, but the local notices which I read avidly were wonderful for the whole production and particularly for me. For the first time I felt that I had been able to give everything that was demanded of me. I felt completely fulfilled playing Beatie. Everything had at last come together. I was the right age, I *knew* the character, everyone else in the play was supportive and superb, it was well written and it was a story I wanted to tell the audience.

*

Toby Robertson had sent me a new French play that he was doing in the very small space of Bromley Little Theatre. He was very excited about it and when I read it, so was I. It was called *The Square*. It had been adapted from a novella by Marguerite

Duras (who I had never heard of then, though she would go on to win an Oscar for *Hiroshima Mon Amour*), and once again it was a part that would be easy to inhabit because I knew her.

The Square was only an hour long, and we were playing it with another short play, not by Duras, called *Dead Letter*. In essence, *The Square* is a conversation on a park bench between a commercial traveller clutching his suitcase and what Duras describes as a maid-of-all-work, a skivvy – the lowest of the low – and their opposing philosophies of life. He knows that he has a tedious, tiring job that will lead nowhere, but he has determined to accept the situation and enjoy the everyday things of life – the sunset on the water, a beautiful town or the first cherries of the season – and is content. Whereas she thinks that if she works to the best of her ability at all the horrible tasks she has to do – washing floors, washing old ladies, carrying heavy loads and putting up with the thoughtless cruelty she's subjected to – she won't become resigned to it. And believes that if she never accepts her lot in life then there's hope that somehow it will change.

Of course, my life hadn't been like this poor girl's, though there were resonances – I knew what it was like to hope for a different kind of life than the one that appeared to be set out for me.

I had no idea that Marguerite Duras was of interest to so many intellectuals, and that because this was the first time she had been performed in this country, the funny little theatre in Bromley would get a very smart audience. It never entered my head that it would be reviewed by the London papers. I simply loved working on it. So it was a great surprise to me when I received wonderful notices in the *Telegraph*, the *Observer* and in particular the *Sunday Times*, where Harold Hobson wrote three columns of adulation for Marguerite Duras's work, and then at the end: 'The only thing I have to add is that the performance of Eileen Atkins as The Girl is up to the measure of Madame Duras's inspiration, still, indestructible, human and superb'. I know that it's very conceited of me to quote that, but it's necessary to make my fury at what followed understandable.

Clearly I had done well, and I thought it a shame that we couldn't do it for longer than the run in Bromley (which was only two weeks). I could see that it was the kind of avant-garde play that wouldn't run in the West End, but I thought that it *would* make a good TV, and so I wrote to the BBC and ITV asking them to please come and see the play. I received no answers.

The play was finished before the end of April and despite those notices, I was once again totally out of work.

It was five months before I got a job. I was meandering down Holborn to the tube when I passed an actress who I knew slightly and stopped to say hello. She was what was known as a Rank starlet – one of the pretty girls J. Arthur Rank put under contract in the hope that they might become film stars.

'You look terrific,' I said (she was very glammed up). 'Where are you going?'

'I've got an interview,' she said, 'for a part in an *ITV Playhouse*.'

I was very surprised. *ITV Playhouse* did serious plays. This girl did not do serious plays.

'Do you know what the part is?' I asked.

'Oh yes,' she said. 'It was a play they did somewhere. It's called *The Square*. It's a two-hander with Michael Hordern.'

I had to stop myself from gasping. I said, 'Oh, really. And who is going to direct it?'

'Stuart Burge,' she said.

So I'd got the bastard's name. We said goodbye and I did *not* wish her well – I covertly followed her. She finally disappeared into what I think were then called the ATV offices and I waited. She was in there for about forty-five minutes. As soon as she came out I shot into the building past a reception area, as if I knew where I was going, through to where I could see there were offices. I said to the first person I saw, 'Could you tell me where Stuart Burge's office is, please?' He actually pointed it out to me and I just barged in without even knocking and exploded at the small, rather sweet-looking little man in the room.

'How dare you,' I said ridiculously, 'how dare you *think* of casting a cute-looking film starlet for the girl in *The Square*. It's wrong. It's terribly wrong. It's my part and I was bloody good in it, and you would never have even *heard* about the play if I hadn't written and let you know about it.'

I was raging. To say Mr Burge, who had never seen or heard of me before, was taken aback was an understatement. I had struck him dumb. He finally stuttered, 'Well, I've just been asked to do it. The casting people are sending the actresses in.'

'That part is MINE,' I yelled at him, 'and I'm not even given a chance to audition.'

He very decently didn't ask for me to be removed from the building, but told me to sit down and tell him why the kind of actress I'd met in the street was so wrong for the part. I told him that this girl must look as if there isn't much hope that anything will change her position in life, and if the girl looks prettily cute, no one watching will believe that. 'For one thing,' I ended bitchily, 'she wouldn't look well fed!'

Stuart as it turned out had scarcely read the play and

certainly hadn't thought too much about it. But he had been handed Michael Hordern, and it was an *ITV Playhouse*, so he had accepted it.

He gave me the part and I did it with Mr Hordern on TV. Nobody was very nice to me, but I guess I couldn't expect that. Stuart, who I worked well with years later on two or three TV productions, including *Sons and Lovers*, really had no idea what *The Square* was about and insisted on putting unnecessary filming in that almost ruined it. All the reviewers who had seen it at the theatre said so, but Michael Hordern and I still came out of it well, though the play had nothing like the impact it had had in the theatre.

Once again my career, such as it was, came to a halt. After the highs of playing in *Roots* and *The Square*, and the fight to do *The Square* on TV and finally getting it, but nonetheless not getting work from it, I began to feel totally despondent. I had shown them what I could do and been hugely praised for it, but somehow I still couldn't take off. I was out of work for nearly a year.

15

Julian's star was rising at the Royal Court Theatre. After *Altona* he had a very good part in *The Knack* by Ann Jellicoe, and then Tony Richardson cast him as the Knight in John Osborne's *Luther*, which was a huge success.

Working at the Court had made him even more political, and we were both members of CND (the Campaign for Nuclear Disarmament), though we never did the walk from Aldermaston – we would join it when it arrived in London.

I believe that demonstrations actually do very little to change things, but the photographs I had seen of what the bombs dropped by America on Hiroshima and Nagasaki had done had so burned into my mind when I was ten years old that I believed no one should ever drop a bomb like that on anyone again, so it would be better to simply not keep nuclear weapons. In retrospect, I now think it likely that there has been no World War III (though we've teetered near it once or twice) probably because we *have* nuclear weapons. But at that time I felt strongly about it, so I went with Julian to a big rally in Trafalgar Square arranged by the Committee of 100 – a group of well-meaning, high-minded people led by Bertrand Russell and including many people who were attached in some way to the Royal Court.

I was very apprehensive. The police had already gaoled Robert Bolt, Arnold Wesker and Christopher Logue for a month because they had refused 'not to breach the peace' at this rally.

We sat there for some hours surrounded by actors and writers that we knew and we were quite nervously jolly. Then the police started carrying people who refused to move and throwing them into police vans. We had been told to go completely limp if they tried to carry us away, to make it harder for them. We heard a cheer and saw John Osborne lifted and carried off. Then there was a shout: 'They've got Vanessa', who was very near us, and I knew that Julian would be next, and he was, and I thought, I'm simply not up for a night in a police cell, and got up and walked away, to the odd 'boo'.

I picked up some crumpets on the way home and felt deliciously relieved, as I munched them with my cup of tea by the fire, that I wasn't in a police cell. Julian came back some hours later. He wasn't at all cross with me and very pleased that he had only been fined twenty shillings. I would have made a hopeless suffragette.

I had been so long without work that when Roland Curram, a very good friend of mine, called me to say that his flatmate, Colin Graham, who was the director of the production of *Twelfth Night* which was playing in repertory at the Old Vic, had to replace his leading lady, the superb Barbara Jefford, who was playing Viola, I vaguely thought, Why is he telling me this?

'He'll see you at the end of the day tomorrow at the Old Vic. I've nagged him into it, so you'd better be bloody good.'

At least it was a part I knew well from understudying it at Stratford. There were two or three men in the stalls. One was Colin Graham and another was Michael Benthall, who ran the Old Vic Company. Roly had told me to prepare two speeches. I did one and they said 'thank you' and then started talking among themselves.

I thought it was rather rude that no one addressed me and I was just left standing there, so I said, 'Do you want me to do the second speech?' Immediately Colin said, 'No, that won't be necessary. Just hold on a minute.' There was some more chatter and then he and Michael Benthall came down to the footlights and Colin said, 'We'd love you to play Viola.' Michael Benthall had seen me play Beatie in Bristol, and apparently before I had even opened my mouth said to Colin, 'I think you've found your Viola.'

Rehearsals started almost immediately. It was a six-month contract. I was also to play Lady Anne in Colin George's production of *Richard III*. I was very happy.

The company who had already been playing *Twelfth Night* for some months were bored at having to rehearse again. But I knew it was annoying, and didn't take it amiss that they didn't go to much trouble to be welcoming. I was just happy to be back in the theatre.

As I was only taking over a part, I didn't expect the critics to come and see the production again, but when I opened I was thrilled to get a notice in the *Sunday Observer* saying that I was 'fresh and original'. I didn't bother to look for any other reviews because I really didn't think that there would be any. But checking for the purposes of this book, I found that there *were* a few others. Apparently I was too keen on the comedy for some, so I'm very glad I didn't see them *then*. I simply loved playing Viola.

Will She Do?

I had only been playing it a couple of weeks when we took the production to Amsterdam for one night and then on to The Hague. This was an incredible experience for me, as no one in Amsterdam knew that I was an unknown actress who had taken over the part – they simply accepted me as a leading player at the famous Old Vic Theatre Company and gave me the full star treatment in their grand and beautiful Municipal Theatre, which was the equivalent of our National Theatre.

I had a massive dressing room with a huge shower and another room for receiving guests, and when I took my call at the end of the play I brought the house down. My dressing room afterwards was packed with Amsterdam's theatre elite, and it was lucky that the management had given me several bottles of champagne or I would have had nothing to give them to drink. When everyone had finally gone, flushed with my success I thought I would go and look for someone to celebrate with. There wasn't a soul in the building. Everyone had left. No one had come to say good night to me as I hadn't had time to make any friends in the company. I was momentarily dashed, and then I thought, To hell with it, I'm going to look round the bars and *find* someone to celebrate with me. I wandered out into the busy streets and finally came across a troupe from our company in a bar who welcomed me with open arms, and I had a riotous night, at last accepted into the bosom of the company.

Back in England, I arranged for my parents to come and see the play. They came backstage and I introduced them to some of the company after the performance. They sat nervously in my dressing room, my father endlessly looking at his watch, my mother tight-lipped, at a loss to know what to say. Both upset that I'd paid for a car to take them home.

*

Just before I had got into the company at the Old Vic, Julian's mother Honor had been in London to see him in *Luther* and come back to have supper with us. I had become very fond of her and enjoyed her visits.

I was probably complaining about the lack of work when she suddenly said, 'Well, when are you two going to start a family?' I know that this will sound odd, but I was absolutely flabbergasted. I had simply never thought about it. Julian too was taken aback and said, 'We haven't even discussed it.' When Honor and I were washing up she brought it up again, and said she thought that it really was time I had a baby, so why not give up the contraception? 'But neither of us has done any-thing much about that for the last couple of years anyway – we couldn't be bothered.' 'And you haven't become pregnant,' she said, clearly shocked. 'You should get yourself tested. If you haven't conceived, there is something wrong with you.'

So I went to the nearest GP. He was a short man, totally bald, with a toothbrush moustache. I told him what the prob-lem was and he examined me behind a small screen. As he turned away when he had finished, I heard him say, 'Now, press-ups, Mrs Glover.' I obediently turned over and started doing press-ups. Who knows with a medical man what action might tell him something revealing about your state of health? I had got to about seven when I heard him say, 'What on earth are you doing?' 'Press-ups,' I said. 'You told me to do press-ups.' 'I said, Now *dress* up, Mrs Glover,' he said with mystified astonishment that anyone could be so stupid. He said he could find nothing wrong with me but that I must go to a clinic for further investigation. I thanked him and went to leave when, suddenly roguish, he said, 'I know who you are, you know.' What in the world did he mean? Surely he hadn't seen *The*

Square on television? If he *knew* me he was the only member
of the great British public who did. 'I'm sorry?' I said. 'You're
Cleopatra,' he said, very pleased with himself, 'in *Carry On
Cleo*. I knew it as soon as you came in.' 'No,' I said, 'that's
Amanda Barrie!' 'Ah, well, you all have stage names, don't
you?' I couldn't be bothered to insist that I wasn't Amanda
Barrie, and left clutching the address of the clinic I had to go to.

After several tests the clinic could find nothing wrong with
me and gave me an appointment for my husband to attend.
By now I had been at the Old Vic for some weeks and had a
late rehearsal call that morning, but hung around hoping that
Julian would get back before I had to leave. He did. 'Well, it's
apparently me,' he said. 'It seems unlikely that I'll ever have
any children.'

Now I know that any normal wife would have thrown her
arms round her husband and hugged him and maybe wept a
little for both of them. But I didn't. I just said, 'Oh, well then –
we'll adopt. That's fine by me,' gave him a quick kiss goodbye
and rushed off to rehearse Lady Anne and give a performance
of *Twelfth Night* in the evening.

On the tube on the way to the theatre I replayed the scene in
my head, and not until I had done that did I realise that Julian
had looked absolutely shattered and that I had said nothing
comforting. But wasn't it better that I didn't make a drama out
of it? Surely that would help him feel it was less of a tragedy? I
don't know. All I *do* know is that I simply wasn't understanding enough.

It wasn't until a miracle happened and Julian had his son
Jamie with his utterly lovely second wife, Isla Blair, that I saw
what not having a child had meant to him. We all know now
what emotions can do to you physically, and I think he was

so very much in love with Isla that waves of happiness briefly changed his physical make-up and made Jamie possible. I was very happy for him.

But back then at Hogarth Road in 1961, Julian and I started the proceedings for adoption. The first thing to do was to get a flat with a second bedroom, and we found a charming attic flat in Bolton Gardens with views at the back overlooking a lot of greenery, and said goodbye to the shunting and screeching brakes of Earl's Court Station.

The next thing to do was to get in touch with an adoption society. At our first interview we had been asked a lot of questions and filled in a long form. The most important question apparently was our religion. Were we Church of England? We agreed to say that we *were*. The other important question was, would we take a coloured baby? (That was the expression used then.) We said that we would happily adopt a baby of colour.

I assumed that they would come back and check where and how we lived and waited to hear more.

One afternoon when I was at home alone studying my script, the doorbell rang. There was no intercom in our flat, and usually we would lean out of the window and try to see who it was and throw down the key for friends. I leaned out but could see no one, and thought that I had better go down.

I opened the front door and there, on the doorstep, was a small carrycot with a tiny brown baby in it. I stood utterly transfixed. All I could think was, They've delivered it. I was so paralysed with fear at what I had taken on that I felt as though my blood was draining out of me through the ends of my fingers.

It must have been only seconds before the baby's mother walked up the steps from the basement and smilingly said,

'Did you think someone had abandoned their baby on your doorstep?' I bought whatever it was she was selling and went back upstairs in a state of deep shock. I had to admit to myself that I couldn't, *mustn't*, adopt a baby. The first thought that had come into my mind downstairs hadn't been, Oh what a darling baby. It had been, That's your life for the next twenty years gone – looking after that baby – and it had horrified me.

I was sick with worry. How could I tell Julian? I was home from the Old Vic that night before he came back from the Royal Court – and I was so distraught at what I had to say to him that I rushed out when I heard him come in and said it on the stairs – 'Julian, I'm so sorry. I'm so sorry, but I simply can't adopt a baby.' He was startled, then his face cleared. 'Oh, thank goodness,' he said, 'neither can I.' We hugged each other with relief, opened a bottle of wine and kept saying, 'But I thought *you* wanted to . . . ' 'No, I thought *you* wanted to', and went happily to bed. I say to bed. Actually it was now two single beds, which I had suggested as my insomnia was worse than ever, and I thought that I would sleep better. I was wrong. Single beds are the first nail in the coffin of a marriage.

I was now playing both Lady Anne and Viola, and in rehearsal for *The Tempest* to play Miranda with Alastair Sim as Prospero. He was famous as a comic actor but had never done a classical play. I was very nervous that with an actor known for being so hilarious, we might tilt the audience into seeing too many laughs that Shakespeare hadn't intended. I was right. The audience didn't know whether they should laugh or not. We were packed because of his name, but the production was a disaster. The director was fired and the Old Vic Company was taken over by Michael Elliott. He had just had enormous success with *Brand* and *Danton's Death* at the Lyric Hammersmith, and came steaming in with his coterie. We were packed off on a long British tour.

Just before we were due to leave, I was offered through my agent (yes, finally, after eight years in the theatre, I had got an agent) a part in a new play with Laurence Olivier. I was ecstatic. I didn't even have to read for it, as Tony Richardson was directing and said he didn't need me to read. There was one small problem – it meant that I could only do five weeks of *The Tempest*'s ten-week tour.

Well, surely they could find a girl to take over Miranda? My agent said they definitely would, our sacked director said he was happy to rehearse someone else into the part, and Alastair Sim said he wasn't *happy* that I would be leaving but he understood what an opportunity it would be for me to act with Laurence Olivier in the West End. Mr Michael Elliott said that under no circumstances would he let me leave. I was to do the full tour. I would be breaking my contract. He wouldn't allow it.

I couldn't believe it. My agent suggested that I ask to see Michael Elliott and beg him to release me.

He was sitting at a table in a room with no other chairs, austere and unsmiling. It was the first time I had seen him, since he hadn't introduced himself to our company, and stood facing him, taut with anxiety and nerves and determined not to lose my temper.

'Yes? What did you want to see me about?' he asked.

'I'm told that you won't release me from my contract, and I've come to ask you to change your mind.'

'Under no circumstances will I change my mind. Have you no loyalty to the Old Vic?' he said with contempt.

I spoke as calmly as I could. 'I did have loyalty to this

company, but you have made sure that the company I am with no longer exists. You are throwing us all out to go on tour with a production which you know is a disgrace but has a star that will make money for you and disappoint theatregoers all over Britain. In the meantime, you have brought your own elite clique into the Old Vic without asking a single member of our company to join your new company here when our tour finishes. Why on earth should I be loyal to a theatre which in reality has just sacked me?'

I was dismissed. I hated him.

A few fury-filled days later I heard that the producer of *Semi-Detached*, the name of the play in question, a Mr Oscar Lewenstein, had offered to 'buy' me out of my contract. I felt terribly grand. A little *less* grand but utterly thrilled when I heard that Michael Elliott had let me go for one hundred pounds. I was actually going to do a play with Laurence Olivier.

Semi-Detached was by David Turner and had been tried out at the Belgrade Theatre in Coventry, where the part that Larry was playing had been played by Leonard Rossiter – this was before *Rising Damp* had made Rossiter a star. Quite a few critics had seen this production and given Leonard amazingly good reviews. But David wanted his play done in London and the producers felt that they couldn't take a chance on a new play with an unknown name. So Larry had accepted to do it. The role was of a lower-middle-class insurance salesman from Birmingham with aspirations to be 'a better class of person' and all the jokes that go with that. I was playing his daughter, Mona Washbourne was his wife, James Bolam his son and John Thaw my boyfriend. Patsy Rowlands, who made a name later in the *Carry On* films, was also in the cast.

On the first day of rehearsals, I really had to make an effort not to be silly. Just being in the same room with someone so charismatic and starry was unsteadying, but Larry (as he asked us to call him) was so purposefully ordinary in the way he behaved, so just like any other actor, that I was amazed how easy it was to work with him.

Sadly the play was a flop, and Larry had some pretty bad notices, but the reviews sometimes exempted me. This was quite embarrassing. In the green room after the first night, Mona Washbourne was complaining about Bernard Levin's review in particular and Larry put his arm round me and said to her, 'But he's not a *complete* idiot, Mona, he noticed how good Eileen was.'

The trouble was, the critics had fallen in love with Leonard Rossiter's performance (it was the perfect part for him, and he *was* a kind of genius) and they were ready to dislike Larry before he had even opened his mouth on stage.

I adored him. My dressing room was above his, and I waited on the landing every night to look down and see which stars had come backstage to visit him, and then as he shut his door I would trot downstairs and accidentally be leaving at the same time. At the stage door his car would be waiting, and the first time this happened he said to me, 'I'm going to Victoria Station (he lived in Brighton). Is a lift that way of any use to you?' 'Oh yes. Thank you very much,' I said, although of course Bolton Gardens wasn't in that direction at all.

So every night I rode to Victoria with him, and during these rides he would tell me his plans for the start of the National Theatre, which would open first as a company in Chichester. He said he was very keen to have me in the company; in fact, there was a part I was right for in *The Workhouse Donkey*, a new play by John Arden in which Peter O'Toole was playing the lead.

For the months that he was contracted to play (and because of him we were packed, even with bad notices) I had a ride with him most nights. One night, as we had just got into the car he asked, 'Where is it that you live?' I said, 'Bolton Gardens' without thinking. 'Then this ride is no good to you at all,' he said. I'd been found out! I quickly tried to cover up. 'The thing is, I have friends who live in Victoria and I stop by and see them most nights.' 'Then Jack' – his chauffeur – 'will take you right to their door,' said Larry firmly. 'No, no,' I said desperately. 'I like the walk.' 'In no way are you to walk about Victoria at this time of night. Jack will take you there.'

I spent the rest of the drive frantically trying to think of someone I knew in the area that I could drop in on at eleven thirty at night.

While I was racking my brains, Larry was telling me that Peter O'Toole had rather fallen for the young actress he was working with and was insisting on *her* for *The Workhouse Donkey*, so there was no part for me after all in the Chichester season, but he would definitely find me something when the company was finally at the Old Vic, which it was taking over. I was so worried as to what I was going to do when he got out that I just said, 'Oh, that's all right, I didn't really want that part anyway,' which of course just sounded rude.

By the time we had reached Victoria Station and Larry had got out and Jack had gone with him to carry some stuff Larry was taking with him on the train, I had decided to tell Jack that I really *did* prefer to walk and refuse his services.

I had got out of the car and was ready with this when he returned. He absolutely wouldn't listen to me. He put me firmly back in the car and said that Larry would never forgive him if he didn't take me safely to my friends. 'So where are we going?' he asked. I should, of course, have just told him the truth – that I had been lying for the past months – but I couldn't. 'I never know the actual address because I walk there,' I parried, still hoping that I would think of a friend I could go to. 'Well, do you turn left or right out of this station?' he asked. 'Right,' I said, wantonly thinking 'Well, I'll think of something.

I *didn't* think of anything, and just kept saying 'right' or 'left', not having a clue where we were until finally I noticed a very narrow entrance to a mews that looked as if it might scrape the car. 'It's down there,' I shouted at Jack. 'Just leave me on this corner.' 'I'm not leaving you to walk down that dark alley – we're driving down there,' and he turned slowly into what turned out to be Holbein Mews.

It was pitch-dark, with no lights on anywhere. Then suddenly a light went on and a door opened, and a woman was saying goodbye to a man. I thought, I'm chancing it, and said, 'Stop, Jack. That's my friend.' '*That* woman?' he said. 'Yes, yes,' I said. He had stopped, so I jumped out of the car and ran towards the woman saying, 'Hi. Hi.' She shut the door. The man was walking towards me, so I said 'hi' to him and prayed that Jack would now move off. Looking at me with some curiosity the man just walked past me, and I saw that, of all things, he was wearing, hanging from his head down his back, the hood and strip of canvas that the men wore at Smithfield for carrying animal carcasses, but Jack was still watching so I had to carry it through. I banged on the woman's door and tried to wave Jack away. The woman opened the door and at last he started to move slowly. With a fixed smile of greeting I said, 'I'm sorry, but will you just speak to me, please?' 'What is it? What's going on?' she asked nervously, peering down the lane, and Jack finally turned the corner and disappeared. I said, 'I had to get away from the man in that car. I'm so sorry to have bothered you,' and I walked as quickly as I could out of the mews and ran to hail a taxi.

When I got home and told Julian we laughed, and I cried a bit from all the tension, and the knowledge that I wasn't going to be one of the first members of the National Theatre after all.

The next evening in our dressing room I told Patsy Rowlands the whole saga. On stage that night we were all sat round waiting for the curtain to rise on the first act, when Larry suddenly shot at me, 'Did Jack get you to your friends all right last night?' 'Oh, yes, yes,' I said. 'Thank you very much.'

Patsy, always ready to be helpful, said, 'Oh, are they those friends of yours who are always having fancy dress parties, Eileen?'

But I saw Larry smile and I knew I'd been sussed.

In the summer of 1963 when Olivier triumphantly launched the National Theatre in Chichester, I was playing Lady Brute in Vanburgh's *The Provok'd Wife* in Richmond in Yorkshire. Restoration comedy is notoriously difficult, but once we were inside this beautiful little Georgian theatre we knew exactly how to play it. Toby Robertson, whose production it was, got overexcited and took us into The Vaudeville, but with no star names, we died an early death.

I was about to sink into the slough of despond again when my agent rang to say that George Devine wanted to talk to me about a play called *Exit the King* by Eugène Ionesco. She was sending me the play to read before I met him, and admitted that she didn't think much of it. I loved it. I had never heard of Ionesco or the Theatre of the Absurd, but I thought the play tragic, ironic and very funny. I had met George Devine a few times at parties at the Royal Court, but only as Julian's wife. I think Tony Richardson must have persuaded him to see me.

There are three women's parts in the play. Queen Marguerite, the first wife of the King; Queen Marie, the second wife of the King; and Juliette, domestic help and registered nurse. I presumed, correctly, that he was seeing me for the part of the last. George Devine had made the English Stage Company at the Royal Court *the* most exciting place for any young actor to want to work. He was known to be almost a father figure to the young playwrights he had encouraged, and I had nothing but huge respect for him and a desire to work at the Royal Court, but after a few minutes' talk about the part, I realised that he thought Juliette was an old woman. 'Oh, but I read her as a young woman,' I said. 'No,' George said firmly, 'she's an old retainer. She's worked in the palace for years.' 'Then why were you thinking of me for the part?' I asked. 'Because people seem to think that you're a good actress,' he answered. 'Well, Mr Devine, I wouldn't want to play her as an old woman for many reasons. Firstly, I always think it looks phoney when a young person plays old and you think, Why haven't they cast someone the right age? Secondly, I think Ionesco's point about the wretchedness of her life becomes more poignant if she's young, and thirdly, I don't want to play an old woman right now, when I'm only *just* about being recognised as a young one.'

Mr Devine pulled at his pipe and said nothing. Then someone knocked on the door to tell him that he was urgently needed somewhere else, so I gathered up my bag to leave.

'Thank you very much for seeing me,' I said. 'Wait a moment.' He stopped me. 'You really thought she was supposed to be young when you read it?' 'Yes,' I replied. 'All right,' he said, 'let's try it then.'

I was very excited. Rehearsals started almost immediately, which explained why George made up his mind so quickly. The cast included Peter Bayliss, Graham Crowden, Natasha Parry, Googie Withers (who greeted me with, 'Ah – the girl who threw up all over me') and Sir Alec Guinness.

To my horror, the minute we put the play on its feet George started telling me to bend my back and drag my feet. I was ready and willing to look tired but to play it bent could only suggest age, and I didn't want to do it. For more than half the play Juliette has to wheel the King round the stage in a wheel-chair. 'You're making that look too easy,' George said, 'you should sigh and look as though you can scarcely manage it.' Then he asked me to lower my voice. I couldn't believe it. He clearly wanted me to play it as an old woman.

At the end of the first week, after the Friday-morning rehearsal, he asked me to stay behind. 'I'm afraid I'm asking you to leave the cast,' he said. 'You're not being obedient and therefore the part isn't working. I can't get anyone else till Monday, so I would be grateful if you came back and did the afternoon's rehearsal.' I said I would and went to a nearby café and had a sad sausage-and-mash lunch.

When I went back to the rehearsal room Sir Alec Guinness was waiting for me at the entrance. 'I hear George sacked you this morning?' he said. I nodded miserably. 'Well, I've persuaded him that that was a wrong decision as *I* think that you are going to be very good. So we've come to an agreement that *I* direct you in the part and George leaves you completely alone. Is that all right with you?' I thanked him and had to bite tears back. I was sure after only one week in his company that he was someone who didn't like tears.

So George ignored me, and Alec would quietly give me notes, and I tried to do everything he asked. The positioning of his wheelchair had to be very exact as the lighting was such that Alec simply wouldn't be seen if I was an inch or two out. I made the person on the lighting board practise with me again and again with a sack in the chair for Alec.

We were opening at the Edinburgh Festival. When I arrived in my dressing room at the Lyceum, to my horror there was a grey wig on a wig stand set at my make-up place. I presumed they expected me to wear it. The designer was Jocelyn Herbert, who was George Devine's partner. I immediately dumped my make-up case down and went out into the street to find a hairdresser's. I found a fairly seedy place quite near the theatre. 'Have you got any really good spray dye?' I asked. 'I want to dye a wig a very bright auburn.' Whatever they gave me did a superb job and I went on for the dress rehearsal with flaming-red hair. Nobody said a word, but I thought Alec had a glint of a smile.

The next evening when I went to my dressing room there was a quite charming turban on the wig stand. 'All right,' I thought, 'I'll settle for that.' Once again, no one said a word.

I happened to mention to Graham Crowden that my digs in Edinburgh were dirty and that the landlord had sealed all the bedroom windows and I hate to sleep without a window open. A few hours later Alec said to me, 'I hear your digs are unpleasant. I've booked a room for you at the Caledonian. You can move in there as soon as you're ready.' He was one of the most generous people I've ever met, always remembering what it had been like for him when he used to walk to drama school barefoot to save his shoe leather.

I've only just recently read all the reviews for this production, all these years later, and it's interesting to see that, although Alec himself had superb reviews, most of the critics thought that George Devine had not directed the play well and clearly had not really understood it. Because I was directed separately by Alec, in many of the reviews I am picked out as the only other actor who had got it right! I did so well, thanks to Alec, that I won the Clarence Derwent Award for best supporting actor, which was a great honour.

Alec and I formed a strong friendship which lasted till his death. He was a complicated man, and we both had quite a temper (mine quick, hot and over very quickly, his a slow, seething burn) and we had quite a few rough patches. But between his repressed homosexuality and his strict Catholicism was someone who really had a great desire to enjoy life to the full in every way. You would have a fabulous evening with him, of flowing wine, of laughter and stories and even dancing, but the next morning you would say, 'Where's Alec?' and the answer would be, 'He's at church. In confession.' And when he returned you'd feel as though a string had been tightened around the bonhomie of the weekend.

While doing this play I had also become friendly with Natasha Parry, a very beautiful and sweet-tempered woman who was married to Peter Brook. 'Ask her to supper,' Julian urged. 'I can't,' I said. 'She would bring Peter, and he would feel awkward being entertained by his vegetation from *The Tempest*, and I would be terrified.' 'I think you're being silly,' Julian said, 'you really like Natasha, she's been generous to you and we've come on a bit since Stratford.'

So they came to supper. I think by then I had progressed from pasta to casseroles. Peter couldn't have been more charming, and halfway through the evening told us the plans he had for a new company that would be very avant-garde called the Theatre of Cruelty, suddenly saying to me, 'I'd love you to come and do the workshops for it, you're just the kind of actor I want to use.'

So I found myself a few weeks later in a large studio with forty or fifty other actors from which Peter said he would choose his company of twelve.

Most of the work was improvisation, which I think should be used sparingly as it can easily become an indulgence. I think it's useful sometimes when you have complex language, as sometimes occurs in Shakespeare, to put the scene in your own words, or sometimes to loosen up a scene that has got stuck in a rut, but other than that I find it mostly a waste of time. Nevertheless, it can be fun to do.

At each session there were fewer actors as Peter whittled it down to the dozen that he wanted. Finally I went in one morning to do a session and found only Glenda Jackson waiting there. I greeted her but she wasn't one for idle chat or social graces then, and she prepared herself in silence. Peter and his sidekick Charles Marowitz arrived, and Peter announced that he had now chosen all but one of his company and he just couldn't make up his mind whether that last person should be me or Glenda. He would make his decision on today's work.

Glenda and I stood side by side in front of him waiting for our first instruction. 'Right, now, are you ready?' We nodded. 'Then would you both take your clothes off.' I took a step towards him as I thought I hadn't heard properly. '*What* did you say, Peter?'

By the time I had said that, Glenda's clothes were in a pool on the floor and she stood upright, stark naked, waiting for the next instruction. 'And that, Eileen,' said Peter, 'is why I'm taking Glenda instead of you. You tend to question things, and I want obedience.'

He was very charming about it and actually took me to lunch, which I enjoyed because I realised that (apart from always wanting to be the chosen one) I was relieved he hadn't chosen me in this case as I don't think that I would have enjoyed the work.

I loved some of the performances that his company gave, but was always glad that I was in the audience and not on the stage. I had no qualms about going on stage naked if the script demanded it. A few years later I played Mary in *Mary Barnes* at the Long Wharf Theatre in Connecticut, and had to appear completely naked, covered in my own excrement. Mary Barnes was a real person who was a schizophrenic, and I knew that she had actually done this and that it was a crucial element in the play.

But Peter was right. I wouldn't be happy to just obey instructions. I don't see the actor as a puppet.

16

In the long patches that I didn't work I tended to get very low-spirited, and also to lose my libido. There was Julian, coming home from the theatre high as a kite on adrenaline and I would often have gone to bed. I couldn't work out whether my inertia made me disinclined to have sex with Julian or disinclined to have sex altogether. We talked about what was happening and sometimes even wondered if we should separate for a while, but we could never manage the logistics and would end up deciding it was just a phase and that we were 'all right really'.

At the end of 1963 Julian had been offered a long tour of South America by our old friend, David William. He was to play the Prince of Arragon in *The Merchant of Venice* and Demetrius in *A Midsummer Night's Dream*, and the company would be led by Sir Ralph Richardson and Barbara Jefford. A few days into rehearsals Julian was asked if he would like to take over from Albert Finney, who was playing Luther to great success on Broadway. He was, of course, terribly excited and immediately called David to ask him to release him. Neither of his parts was very big and he could have been replaced without upsetting things too much. David was as adamant as Michael

Elliott had been with me. I said, 'Break your contract,' to Julian, as he had played Luther at Dundee Rep and had superb notices, and just to appear on Broadway would be a huge boost to his career. But I think, quite rightly, he didn't want to get a name for behaving badly or, indeed, be sued. So he went on the tour and I think he had a very good time with his pal Alan Howard, but will always wonder what difference going to America might have made to his career. He was away for about four months.

As Julian left I was offered a six-part TV serial called *The Massingham Affair*. I was the young leading woman and would be in all six episodes. It was a period piece, and that is the only thing I can remember about it, other than that most of the scenes were with an actor called Lyndon Brook, who was the star.

Lyndon was the son of Clive Brook, who had been a *big* star and played in many Hollywood movies, and it was hard for Lyndon because he just hadn't done as well as his father. This was mainly because, although he had wonderfully classical features, he had been born with a slight deformity of the spine, which not only made him short but also gave him quite a lot of pain, and the pain had etched itself onto his face. So he wasn't the success his father was, and he didn't have the easy affability his father apparently had.

We were the love interest in the story, and I realised immediately that he had a huge consciousness of his lack of height as, when we were introduced, he said, shaking his head, 'It's all that milk they gave you at school', and several times in the first week he referred to my height. Finally I said, 'You would be so much happier if we did these scenes lying down, wouldn't you?

What a pity it's a costume drama.' I knew that I had taken the sting out of the remark by saying it quite flirtatiously and he suddenly smiled and said, 'I'm being grumpy, aren't I? I'm sorry.' And that was the start of the affair.

He told me that he had a wife and two daughters in a house in Sussex and had always kept a flat in London in Jermyn Street, but now because he simply couldn't afford this any more, they were selling both and the whole family would live together in a house in Fulham. He had spent his childhood in great style in Hollywood, New York and London, and he gave this information with an ironic contempt for his failure to be successful and to end up in Fulham – not the upmarket place it is today. He told me all this on the first evening that we had dinner together in a restaurant in Jermyn Street.

I told him that Julian was away on tour and that we had problems because I seemed no longer interested in sex.

The information hung in the air. We both knew that that evening I was suddenly very interested in sex.

So we went back to his flat.

I'm pretty sure that he wasn't a serial adulterer. I just happened to catch him when domesticity had eaten away at the romance he and his wife had had in their marriage and he was about to lose his bolthole in London.

He was eight or ten years older than me – cultured, sophisticated and with this vulnerable streak of melancholy about his 'crook back', as he called it, which was hardly 'crooked' at all. I made him laugh. It gave me enormous pleasure to make him laugh.

Although I realise that today disloyalty in marriage is not to be tolerated, this was 1964 and all the rules on sexual behaviour were in a state of transformation, and I certainly didn't feel that I had done anything very dreadful. I'm sure that much of the sexual attraction was to do with it being illicit, but there was a great deal of affection between us. We had a very good time together; we were immensely discreet and his wife never found out. Julian was coming home, Lyndon's flat was sold and we had one last evening together and said goodbye.

While I was doing *The Massingham Affair* Peter Dews asked me to join a company he was taking to America. A group of very rich people had been such admirers of *An Age of Kings* (Peter's adaptation of Shakespeare's histories on TV) that they had put up the money themselves for a Shakespeare Festival in their home town of Ravinia, just outside Chicago, and asked Peter to bring his company. I was to play Ophelia in *Hamlet* and Viola in *Twelfth Night*.

Julian came back bronzed, handsome and looking as though he had had a good time in South America, and we decided to squeeze in a week in Corsica for my thirtieth birthday before I had to go to Chicago, the idea being that maybe it could be a renewal of what we originally felt for each other. We knew we were drifting apart.

As the plane was landing on the island Julian said, with enthusiasm, '*Look* at those mountains.' And I said, 'It looks just like Wales to me.' Yes, I put a damper on the holiday from the beginning. We were in a lovely little hotel in a beautiful bay where every afternoon there was a convenient short thunderstorm when every couple apart from us went to their bedrooms and copulated along with the storm, while we sat in our room reading, with me occasionally whining that at thirty my life was over and that I obviously was never really going to get anywhere, while Julian sat there tight-lipped. I behaved very badly in Corsica. I think I even told him about Lyndon (which was unforgivable of me), and I'm lucky that Julian didn't strangle me. I suppose that unconsciously I was making it worse in the hope of somehow making it better. I probably wanted a quarrel. I'm told psychiatrists say that it's very hard to leave a marriage unless you quarrel. We were both glad to get back home, and in no time I was off to America.

The first shock when we arrived in Ravinia was that the theatre was huge, with a roof shaped like a tilted saucer over several solid pillars with no walls, and right alongside it ran the main railway line. We were doomed to play Shakespeare with the whistle, hoot and clanking of a train charging through every so often. There was nothing to be done about it, as the local people who had so kindly paid for us to be there saw nothing wrong with the interruption. They had held many concerts there and it had never worried them. The stage was so enormous that we would have to make our entrances well in advance. The whole Court had to creep on while the ghost was still speaking in the first scene of *Hamlet*, which rather spoilt the effect, and I had to wander on as Ophelia in the middle of Hamlet's 'To be or not to be' speech.

Highland Springs, which was where we all stayed in one hotel, was simply an area of estates owned by the multimillionaires who had invited us, and they were ready to give us a warm, generous welcome. What no one could foresee was that the women would fall so utterly in love with all our long-haired actors. Not only was it the fashion in England in 1964 for young men to have long hair, but the actors in our company had grown theirs luxuriantly for the Elizabethan period in which all the plays were staged.

The local women fell upon the boys in our company as

if they had never seen men before, and the local men, who were mostly conservative jocks with near-shaven heads, were stunned and mystified that their wives and daughters could in any way find these skinny, long-haired creatures with no muscles attractive. So the women gave endless all-day pool parties while the men glared and wished that they hadn't spent so much money bringing these weird but worryingly enticing Brits to their town.

The whole company became completely out of hand, our hotel palpitating with all the sex that was going on and heads spinning at all the luxuries that they were being plied with. Several of the actors were loaned cars for the season, dollars seemed to be flying in the air and with the hot sun shining down there were days when I thought, This is Babylon, and we're never going to get the plays on at all.

Not to be left out, I slept with my Laertes, and when he moved on to one of the local lovelies, I found myself sleeping with someone that I had scarcely known was in the company and thought, This is silly. You're just doing this to feel part of this carefree, rollicking, possibly actually rocking, hotel. So I moved my room to a tiny tree-covered extension at the back of the hotel and calmed down.

The season wasn't a disaster, but it could hardly be called a success. I did have a treat, though, in the middle of it. Robert Morley turned up to see his son-in-law, Robert Hardy, who was playing Hamlet, very much our leading man and the only actor with short hair and who didn't stay in the hotel with the rest of us. Having done his duty and seen a matinee, Morley asked if there was anyone in the company who wasn't in *Henry V* (also played by Hardy) that evening who would like to go to the pony-trotting races with him in Chicago. I put my hand up and had an enormously enjoyable evening. He gave me ten dollars to bet with and I won a hundred dollars, and disgracefully didn't think to give him his ten dollars back. This win meant that I had enough money to fly to New York for my weekend off, and I had the audacity to leave a message at the theatre where Alec Guinness was playing in *Ross* at the time, a play about Lawrence of Arabia, telling him I was coming. As I impertinently expected, he sent a telegram saying, 'You must stay with us'.

I had a wonderful weekend with him and his really sweet wife, Merula, who were renting Sybil Burton's fabulous apartment overlooking Central Park, and realised that New York was the America I had dreamed of – exotic, noisy, exciting, dangerous and very attractive to me. Alec had to do three shows that weekend, but I wandered around on my own and with Merula, and we both infuriated Alec by each buying a painting from a blind man in Greenwich Village. They *were* very bad paintings, and Alec kept saying, 'But WHAT made you buy paintings from a blind man?'

When I got back to Ravinia a gay actor called Terry Scully, who I was very fond of and loved to dance with, told me that a producer of floor shows had noted our dancing at a party and offered us a job touring America as demonstration dancers. Terry was keen to stay and see the country, but I said it wasn't for me. He said he thought he would stay anyway and I found myself saying, 'Will you rent your flat in London to me then?'

It was difficult to make calls to England, but I had to tell Julian what I was thinking of doing. There was a long pause, then he said, 'Don't do that. You won't be happy in Terry's flat. You'll get depressed. Come back home.' So I said, 'All right then.'

On the trip back to London our plane made three terrifying attempts to land in a fog at Heathrow and everyone had sat gripping the hand of whoever they were sat next to, waiting for the plane to crash, until the pilot gave up and took us all to Copenhagen for breakfast. Never has there been such a joyous celebration as we had in Kastrup Airport. We drank a great deal of champagne, and more than half the company admitted that they had thought they were going to nosedive straight into hell.

Julian and I just picked up our lives together, and my attempt to leave was never spoken of again.

On arriving home, my agent told me excitedly that Binkie Beaumont and Noël Coward wanted to see me with a view to playing Monica in *Present Laughter*, with Nigel Patrick playing the leading part. I read the play and was very disappointed. Monica was the leading man's secretary and had worked for him for years; she should obviously be as middle-aged as Nigel Patrick was. So now, at thirty, was it all over for me? Would I never play Rosalind or Beatrice, the Duchess of Malfi or any of Chekov's Three Sisters? (I never did play Beatrice, but I managed the others.) Was I being considered now as a middle-aged supporting actor? But Binkie Beaumont was a horribly important man in the theatre world and I wanted to meet Noël Coward, so I thought I would dress as youthfully and glamorously as possible and hope that they would see that I was wrong for the part, and then I might make an impression on them for a younger role in the future.

I borrowed an expensive fur-collared coat (even though fur was against my principles) from a good friend, Ann Firbank (another Rank starlet), and I thought I looked tremendously chic. It had a tie belt and was the new short length, to show my good long legs, and I did the best hair and make-up that I could manage.

All three men were sat at a table, and as soon as I entered and sat down, Noël Coward said, 'This is absurd. She is far, far, far too young to play Monica.' The others appeared to agree with him. He apologised for wasting my time and became charmingly chatty. I relaxed, thinking, It's worked — now they'll think of me for something younger in another play some time. Coward made me laugh so much that gradually the belt of my coat came undone and displayed my very cheap skirt and sweater. Suddenly he said, 'You know what? She would make a marvellous Miss Erikson.' Miss Erikson was the Swedish cleaning lady. I was completely deflated and said I couldn't do it. But Coward was insistent that I must go to a dressing room, look at the script and come back and read for them. He was sure I would be wonderfully funny in the part. I took a script with me and decided just to leave the theatre and not go back. It was all too depressing. Not only would I have to look middle-aged as Miss Erikson, but it would enhance the part if I made myself look jokily unattractive as well.

I wandered down Shaftesbury Avenue and noticed a telephone booth and thought, I suppose I should tell my agent what I have done. I now had an agent called Larry Dalzell, who was a simply lovely man who I was with for over thirty years. He almost yelled at me. 'Get back. Get back to the theatre *at once*. Have you *no* idea who you're being rude to?' So I went back and read and they offered me the part and Larry got me gracefully out of it.

*

One of the bright young things at the Royal Court, Peter Gill — a clever Welsh boy who looked about twelve — offered me a play he had written called *The Sleepers Den* that he was going to direct. It was to be done for a few weeks at the Royal Court Upstairs — a tiny theatre they had made for experimental work at the top of the building.

Although I was to play an exhausted, depressed woman in her forties, based on Peter's mother, I thought that the part was really good and I was longing to work with Peter. So all thoughts of youth and glamour were forgotten, and we had a wonderful time working on that play, though Peter never forgave me for the reviews I got. He felt they obliterated the brilliance of his work — playwrights are tortured creatures.

While I was doing Peter's play at the beginning of 1965, there was an uproar about a TV play I had recorded when I came back from Chicago called *Fable*. It was written by John Hopkins, who had made his name with *Z-Cars*, and directed by Christopher Morahan. It was called *Fable* because it was an imaginary Britain where nearly everyone was black and only a small minority was white. It showed exactly what it was like in 1964 to be black in a white community by reversing the colour of the skin. Ronald Lacey and I played the only white characters in it and were subjected to degradation and police brutality. It was a tough, brave piece of work.

It was supposed to air on 20 January, but the BBC delayed it for a week because there was a by-election in Leyton and they felt that what was known as 'the colour problem' was a big issue in that area. The play was a plea *against* intolerance, but it was feared that racial rabble-rousers would falsify the message and it would be misinterpreted, so it was to be shown after the election.

This action by the BBC made headline news in many newspapers, and the play was certainly misinterpreted by my mother, who, happy that I was at last in something that was being talked about in the newspapers that were read in Courtman Road, Tottenham, with a photograph of me being beaten by a black policeman splashed across them, said, 'Well, you showed them. *That's* what it would be like if ever the blacks took over.'

'Mum,' I said despairingly, 'it was ironic. It showed you what it's like to be black in this country.'

'Yes,' she said, 'a lot nicer than where they came from.'

My mother was not a vicious woman. She was racist because she was ignorant. She was only repeating what the tabloids said.

In March Larry Dalzell called me to say a script was coming to me of a new play and that I had an appointment to audition for the director, Val May, and the producer, Michael Codron – the play was called *The Killing of Sister George*. I was intrigued. I was even more intrigued when I read it and found it was about lesbians. This was the first time the subject had been talked about openly in a play. There had been Lillian Hellman's *The Children's Hour*, but that was American, and in that there was a sexual relationship that was only referred to obliquely. This play made it quite clear what the relationship was between the two main women and I thought it edgily funny. It wasn't a great play, but in 1965 it was a brave one. It's a pity, I thought, that I'm so very wrong for the part of Childie. It seemed to me that she should be a small, pretty, childlike creature who looked as though she could easily be bullied by her tough, mannish partner, George. For this part they had already cast a stand-up comedienne called Beryl Reid, and she was quite short. I would tower over her and it would look ridiculous.

Thinking I didn't stand a chance anyway, I went to the

audition in a trouser suit and read the part for Mr May and Mr Codron. Mr May asked me if I would come back the next day in a pretty dress and read again. I said yes, I would, thank you very much, and went home thinking, I'll still look too tall.

I had a new short minidress with a Peter Pan collar and arrived in that the next day. I read again and the two men talked quietly together. I suddenly interrupted: 'Excuse me, but you know I'm not really right for this part. You should cast a tiny, pretty little girl who looks like a porcelain doll.' 'We know that,' said Mr Codron, 'but we can't find anyone looking like that who can act. So we're trying to decide whether to take a chance on you.'

I thought they were crazy, but they cast me.

I needed the work, but I had never started rehearsing a play with less enthusiasm. I just felt I wasn't right.

We were to try the play out at the Bristol Old Vic, the lovely theatre where a few years earlier I had played Beatie in *Roots*, the idea being that we would get wonderful notices and transfer to the West End. I thought quietly, It will be a quick three weeks, then it will all be over.

On the first morning that we gathered together on the stage of the Old Vic, I played a silly joke on Beryl Reid. As I introduced myself to her I added, 'Oh, and could you let me know where you're staying, because of course I'll be moving in with you. I'm a method actress.' I was told by Val May afterwards that Beryl had rushed straight to him and said, 'You'll have to keep that weird girl away from me. I'm not doing any of this method stuff.'

There were four women in the play. Beryl and I had the big fat leading parts, and then there was the part of the BBC producer, a good supporting part played by Lally Bowers (who had complained about the colour of my costume at the Oxford Playhouse), and the small part of a clairvoyant called Madame Xenia, played by a foreign-looking actress whose name I can't remember.

Beryl Reid was odd to work with. It was only the second play she had done – the first was something unmemorable at Worthing Repertory Company – and whenever Val May and I tried to discuss the scene she and I were having together, Beryl would say, 'Well, if you two want one of your little talks, I'll go and make some phone calls,' and she would leave the stage. She seemed to have no idea that acting was an interactive affair. But Val May did an excellent job of pulling us all together and I began to think that maybe it wouldn't be so bad after all.

We were *not* a success. You might even say we were a disaster, as every night we would hear rows of seats banging as people left in disgust. Bristol was not amused by the play and the local reviews reflected this opinion. We were all expecting to be told that Bristol would be the end of the play when, to our amazement, Michael Codron held a meeting on the last Saturday to say that we were having a few days off and then going to Hull for a week, and he still hoped to take the play to London. The only difference he was going to make was to replace the actress who was playing Madame Xenia.

That evening after the show as we all packed up our dressing rooms, I suddenly smelt smoke. So did Beryl. We met in the corridor and saw that flames seemed to be flickering in the room of the actress playing Madame Xenia and there were strange noises coming from it.

We opened the door on the extraordinary sight of this woman in her sixties or seventies, stark naked, dancing round the room, which was blazing with candles which had set fire to the curtains, as she shrieked some chant and stuck long pins in what was clearly meant to be an effigy of Beryl.

We were very relieved she wasn't coming with us to Hull.

The second morning we were there, having played again, the night before, to seats banging as people left the theatre, Beryl turned up at my dreary digs. There was a shop she had found that excited her and she was longing to take me there. Had she found an undiscovered Mary Quant, or a Northern Biba? No. The shop that we went to fascinated Beryl because it sold, among bric-a-brac, second-hand false teeth. I spent the morning helpless with laughter as she tried on different pairs of teeth with impromptu characterisations. I think that was the day we bonded. She never liked the other two. Margaret Courtenay took over Madame Xenia and Beryl loathed her, and as the play progressed she grew to really dislike Lally. I got on well enough with them both, but I adored Beryl – we couldn't have been more different and we couldn't have got on better.

Michael Codron came to Hull to tell us that we would open at the Duke of York's Theatre in London on 15 June. We truly thought he had gone out of his mind or maybe, for some tax reason, he wanted a big flop.

The week we opened, there wasn't much to excite the critics. There was a somewhat disastrous *Mother Courage* on somewhere, and a couple of other plays that didn't come up to expectations, and I doubt if they had *any* expectations of us. The only known name or star was Beryl Reid – 'What on earth was she doing in a straight play – and apparently a play about lesbians!' – and they didn't find the prospect enticing.

We all rather dreaded the opening night. You are always terror-struck, but there is also a small voice saying it just *might* go wonderfully well. There was no such voice for this production. I just thought, Well, it's going to be a train crash, but I expect you'll get over it. The curtain inevitably rose.

We had hardly got a few lines out when they started to laugh. Beryl and I were stunned – we hadn't heard a single laugh in Bristol or Hull. The laughs continued, and got louder – it was amazing that we managed to time them and didn't walk through our lines, they were so surprising. When the curtain came down for the interval, Beryl rounded on me furiously. 'What are you doing behind my back?' she said. 'I'm not doing anything, Beryl.' She looked bemused. I said, 'It's the play. We've forgotten it's funny.' In the second half there were more gales of laughter, but also a wonderful hush for the touching moments between the two women.

When the curtain finally came down we received a rapturous ovation, and the reviews the next day in the newspapers were all superb. We had had a huge hit.

Michael Codron had played a cool hand and been very clever. Our first night was carefully packed with as many camp people as he could find to lead the laughs, and he had gambled that a London audience would be much readier for the play than a provincial one. His gamble had paid off. It played, with only one change of cast, for over two years at the Duke of York's.

Everyone who was anyone came to see that play. When Noël Coward came he said, '*What* a clever girl to turn me down and wait for this part.' And I was at last that magic thing – KNOWN. I had a lot of notice taken of me suddenly, as not only was my acting admired, but for the part I had been made to look as attractive as possible. They had sent me to Vidal Sassoon to have my hair cut by Vidal himself, and dyed blonde, and in the progress of the play I had to appear in a pretty mini-dress, tight pedal pushers, a shorty nightie and at one point in just bra and pants. I was suddenly seen as glamorous as well, and the play did more for me than anyone else because I was young enough to make the most of all the attention. I'm happy to add that Beryl was taken seriously as an actress for the rest of her career, rightly winning a BAFTA for her performance in *Smiley's People*.

That summer after I had opened, Julian went to Ireland to do a film called *I Was Happy Here* with Sarah Miles, which was a wonderful opportunity for him as he longed to do movies. I was so caught up in the excitement of my life that I failed to notice when he came back that there was anything wrong; when he was filming and I was playing in the theatre he often slept in the spare room and we hardly saw each other.

Then I had a call from an actress asking if she could come and see me. I knew her a little and, wondering what on earth she wanted me for, said, 'Yes. Come today.' I greeted her warmly but she quelled me with a very serious expression and refused the tea I offered her – and I *still* couldn't think what she had come for. She then told me that she had been on the film with Julian in Ireland, and did I know that he was having a flagrant affair with Sarah Miles? 'Everyone knows it,' she said, 'they're being quite open about it, and I just wondered if you knew.' I said, 'No, I didn't know,' thanked her and got rid of her as soon as possible.

I was utterly enraged and wanted to kill Julian. Not for the infidelity. My fury was about the way the deed was done rather than the deed itself. After all the talks we had had about quietly splitting up with no fuss; after him persuading me back when I'd suggested I go and live in Terry Scully's flat – how could he do this? Sarah was a huge star – it would be in every newspaper.

When I came back from the theatre that night I charged into the flat ready to pull him out of bed, if necessary, to ask if it was true. But he was waiting for me and got in first, and said he had fallen in love with Sarah. I was very, very angry and there was one hell of a scene where, Julian tells me, I came at him with a knife, but I don't remember that. Maybe I did. It was an ugly affair – they always are. We finally crawled exhausted to our beds in separate rooms. The next day he'd packed a small bag and told me he wouldn't come back after that day's filming. I was over my anger and was just sad and cried. And he left.

Within forty-eight hours it was in all the papers. The two of them at some big party, he looking handsome, she looking fabulous, and a small photo of me in the bottom right-hand corner looking like Mrs Danvers. In every paper that reported the affair the photograph of the 'deserted wife' always made me look hideous. The newspapers took stills from *The Sleepers Den* on purpose – there wasn't one picture of me from *The Killing of Sister George*.

I called Julian and asked him to please stop giving the press such opportunities, and he came over as soon as he could and was very apologetic and we talked for hours, but I could see that he was utterly under Sarah's spell. In my heart of hearts I knew that it had probably needed something brutal like this to make us see that our marriage really was no longer a marriage.

As Dr Greasepaint healed my wounded pride – because that's all it was now, really – I thanked God we hadn't had any children and came to see our nine-year relationship as hugely enjoyable and of great advantage to both of us – certainly to me.

His affair with Sarah was over in three months. Our divorce two years later was probably the simplest ever. He arranged a charade where he was caught and photographed in a hotel bedroom with a girl (as in those days there could be no 'agreed' divorce). I kept the furniture. He took the car, and we had saved four thousand pounds which we split precisely in half.

He and his wife, Isla Blair, are two of my dearest friends.

I not only got a lot of sympathy at the theatre because of the very public break-up, but on hearing that I was now a free woman I had quite a few admirers turning up in my dressing room and had the odd enjoyable affair, the best being with George Baker. George had a wife and children in the country, a long-time mistress in London and was seeing Brigitte Bardot every so often in Paris. That's how it was in the 1960s. Not only was he totally delightful to spend time with, but he always cooked us something utterly delicious afterwards.

I won the Evening Standard Award for Best Actress, and Mr Codron put my money up by ten pounds. I was now earning sixty pounds a week and bought my first Mary Quant dress, a cute little black crêpe number that I wore to the grand Christmas party that was given every year by the great wig-maker, Stanley Hall – if you were asked to that party, you knew that you had made it. I had never been announced by a flunkey on the threshold of a party before, and stood feeling a million dollars in my Mary Quant as he intoned my name. Stanley himself, after shaking hands with me, took me across to the bar for my first drink. The young man at the bar leaned forward on his elbows, grinning up at me. ''Allo, Auntie Eileen, I'm Dorrie's youngest, Sid. What about you then, eh? What're you gonna 'ave, then? It's all on the 'ouse.' Stanley shrank away in horror and I heard him say, 'The barman is a *relative* of hers.'

Suddenly a short bullet of an American shot to my side.

'Hi. I'm Larry Kramer and I'm crazy about you.' He was

about my age and hadn't yet reached fame as a playwright, AIDS activist and miraculous survivor of HIV. As I turned to talk to him, I said to Sid:

'Say hello to your mum for me.'

'You know the bar boy's *mother*?' said my astonished new friend.

'Yes,' I said wearily, 'I'm a fully paid-up member of the working class.'

'You're *first* class, kid, and don't you forget it. When is the play coming to Broadway?'

'In September.'

'You'll love New York – and New York will love you.'

And I did. And it did.

And, at last, I would do.

And after that . . .

Eileen Atkins' Broadway performance in *The Killing of Sister George* earned her the first of four Tony Award nominations for Best Actress and also *The Evening Standard Award* for Best Actress. She has continued to work on both sides of the Atlantic in theatre, film and television.

A three-time Olivier Award winner, she has been on the UK stage for over sixty-five years, most recently in her one-woman play, *Ellen Terry*, and in *The Height of the Storm*.

She's appeared in many films including *Equus*, *The Dresser*, *Gosford Park* and *Robin Hood*.

Her screenplay for the film *Mrs Dalloway* won an *Evening Standard* Award.

For television, she co-created *Upstairs, Downstairs* with her friend Jean Marsh. She won a BAFTA and an Emmy for her part in *Cranford*. She played Queen Mary in the Netflix television series *The Crown* and for years has appeared in *Doc Martin*.

Appointed Commander of the Order of the British Empire in 1990, she became a Dame in 2001. Later she received an honorary Doctor of Arts from City University, London, and was awarded an honorary Doctor of Letters by Oxford University.

In 1978 she married the film and television producer Bill Shepherd, who sadly died in 2016.

Acting has given her huge fulfilment, she says: *'I've realised my destiny and I've had a very, very good time doing it.'*

Acknowledgements

I would like to thank my brother Ron for sharing his recollections of our childhood.

Many thanks to Janet Macklam, who had to translate my scribblings into her computer, for never complaining and for encouraging me by always looking forward to the next chapter.

I cannot thank my ex-husband Julian Glover enough for not only giving me support but for having painstakingly made a scrapbook of my work up to 1965.

I'm grateful to Ian McNeice for giving me a list of every play, TV show or film I've ever done.

Special thanks to Oliver Soden for his wise counsel.

Above all, I thank Lennie Goodings, who first asked me to write for her in 2010, over ten years ago, and has continued to prod me gently ever since, and for her trust, guidance, advice and support.

Credits

All efforts have been made to trace the copyright holder of images, but in the case of certain photographs, no copyright holder could be identified. Little, Brown welcomes any information regarding this.

Plate Section II

Page 1
Top left: Alastair Muir/Shutterstock
Bottom: ANL/Shutterstock

Page 4
Bottom: Joan Marcus

Page 5
Top left: BBC Photo Library
Top right: Desmond Tripp/University of Bristol/ArenaPAL
Bottom right: © Sandra Lousada/Mary Evans Picture Library

Page 6
Bottom: George Elam/Daily Mail/Shutterstock

Page 7
Middle top: BBC Photo Library
Middle bottom: BBC Photo Library
Bottom: George Elam/ANL/Shutterstock

Index